W9-AFV-361

BIKE RACING
101

Kendra and René Wenzel

To Tim -
Best Finishes,
Kendra Wenzel
R. Wenzel

Human Kinetics

Library of Congress Cataloging-in-Publication Data

Wenzel, Kendra, 1967-
  Bike racing 101 / Kendra Wenzel, René Wenzel.
     p. cm.
Includes bibliographical references and index.
    ISBN 0-7360-4474-4 (soft cover)
    1. Bicycle racing.   2. Bicycle racing--Training.   I. Wenzel, René,
1960-   II. Title.
    GV1049.W45   2003
    796.6'2--dc21   2003000446

ISBN: 0-7360-4474-4

The Web addresses cited in this text were current as of February 14, 2003 unless otherwise noted.

Illustrations on pages 112, 116, and 186 reprinted, by permission, from Eddy Borysewicz, 1985, *Bicycle Road Racing* (Brattleboro, VT: Vitesse Press), p. 131, 133, 185. © Jude Roberts-Rondeau.

Acquisitions Editor: Edward McNeely; **Developmental Editor:** Julie Rhoda; **Assistant Editor:** Carla Zych; **Copyeditor:** Jacqueline Blakely; **Proofreader:** Kathy Bennett; **Indexer:** Nan N. Badgett; **Graphic Designer:** Nancy Rasmus; **Graphic Artist:** Francine Hamerski; **Photo and Art Manager:** Dan Wendt; **Cover Designer:** Keith Blomberg; **Photographer (cover):** Casey B. Gibson; **Photographer (interior):** Noted next to photos; **Illustrator:** Roberto Sabas; **Printer:** United Graphics

Chapters 5, 6, 7, and 8 were written with help from Scott D. Saifer

Photos on pages 22 and 43 shot by Dan Wendt at Spin City Cycles in Decatur, IL. Shop owner and model: Kyle May.

Human Kinetics books are available at special discounts for bulk purchase. Special editions or book excerpts can also be created to specification. For details, contact the Special Sales Manager at Human Kinetics.

Printed in the United States   10   9   8   7   6   5   4   3   2   1

Human Kinetics
Web site: www.HumanKinetics.com

United States: Human Kinetics
P.O. Box 5076
Champaign, IL 61825-5076
800-747-4457
e-mail: humank@hkusa.com

Canada: Human Kinetics
475 Devonshire Road Unit 100
Windsor, ON N8Y 2L5
800-465-7301 (in Canada only)
e-mail: orders@hkcanada.com

Europe: Human Kinetics
107 Bradford Road
Stanningley
Leeds LS28 6AT,
United Kingdom
+44 (0) 113 255 5665
e-mail: hk@hkeurope.com

Australia: Human Kinetics
57A Price Avenue
Lower Mitcham,
South Australia 5062
08 8277 1555
e-mail: liahka@senet.com.au

New Zealand: Human Kinetics
P.O. Box 105-231,
Auckland Central
09-523-3462
e-mail: hkp@ihug.co.nz

—for Katrine

Contents

Part III Racing Skills

Part IV Racing Strategy and Tactics

Foreword

I was lucky to have learned the basics of cycling from my father, a national caliber racer in his native Colombia. I was 12 years old when I started cycling, and my dad was an excellent mentor and coach in those early days, but getting in to bicycle racing was not as easy as, say, getting into baseball. A book like this one could have saved us time and energy in the early years as we worked to figure out my training, strategy, and seasonal planning.

I was 16 years old when I first met my coach René Wenzel, who had just accepted a position as the National Junior Coach at the United States Cycling Federation (USCF). I had had a terrible winter with injuries and sickness and came to René's spring camp very much out of shape. A lot of coaches with no predisposition and firsthand knowledge of me as an athlete would have written me off, or at least taken me out of the upcoming racing trip to Europe. However, René took a step back, looked at my results from the previous year, and then told me that I'd better lose some weight and get serious if I was interested in a future as a professional bicycle racer or in remaining with the National Team.

René's coaching style differs from other coaches in that he appreciates hard work and sacrifice, but at the same time he never forgets that he is dealing with human beings. He coaches with heart and always takes on each athlete's goals as his own. René feels as if he is part of his athletes, and he makes athletes feel that they make a difference. He was never afraid to tell us when or if we made mistakes. He never let anything slide, but at the same time he would reinforce our strengths and make us believe that we could be the best and nothing less.

Working with René, I won Junior National Road Championships (1991), the silver medal in the Team Time Trial Junior World Championships (1991), and several races while racing for Saturn which helped me make the leap to a level I professional team in Europe. As a Euro-based pro, I have managed wins in the Tour of Suisse, Tour of Luxembourg, and other events abroad. Recently I have managed to win the U.S. Professional Road Race Championship twice, and in 2002 I was second in both Milan-San Remo and Gent-Wevelgem. I intend to better both results with René's continued support.

René has now worked through all basic levels of the sport of bicycle racing—as a junior, track, and elite road racer for 22 years, as Denmark's first sport director for a professional team, and as a coach. He and his wife, Kendra Wenzel, now operate the successful cycling-specific coaching operation Wenzel Coaching.

The winning mentality that René instilled in me as a junior racer has helped me throughout my career. He and Kendra together have the mental muscle to give anybody the tools to find the driving force behind their own talents. I would encourage anybody interested in cycling to listen carefully when the Wenzels speak.

This book will get you on the right track, from choosing your first race to becoming a more knowledgeable fan of the sport.

Fred Rodriguez

Preface

There's nothing like pushing yourself to the limit on a bicycle: pounding up a long hill, hammering into an unrelenting headwind, or straining to break your personal best on a favorite loop. Anyone who has ever ridden a bike has felt the rush of going faster than ever before. But some dream of taking it a step further. Maybe you're one of the lucky few who long to push themselves, driving to the limit and crossing a finish line with hands raised, pumping the air in victory.

Road bike racing is one of the most storied, beautiful sports in the world. It's no surprise that the sport's most famous race—the Tour de France—was established by French journalists who wanted to create a spectacle newspaper readers could understand. After all, everyone rides bikes. And that's why anyone can be a bike racer. The daily routines of racing a bike are not much different from the youthful days of racing your Schwinn™ around the block, and the health benefits are the same. (You'll never be more fit in your life than you are the day of an important bike race.) But the best benefits are not physical—you'll revel in the sense of accomplishment and achievement that can come only from having a competitive goal. And you'll have a blast doing it.

The absolute best part about cycling is that anyone, with the right amount of determination and motivation, can succeed. Our sport does not limit based on body type, background, age, or ability. Some of the best professional cyclists are those with average talent who also have a fanatical love of cycling. It's a sport that draws you in, bit by bit, carefully opening your eyes to the thrill, the sense of accomplishment, the cool gadgets, and the camaraderie.

Becoming a cyclist is easy: you buy a bike, and you ride a lot. But if your ultimate goal is to become a road racer, learning a few basics will get you started right. Cycling rewards patience and careful planning—it's as much a sport to be learned as it is one to be practiced.

We won't lie—becoming a road racer is intimidating. If the jargon doesn't make your head spin, then the fast corners and bright, tight clothing will. Road racing is a sport with rich traditions and cultures, but it takes time to learn them. It also takes time to learn not only how exactly to be a road racer, but how to be a successful one.

As with anything else in life, a learning curve exists in road racing. Whereas most new racers struggle through, picking up tips here and there, making numerous mistakes along the way, this book can considerably shorten your learning curve. Following our tips and advice will keep you on the right path during your journey. And these tips are not just for new riders—you'll find yourself constantly reviewing the lessons as you progress as an athlete.

You may have picked up this book because you caught the cycling bug the very first time you rolled out the driveway, or perhaps you've been contemplating racing for a while now. You may even be a refugee to cycling from running or another higher-impact sport. Regardless of your experience, this book will guide you through the moment you consider your first race to after you cross the finish line and start the preparation for your next event.

Unique to this book is the how-to aspect for the beginning racer. We skip the true beginner cycling setup and assume that you have a certain level of riding proficiency. (For example, lengthy explanations of riding position are left to shops and professional bike fitters; the focus is instead on hand and body position and motion during racing and training. Things like basic traffic hand signaling are left out, while signals that would be useful to a racer in a pack-riding situation are included.) The focus is on racing and pack riding, and not just on basic riding. This book also contains more basic strategy information than any other road racing book available.

We've organized the lessons here with an introduction to the sport of cycling and the equipment and training that will take you to your first race. We'll roll you through a race from the night before to beyond the finish line. Finally, we've followed up with lessons about bike racing itself. We warn you, though: if you absorb the lessons of this book and enter your first bike race, you may become a lifetime road racer, a condition curable only by more racing.

Acknowledgments

Many people deserve recognition for their contributions to this project and for providing us with the experience to write a book like this. In fear of forgetting some, we have mentioned only the nearest and closest here, but we thank all those who have touched this book in some way.

Thanks first and foremost to Scott Saifer for writing the basis of several chapters and providing most of the physiological information for this book. Thanks to Ed McNeely at Human Kinetics for proposing the project and believing in us, and thanks to editor Julie Rhoda DaGiau for her attention to detail and countless back and forth e-mails. Thanks to John Foster for his writing and to Karen Bliss for proofreading numerous chapters. This book wouldn't be complete without the photos contributed by Dave Beede, Tony Halford, Jim Safford, and Susan Yost.

We thank our parents, Kathie and John Kneeland and Inga Olesen, for countless hours of babysitting and support; and finally, we thank late dad Wenzel Jorgensen for the foundation of much of the knowledge put forward in this book.

Part I

Getting Ready to Race

Preparation is the key to your successfully starting to race. The next few chapters will help you ensure that you are ready to race—you'll learn what you need to do to get your racing license, what types of racing are available to suit different strengths, how to set goals and choose your first race, and how to get the racing gear you need.

Chapter 1

The Individual Team Sport

When you enter a bike race, you join a long tradition of cycling in North America. Most riders don't realize that in the late 1890s and early 1900s bike racing was one of the top sports on the continent. Venues such as Madison Square Garden hosted indoor racing for thousands of fans, and weekly racing all over the United States drew spectators to crowded local racing tracks. During that time, the United States had several world champions, including one of the country's first black professional athletes, Marshall "Major" Taylor. It took the automobile, two World Wars, and fixed gambling races for cycling to lose its popularity. A century later, road racing is steadily growing once again, with more North American heroes than ever placing in the top races in Europe. Today, the lure of the grueling mountain stages of the Tour de France captures the imagination of most racers, with the idea of conquering Alpe d'Huez ahead of a pack of chasing racers as the ultimate dream.

You've probably picked up this book because you have your own dream of getting out on the road and competing in a bike race, but you may be worried about showing up to the line and being the only one who is maybe a little too "round" or riding a bike that is a little too old. But you need not be worried; you don't have to be super-fit to enter your first bike race, nor do you have to have the very best equipment. Everyone has to start somewhere in bike racing, and the sooner you start, the more quickly you will become even fitter.

Regardless of what fitness level you begin with, you will need to complete a few steps before entering your first race. This chapter

Photo courtesy of David Beede

Every professional rider can still recall her first time at the start line of a bike race.

outlines those steps and paves your entrance to the long, winding journey of bicycle road racing.

Getting a Racing License

The paperwork involved in bike racing can't be overlooked. You will need a racing license to present to a registration desk each time you enter a race. Racing licenses track the ability levels of competitors in a sport where numerous riders race together at once. They also help to ensure safety and fair racing so that beginners aren't up against seasoned pros.

The majority of road bike racing in the United States is overseen by the United States Cycling Federation (USCF), a branch of the national governing body, USA Cycling. USA Cycling is the organization responsible to the United States Olympic Committee for preparing and sending athletes to the Olympic Games and organizing the National Cycling Championships, as well as sanctioning most bike racing around the country, including professional, collegiate, and recreational racing. USA Cycling is also affiliated with the international governing body, the Union Cycliste Internationale (UCI), which regulates international cycling and sanctions the World

Cycling Championships, as well as the cycling portion of the Olympic Games. (Information about USA Cycling and other international cycling federations is included in the resources section, page 215.)

The USCF, through USA Cycling, is the main issuer of bike racing licenses in the United States. A one-year USA Cycling license for road racing costs $50 for an adult and $35 for a junior. (A mountain bike racing license can be added for an additional $25.) One-day licenses are available at a reduced cost of $5 for those who want to take a stab at racing without committing to the full year's license, but a full year's license is the way to go if you plan to race more than a few times. Purchasing a USCF/USA Cycling license affords you a "membership" that entitles you to some other perks, such as secondary medical insurance in case you crash in a race or organized training ride, discounted air travel and car rentals, as well as the federation's bimonthly magazine. You may also purchase bicycle insurance through USA Cycling. All riders age 10 and over are eligible for a racing license.

While the USCF sanctions most road racing throughout the United States, several smaller regional organizations around the United States cater to their local racing populations by sanctioning their own racing and issuing their own racing licenses. Whether you will need a USCF license, a regional federation license, or both depends on where you live and whether you plan to race outside of your home area. (More information about regional federations is in the resources section, page 215) Race flyers and advertisements usually denote which cycling federation is sanctioning the race. Obtaining a racing license through any of the bike racing associations is most often a simple process of filling out an application form, usually found in local bike shops or on the organization's Web site, and then sending in the annual fee.

If you are a U.S. resident planning to race outside of the States, you will need an international license (also available through USA Cycling). An international license also allows you to participate in any domestic event hosting an international field.

What Category Are You?

Your bicycle racing license includes the basic information a race organizer needs to make sure you are racing with riders of equal caliber. Most important, it shows the ability and age categories you qualify for (see table 1.1). USCF race categories go from beginners in category 5 to elite riders in category 1. Most riders talk about their

Table 1.1 USCF and United States PRO Categories

Women	Men	
Category 4	Category 5	New licensees
	Category 4	Novice riders in their first or second season
Category 3	Category 3	Intermediate riders with one to three years' experience
Category 2	Category 2	Advanced riders with several successful seasons of experience
Category 1	Category 1	National-caliber amateurs who often compete in the same races as professionals
Professional	Professional	Member of a UCI-registered trade team in the United States

Adapted from USA Cycling 2002

category by shortening the word *category;* a category 5 racer is a "cat 5," a category 2 racer is a "cat 2," and so on. Professional racers in the United States are required to take out a separate U.S. Professional Racing Organization (USPRO) license.

In men's racing, all new licensees ages 19 through 29 automatically begin as cat 5 racers, racing against other first-timers. Female beginners 19 through 29 start as cat 4 racers due to smaller overall numbers in women's racing. Riders 18 and under are junior racers, while riders 30 and older qualify as master racers. Most areas offer master racing only to riders ages 35 and above, even though the USCF offers a 30-plus category.

Juniors and masters are usually divided into age groups at most races, even though they will also have a category on their license. Junior racing is divided in two-year age groups, while master racing is divided into five-year age groups, although most will never race against a field made up of *only* their age group unless they are at a national championship race. For most other races, two or more age groups close together will be combined to make bigger fields. Stronger junior and master riders may also choose to race in the regular cat 1 to 5 racing designation when the race doesn't prohibit it.

Riders attending U.S. colleges and universities have an additional racing outlet available: the collegiate bike racing system. Bicycle racing is considered a club sport by most colleges and universities, allowing all riders—regardless of age or number of years in school—who are currently enrolled as full-time students to be eligible for their college team. Collegiate racing, overseen by USA Cycling through the National Collegiate Cycling Association (NCCA), is made up of 10 regional conferences and two divisions for larger and smaller schools. Regular intercollegiate events are scheduled throughout the year, in which schools race mostly for conference points. Riders entering bicycle racing through the collegiate system are also categorized according to ability and racing experience (table 1.2).

Table 1.2 USA Cycling Collegiate Racing Categories

Category D	New licensees
Category C	Novice riders in their first or second season
Category B	Intermediate riders with one to three years' experience
Category A	Advanced riders with several successful seasons of USCF, National Off-Road Bicycling Association, or NCCA experience

Adapted from USA Cycling 2002

Collegiate riders who already have USCF race experience can generally choose their collegiate category within the following limitations: All category 1 or 2 or pro riders must be category A riders, all category 3 riders must be at least category B riders, and category 4 riders must be at least category C riders.

Determining Your Racing Age

Just as all riders have a category listed on their license, each also has a "racing age" listed—the age he or she will be as of December 31 in the given year. While this is a relatively easy way of dividing age categories, it has both drawbacks and advantages for those riders born near the end of the year. For instance, a junior racer born in

January who is turning 15 this year will have the same racing age as a racer born in December who is turning 15 this year, giving the older rider almost a full year of growth ahead of the other. In the same way, a rider entering the master category at racing age 35 who is born in December will actually be racing most of the year at age 34, having a bit of an advantage in the opposite direction. Once you've raced long enough, you may find yourself giving your *racing* age to anyone who asks your age rather than your real age!

Race promoters may combine races for categories that are too small to make big enough racing fields. For instance, a race may have combined categories such as "women's open," "junior 15-18," or "master 35-plus." A larger field of riders is usually more fun to race with, makes for a better race, and is easier for the officials to keep track of on the course. However, the downside is that a beginning rider in the women's open race may find herself racing against cat 2 female riders. Although this happens less frequently as bicycle racing grows in popularity, it still can be frustrating for a beginning racer. When race fields are combined to make larger groups, the different category finishers may be combined into one race placing or picked separately, so that the race may have more than one winner and, in that way cater, to all categories participating.

Upgrading

All riders are eligible to upgrade their categories by earning upgrade points based on placings in races. When riders earn enough upgrade points to move up a category, they contact their USA Cycling regional representative and request the upgrade. (Visit www.usacycling.org for upgrade requirements and a USA Cycling regional representative listing.)

Joining a Club or Team

Worldwide, racing is mainly supported through the club system. Whether you live in Arkansas or Italy, the best way to become involved in racing is to join the racing team of a local bicycle club. Clubs provide an organizational and social structure to racing, holding club meetings, providing rides to races, and organizing races. Finding a club in your area is as easy as asking around at the nearest racing-oriented bike shop, asking other riders about their clubs, or surfing the Internet to find lists, contact numbers, or home pages of clubs near you.

There are many clubs in the United States, so look around to find one that supports beginning racers and welcomes you as a person. Clubs can be all-inclusive or focus on a particular section of racing, such as offroad, track, women's, master, or junior, for example. Some clubs have several teams within them. Teams may be even more focused, centering on groups such as police organizations, colleges, military branches, corporations, or other common interests. And if you still have a difficult time finding a team to fit into, it's only a matter of filling out paperwork and sending it along with a fee to your applicable cycling federation to create your own.

Clubs can also be a link to obtaining affordable race equipment and supplies through sponsorship agreements. Most organized clubs have at least an agreement with a local bike shop for a small discount on merchandise and even repairs. Some clubs have agreements with bike industry suppliers for you to purchase such items as tires, energy bars, eyewear, and other necessities at a discount.

Your club may be one that accommodates both racers and nonracers, or it may be a club that is made up of a racing team only. Regardless, take advantage of your team to find riders to train with, to learn from, and to travel with to races. Club members or teammates are the best avenue for discovering the local racing scene. And following their example is the best way to learn good training habits. Well-organized teams may even have a club coach to whom you can direct your training and racing questions. Ask questions and follow the most respected riders during rides, and most riders will be happy to share their experience with you.

Club rides are the backbone of club existence. Most clubs host at least a weekly club ride that meets in a consistent location and can serve as a social ride, endurance-building effort, or race simulation,

Technical Stuff

USA Cycling sanctions clubs and professional trade teams. Unless you are a professional rider racing for a registered trade team, USA Cycling will recognize your team as a club. If you don't register with a club, your racing license will list you as "unattached." Only riders belonging to clubs are allowed to have sponsorship, meaning that riders who are unattached must compete in race clothing that bears no sponsorship identification.

Photo courtesy of Susan Yost

Riders of all ages and abilities can benefit from participation in a supportive local cycling club.

depending on the time of season. Using these rides wisely can be a major part of your training and skill building for racing successfully. Some riders train all year long just to ride well during club rides. Rides also may familiarize you with the local bicycle racing scene and introduce you to local and national stars of the bicycling community. Regardless of what your goals are, you are bound to find a team or a club with group rides that suit you.

Club racing teams are identified by their identical uniforms, namely matching jerseys. Besides the social and training benefits, teams exist to benefit from group strategy. Using the elements of drafting and aerodynamics, riders can work together to save energy during races. Even two riders can take advantage of team tactics to work together. It may seem strange that a rider can actually assist another rider in a race without physically pushing or towing another. However, when riding in wind, for instance, it is advantageous to ride behind another rider to be shielded from the direct wind. Having a teammate let you into their draft rather than forcing you onto the windy side can make a world of difference for both riders, as you can trade off being in the front and therefore spend only half as much time fighting the wind. Later chapters explain in detail how to take advantage of drafting and teamwork during races.

Well-organized teams collect together before the race begins, warming up together or meeting to discuss the team's strategy for the race. The higher category of racers, the more important team strategy becomes. Most category 5 and 4 racers will have a difficult enough time just mastering racing skills and getting fit to compete without worrying about teamwork. But as a rider progresses, it's easy to see the value of working with teammates. While only one rider can actually win the race, nothing prevents teammates from sharing prizes and taking turns helping each other during races.

Understanding Road Racing Events

Understanding road racing is as important to a racer as owning a racing license or belonging to a club. Getting a grasp of the events of road racing will make you both a better rider and a better fan. Understanding the structure of road racing can also make breaking into the sport much less intimidating and can help you find races in your area that are suited to your talent and experience level.

Three main racing event types make up road racing: the *road race*, the *time trial*, and the *criterium*. Table 1.3 on page 11 gives typical distances and completion times for these events. Other events usually combine two or three of these main formats. We break down the three main types here along with the main event that combines them, *stage racing*.

Road races. While the term *road racing* encompasses all cycling events that take place on pavement, the road race itself is one mass-start event on challenging terrain over a set distance, usually from 10 miles to 150 miles (16 to 243 kilometers). The premise of the event is simple: The rider who crosses the finish line first wins. Riders compete directly against one another as teams and individuals, riding within close proximity for aerodynamic reasons and to keep an eye on each other strategically. (See also chapter 15.)

Time trials. The *time trial* is the simplest and most straightforward of all bike races. It's also the most individual. In a time trial, racers take off from a start line one at a time at intervals, racing over the course as quickly as possible against the clock. The rider with the fastest time

Table 1.3 Typical Race Distances and Approximate Times to Complete Them

Age group	Road race		Time trial		Criterium	
	Distance (miles/km)	Time (min)	Distance (miles/km)	Time (min)	Distance (miles/km)	Time (min)
Junior women 17-18	20-45/32-73	55-135	1-12/1.5-18	2-38	12-18/19-29	30-50
Junior men 17-18	20-75/32-121	55-180	1-15/1.5-25	1.5-57	12-25/19-40	30-75
Under-23 women*	25-65/40-105	75-180	1.5-25/2-40	3-60	15-25/24-40	35-75
Under-23 men	25-95/40-154	60-240	1.5-25/2-40	2.5-56	20-35/32-57	60-90
Cat 3-4 women	20-50/32-81	60-150	1.5-25/2-40	3-70	12-25/19-40	30-60
Cat 1-2 women	25-85/40-138	75-240	1.5-25/2-40	2.5-59	15-35/24-57	45-90
Cat 3-5 men	30-65/49-105	60-300	1.5-25/2-40	2-54	25-50/40-81	60-120
Cat 1-2 & pro men	40-150/49-243	90-390	1.5-35/2-60	2-53	25-60/40-97	60-120
Master women**	20-45/32-73	60-135	1-15/1.5-25	3-40	15-20/24-32	45-60
Master men**	20-55/32-89	60-165	1-15/1.5-25	3-37	15-25/24-40	45-75

These are only estimates and are for some of the most common race categories only. Race distances and times will vary according to terrain and conditions.

*Under-23 women are most often combined with category 1-4 women's races.

** Typical maximum miles for master racers depend on age group and field combinations.

wins. There is no drafting and no teamwork. It's only the rider versus the road and conditions—and how the other competitors fare by time on the same course. For that reason, the time trial is often called "the race of truth." A variation of the time trial is the *team time trial,* where each team of two or more riders covers the distance together using drafting and pacing against one another to try to beat the clock. (See also chapter 16.)

Criterium. The *criterium* (often called a *crit*) is the event of choice for speedsters and sprinters. Short courses .5 to 1 mile long (.8 to 1.6 kilometers) made up of turns, flat fast pavement, or short hills, descents, and other technical delights, make for fast laps and spectator-friendly racing. Criterium events are usually anywhere from 10 to 50 miles (16 to 80 kilometers). A typical race might be 30 laps on a .8-mile (1.3-kilometer) course for a total race of 24 miles (39 kilometers). (See also chapter 17.)

Stage race. People all over the world have heard of the Tour de France, but few outside of the race's fans really understand what it is. "Le Tour," as it is known in the racing world, is a multiday event made up of daily races; the finishing time for each racer each day is combined for an overall time to find the winner—the rider with the lowest cumulative time. Stage races are the all-around racer's paradise, combining all the elements of racing into one extended race. For example, a two-day weekend stage race might combine a road race one day, a time trial the next morning, and a criterium or hill climb in the afternoon. (See also chapter 18.)

The offerings in road racing are only a portion of the kinds of bicycle racing available. Many of the skills and rules learned on the road will also apply to mountain bike racing, cyclocross racing, and velodrome (track) racing and vice versa. Riders who don't find their particular talent on the road may find the twist of a related offroad event better suited to their abilities. These events can also provide good offseason training during parts of the year in which there aren't road races in your area. Learn more about racing on the dirt or on the velodrome with the suggested reading in the resources section of this book or by asking around at your local club or bike shop.

Chapter 2

Racing Equipment and Accessories

The sleekness and beauty of cycling equipment draw many cyclists to the sport. You aren't alone if you've ever gone to sleep with your new bike leaning against the wall of your bedroom the night before its maiden voyage, gazing at it by the moonlight coming through the window.

Magazines, bike shops, and the Internet all tout this frame or that set of wheels and tell you why you need the latest, greatest, lightest component if you want even a *chance* of ever winning a race. It's confusing, even for the experienced cyclist. The professional riders may have the best stuff, but they were fast enough to become pros even before they had their pro equipment. And some professionals may not even have the best equipment, riding whatever they are contracted to ride by their sponsors but getting results regardless.

Your bike and accessories are tools for a task—and when you think of them that way, buying bike equipment becomes much easier. Our advice: Buy the nicest possible equipment you can reasonably afford, but avoid going overboard. The returns on expensive equipment are quite low, and by buying more affordable equipment you can put more money toward traveling to more races, where the experience you gain contributes more to your improvement and success than any equipment you could buy.

Your Bike

Although a bicycle may seem like a single unit to the casual onlooker, racers usually look at it as having three main parts: the *frame and fork combination*, the *components*, and the *wheels*. The features of the frame and fork include the materials and the weight, the angles, and the finish. The components include all moving and nonmoving parts, from shifters and derailleurs to the brakes, handlebars, and seat post, for example. Finally, the spokes, hubs, rims, and tires make up the wheel combination.

The right combination of frame and fork, components, and wheels makes a good racing bike if it also is reasonably light, fits you well, and is dependable. If you check out your favorite European cycling magazine, you'll notice that many of the best teams ride light and strong but still plain old 32-spoked wheels in most races instead of wheels made from high-tech composite minimal tri or quad spokes. Some of the best pros in the world don't ride custom frames but rather stock frames from their sponsors.

The important part of the bike is you, the engine. Keeping that engine tuned and running strong means making sure the bike fits, is well maintained, suits your goals, and will hold up well over a season or more, if necessary. We cover general road racing and training equipment in this chapter. For specific equipment you'll need for time trialing, check out chapter 16.

Finding a Good Frame

There are three main avenues for finding a quality racing bike frame—at a local bike shop, through catalogs, or on the Internet.

The Internet is a fantastic resource for gaining knowledge about new and existing products, reviews, and pricing (the resources section on page 215 provides some suggested Web sites). Frequently, though, the knowledge is packaged in a way that is most useful to people who already know what they are looking for. Occasionally you can pick up a fantastic deal on a frame on the Internet. In the same way, you can find some great buys in catalogs. However, the same items can be found at a bike shop, which offers the added benefit of having people there to answer questions and owners to talk to if you later run into a problem with your purchase. You can also take a bike for a spin around the block and know without a doubt what you're getting. A good frame should last at least two seasons, barring any major crashes or traveling incidents.

Assess the Frame Materials

Although it isn't necessary to buy an *expensive* frame, it is necessary to buy a *nice* frame. Look for clean welds at the tubing joints and deep paint as well as more practical issues: Are there chips where the headset and bottom bracket meet the frame? (Missing paint might signify a frame that isn't built proportionally.) Do the wheels slide in and out of the dropouts smoothly and quickly? When you grab the brakes and rock the bike back and forth, does the fork flex no more than a centimeter or two?

Whether made of lightweight steel, aluminum, titanium, or carbon fiber, racing frames are made of high-tech materials these days and are lighter and stronger than ever. But if you check out photos of racers from the 1950s, you'll see that the actual frame design—its angles and shapes—hasn't changed much. The best frames combine tried-and-true design with the most tested new frame materials. The merits of various tubing materials aside, a little secret about bikes is that all different frame materials work equally well in racing and training for most riders. Some may be lighter, some may feel stiffer, and some may be longer lasting. But unless you are an extremely large or small racer needing an exceptionally strong or compact frame, the frame material choice is mainly an issue of personal preference. You won't lose a race because you were riding steel and someone else was riding aluminum, but you might lose a race if your bike doesn't fit you well.

Fork Specifics

Forks for most entry-level racing frames come standard with the chosen frame. You may have a choice of materials or paint, but for the most part, the shape and angling of the fork will be standard with the bike. A good fork is light but feels solid and rigid. Most shops are required to sell bikes these days with forks that have the feature (or nonfeature, depending on your point of view) called *lawyer lips*. Lawyer lips are edges added to the dropouts of the fork so that even if the quick-release mechanism on the wheel is slightly loose, the wheel has a difficult time falling out. These edges were added as bike manufacturers attempted to lessen their liability for improperly tightened quick-release levers. But the main effect they've had on racing equipment is to make wheel changes slower by requiring you to loosen the quick-release even more to clear the extra edge. Most racers file these edges off to speed up tire changes. If you choose to file off your fork's lawyer lips, have a qualified mechanic do the work for you.

Find a Fit You Like

Each company produces a line of progressively expensive and higher-quality frames (to a point), but the fit tends to be pretty consistent from model to model. If you are a rider with a relatively long torso, you may want to seek out a bike that is known to have a longer top tube. Riders with shorter torsos will seek the opposite. You also want to make sure that the bike has a seat tube length that provides decent stand-over height. Some bike manufacturers make frames only in even or odd sizes, so their frame sizing may jump a couple of centimeters at a time, leaving fewer options for riders between sizes. Most quality racing shops have a salesperson who can help you find a bike that fits. (See the fit section later in this chapter as well, pages 21-23.) Be wary of any salesperson who pressures you toward one bike or suggests a particular special part that "makes this bike the perfect setup for you." It may be that the shop is trying to clear the floor of a particular model or brand. Once you find a company whose bikes fit you, then it's time to start thinking about frame materials, components, and colors.

Proper bike fit and a good feel for handling the bike are advantageous in tense racing conditions

Photo courtesy of David Beede

Often new racers find out too late that the precise geometry of the frame can be important over many miles. The angles where the top tube meets the head tube and the seat tube are important to how a bicycle fits and how it rides, especially in corners. The range of angles on road bikes is quite small—71 to 78 degrees. The lower the number, the more laid back the frame—meaning the more the seat tube leans back, making the bike more relaxed and comfortable. The higher the number, the steeper and more aggressive the frame, meaning the bike is quick and responsive but more likely to transfer the shock of even small bumps in the road straight up to your hands and rear. A touring bike is usually around 71 degrees, while a custom bike built for a devout criterium specialist might be 75 or even 76 degrees.

Since most riders race both longer road races and criteriums, the goal in frame angle is balance. The most common angle, for both head and seat tube, is 73, with some bikes a bit different in either direction depending on the theories of a particular manufacturer.

Take a Test Ride

You can't determine whether a bike fits you until it has been adjusted for you and you've ridden it more than a few minutes. When you test ride, try to include some hills, sprints, and fast turns, because these are the challenges that really distinguish a good bike for you from a bad one. Feel for how much the bike flexes or doesn't flex, how confident you feel in the turns, and how the reach to the various handlebar positions feels.

Read magazines, bike company catalogs, and Web sites with an eye that discerns real information from hyperbole. The information from these sources will give you ideas about what you like and don't like and give you options to think over. The most important part of shopping for a bike will always be the test ride. If another racer near your size in your club has a bike that you really like, see whether you can borrow it for a day (with your saddle and pedal combination) and take it out for a real ride. There is always a little guesswork in finding the perfect frame, but doing your homework can help you avoid the headache of committing to a frame and then finding out it definitely won't work for you.

Choosing Your Components

The smaller components on your frame may be the most important parts. Derailleurs should be dependable and easy to tune. The choice of derailleurs by most racers is considered limited to the brands

Campagnolo and Shimano because they have been the lightest and most dependable over many years. Most racing derailleurs work with 9-speed rear cog sets, although Campagnolo offers a 10-cog rear derailleur that requires a special chain and a special wheel hub. The more cogs available, the wider the range of gearing available and the closer the gear ratios will be from gear to gear, making for smoother transitions and greater precision in the choice of gear at any given time. Be aware, however, that if you show up at races with 10-cog wheels, you should have 10-cog wheels in the follow vehicle in case of a flat tire. A 10-cog derailleur can accept a 9-cog wheel, but not as smoothly as a 10-cog wheel made for the setup.

Many riders buy both their derailleur and brakes in the same brand set, called a *grupo*. If you buy a quality derailleur grupo, the brakes that come with it are likely to be quality also. Before you buy, flip open the brake release on a model of the brakes you are considering and see whether you like the mechanism with which they open and close again. Is it easy to operate? Does it require little force to open and close? Test ride the setup and see how the reach is from your hand on the bar drops to your fingers on the brake lever. Riders with shorter fingers (such as many women and juniors) may want to look into brands that offer a version with a shorter reach to the brake lever. Give the brakes a squeeze to see how responsive they are, and check to see what kind of tension adjustment is available.

If the gear shifters are also part of the brake lever, try shifting them with your hands positioned on the brake hoods and in the drops. Can you shift comfortably while on flat terrain, on a hill, or while sprinting? Flubbing a gear shift on a climb or in a sprint can potentially cost you a race win. Make sure you can shift smoothly and comfortably; eventually you want to be able to shift without even thinking about it. Components such as brakes and derailleurs should last at least two to three seasons, barring a crash or travel crunch, as long as cables and pads are replaced as needed (see table 2.1).

While it's true that your bike is a tool for achieving your goals, all tools must be maintained. The best way to keep your bike in its best condition is to find a mechanic you trust and use her not only for skills, but for knowledge. If your bike needs a repair or regular maintenance and you don't feel 100 percent comfortable doing it yourself, take the bike to your favorite mechanic and ask whether you can watch while she performs the work.

Table 2.1	Routine Preventive Maintenance
Daily	Make sure tire pressure is between 90 and 120 PSI. Tighten brakes and adjust derailleurs as needed. Be attentive to unusual noises.
Weekly	Clean chain and gears thoroughly, then relube. Make sure wheels are true; feel for loose spokes. Inspect tires for cuts and wear.
Monthly	Check all nuts and bolts, and tighten as needed. Check headset, bottom bracket, and hub bearings adjustment. Check chain for stretching and wear.
Semiannually	Replace bearings in headset, bottom bracket, and hubs. Replace pedal cleats on shoes. Check frame, fork, and wheels for cracks and damage.
Yearly	Replace brake pads. Replace cables and housing. Remove all bolts and reinstall them with new grease.

Choosing Stems, Seats, and Handlebars

A stem that is light, strong, and easy to adjust makes your bike easier to handle and to dismantle for packing if you travel with it. A quality seat keeps you comfortable. The right bars fit your hands and are strong for the season to come. One trick for finding affordable quality racing equipment is to check out what the second- and third-tier pros ride, because what is on their bikes is reasonably affordable and will last through a season or two. When looking at the catalogs, compare the most expensive bars or stems to the second-most expensive. Fifteen grams lighter isn't going to make a difference in your race, but by saving 40 dollars you'll be able to afford one more weekend of racing.

Seats are similar, and the most expensive isn't always the best. Your local shop should have a big box of old seats for you to try. Once you find a shape you like, look for a new saddle with the same shape and with titanium rails. Titanium rails are best because they will last an entire season, and because the extra flex will keep you more comfortable on long rides. We could go on and on about saddle width, saddle shape, or whether to buy a saddle with a hole cut out in the middle. But all that matters is that you try a saddle before you buy it and that it's still comfortable after a couple weeks of consistent riding. Any saddle will be a little uncomfortable in the very beginning, but if after a week or so it still is, see whether your local shop will exchange it for you.

Above all, keep in mind that stems, seats, and handlebars are "safety" equipment, in that a breakage due to extreme lightness or lack of quality can cause crashes and therefore serious injury. Because of that, we recommend strength and solidity over design and lightness for these parts.

Choosing Wheels and Tires

When just starting out in the racing world, many racers use the same pair of wheels and tires for both racing and training. Once the racing bug has been caught, however, investing in a quality pair of racing wheels is one of the first solid steps a budding racer can take, equipment-wise, into the serious racing world. Having a separate pair of wheels for training and racing can help you prepare your racing routine and ensure safe, fast racing when it counts.

Training Wheels

Simply put, use simple wheels. For training, nothing works better than a 32- or 36-hole midrange hub, laced with straight-gauge spokes and brass nipples to a durable rim. If you build your training wheels right, they can be a fantastic value, because they will last many years. If you order training wheels through a catalog or Web site, be sure to have an experienced mechanic go over them to fine-tune the truing of each wheel.

The tires you train on should be "clincher" style with rubber tubes inside; these will save you dollars on the flat tires you will inevitably get during training. Also, it is relatively easy to change a tube of a clincher tire on the go, but if you're riding tubular tires (also called *sew-ups*), changes are messy, difficult, and relatively unsafe. Training tires should be wide and thick, and impervious to glass, thorns, and wear. You don't find those tires on the shelf in the shop showroom— you find them hanging on a hook in the back of the shop. They are cheap, and they last for thousands of miles. Save the showroom tires for your racing wheels.

Racing Wheels

More than any other piece of equipment, the wheels themselves can have massive effects on how you race. On a flat, fast, moderately windy day, a pair of aero wheels with a deep-dish rim can give you an extra mile per hour. On a course with a lot of crosswind, really deep section rims can become unrideable. On a hilly course, a lightweight pair of box-section tubulars will float you up a climb. An ideal bike racing stable would have both kinds of wheels, but for most people the cost of two such sets is prohibitive. If you have to choose, go with the most generally useful pair of wheels you can find. For most racers, this is the lightest wheel set you can find with a moderately deep rim.

Also, although the easiest tires for training are clinchers, clinchers can't quite compete with tubulars for quality race wheels. Racers have been arguing the merits of cornering with and riding clinchers versus tubulars since lighter and higher-quality clinchers have come into the market, but pros choose tubulars over clinchers every time for racing. The tubular rim, with its lack of a flange at the top, shaves a significant number of grams over a comparable clincher rim, and the higher profile of the tire itself gives a more comfortable ride with better traction. Tubulars are more expensive, but for racing, the lightness and performance in extreme conditions make them worth it. However, don't worry if you can't afford tubular race wheels in your first years of racing. The majority of beginning racers race on clincher tires. You can always build your racing equipment stable bit by bit as you get more serious about the sport.

Achieving Proper Fit

We often hear about a bike's fit—that's frame fit, crank length, and cleat position on the shoe, as well as proper adjustment of the seat and stem—and how the difference between a good fit and a bad fit can make all the difference in the world. How, though? Why is it so important for a bicycle to fit a certain way?

It's simple: you'll ride on it for hours at a time, so it had better be comfortable. Plus, you aren't just cruising along. You need to be able to keep pushing hard in a low, aerodynamic position without any distracting discomforts (see figure 2.1, a and b).

You'll know your bike fits properly when these three simple rules are met:

1. Your back is relatively flat. In all positions—upright, on the hoods, and in the drops—your back is at a variety of angles. Most riders have a certain small amount of "hump" in the back, but a good fit minimizes it. If you have a major hump

© Human Kinetics

a   b

Figure 2.1 Hands on the brake hoods *(a)* is a comfortable and responsive position. Hands in the drops *(b)* gives extra stability, power, and aerodynamic advantage during fast racing.

in any part of your back while in any of those riding positions, your stem length and height are probably off. The best place to start is to put a flat dowel or level on your seat so that the tip is directly over your stem. If the height is right, most men will have about 4 to 6 inches (10 to 15 centimeters) between the dowel and the stem, and most female or smaller male riders will have 3 to 4 inches (7 to 11 centimeters). Another good rule of thumb involves determining the distance between the nose of your saddle and the end of your stem. That measurement should be roughly the same distance as that from the center of your bottom bracket to the top of your seat tube. The seat itself should be nearly level so that when you are riding you feel balanced in it and are not sliding off either the front or the back.

2. Your neck and lower back and all other parts of your body should be free of pain and strain during normal riding. If your reach is too long, you feel stretched in the backs of your arms and perhaps across the middle of your back. If your reach is too short, the pain will center on the back of your neck and the tops of your shoulders. If you cannot comfortably ride in the drops, you may need to raise the bars temporarily to practice stretching enough that you can eventually get lower.

3. When your leg is fully extended, you should have a slight bend in the knee. Some cyclists aim for a full extension, but that's begging for trouble. As we ride longer and longer on any given

day, our muscles fatigue and tighten. A bike with a seat that is too high can cause a lot of strain—and possibly injury—to those tight muscles and tendons, especially the hamstrings and back of the knee. Conversely, if your saddle is too low, it puts a different strain on your knees, but one that is even more insidious. When your knee is not allowed to extend enough, the cartilage crunches together thousands of times an hour. Our legs are designed to extend while at work; you have to give them a chance to do so.

Doing a rough check of the saddle height on your bike is easy. Simply sit on the bike in your cycling shoes and shorts. Make sure one crank arm is all the way down (at a 90-degree angle to the floor), and allow that leg to dangle toward your pedal. Your leg should feel stretched out, and your foot should just graze the top of the pedal. To test this, try pedaling the crank backward a rotation. If the height is right, the middle of your foot should be able to stay on the pedal with just enough hold that it won't fall off the top of the pedal at the bottom of the stroke while you sit straight and balanced on your seat and avoid leaning or reaching to either side. Raise or lower your seat to reflect this proper leg extension. Once you reach the proper height and you click your foot into the pedal as usual, you should feel that you are able to apply power to the pedals in every part of the pedal stroke—without bouncing, shifting your rear back and forth, or feeling as though the up-and-down motion of your legs is interfering with your breathing or steering of the bike.

Of course, this kind of fitting is only a starting point, a system based on experience in eyeballing correct position. Today there are several good scientific systems that can be explored online or at your favorite bicycle shop. However your fit is done, be patient. It takes time to get used to a new position, and even though it may feel strange and awkward at first, that does not mean that it is not correct—or at least better than before!

Other Gear

In addition to the bike and its components, the following items are mandatory for anyone training to race.

- *A small bag that fits behind your saddle.* It should include a patch kit, two spare tubes, three tire levers, and a five-dollar bill. (The money can be used between your tire and tube if you get a big cut, or it can buy a snack to get you out of a bonk.) In addition, it's a good idea to carry a small multitool that includes a variety of Allen wrenches and a chain tool. If you train on sew-up tires, you will also need to carry a whole spare tire.

- *A pump.* There are two basic kinds of portable pumps. One is called a *frame pump,* and it fits under your top tube. These pumps are the most effective for moving large amounts of air in a small amount of time. The other kind is called a *mini-pump,* and it can be attached to almost any part of your bike or carried in your jersey pocket. These pumps don't move as much air, but some do almost as well as a regular frame pump.

- *Water bottles and water bottle cages.* Your shop should have a wide variety of cages, but skip the very cheap and the very light. Buy something sturdy that holds your bottles well so that they don't fly out when you cross railroad tracks. Be sure you buy more than two bottles. Eventually you will reach a point when you'll have enough water bottles to fill a small house—that's because you can never have enough. You might also consider a backpack hydration system. While some road racers look down their noses at these devices as being strictly for mountain bikers or tourists, hydration packs are the most effective way to carry large amounts of water if you don't have a place to stop and refill during a ride or a person to hand you bottles during a race.

- *A bike computer and heart rate monitor.* These two tools may be the most important additional pieces of equipment you will use as a bike racer. Neither needs to be fancy or expensive; they just have to work well and be set up properly. A computer should have an easy-to-read screen and at least three main functions: speed, trip distance, and trip time. The heart rate monitor can be even simpler—the only function you truly need is heart rate. If you decide to spend more money on a heart rate monitor, however, look for one with the ability to program different heart rate zones such that the monitor records the time that you spend in those zones. Also look for the ability to download saved information from your monitor to a personal computer. This allows you to compare workouts or e-mail information to your coach.

- *Rollers or an indoor trainer.* Inevitably the weather will make it impossible (or crazy) to ride outdoors. No one gets fast by skipping workouts, so having the option of bringing your ride inside assures a stable training schedule. It doesn't have to be fancy—in fact, some of the best models are very simple and durable.

Another item that advanced racers mention is a wattage monitor. These devices are installed in place of a usual piece of your drive train (the hub, a link of your chain, or the cranks) and measure how many watts you churn out. This is a useful training tool, however, these devices can cost from $700 to much more if you add in the software to analyze all the information. The information they give is simple, but difficult for the inexperienced to apply. If you decide to purchase one of these monitors, consider hiring a coach who can teach you the best ways to use it effectively.

Clothing

Cycling clothing takes a great deal of abuse from sun, sweat, and repeated washings. If there are only two pairs of shorts in your closet and you're training seriously, you'll wear the shorts out in half a season. That's fine if you're willing to let the Lycra wear down to the point where your buddies riding behind you can see things they will wish they had not. (Cycling shorts are *always* worn without underwear to minimize the risk of chafing.) Otherwise, pick up a few more pairs.

The basics of what you need are simple:

- Several short-sleeved jerseys with back pockets
- Several pairs of riding shorts
- A pair of arm warmers
- A pair of leg warmers or tights
- A windproof vest that easily fits into a jersey pocket
- A windproof jacket
- A good pair of cycling shoes
- A pair of cycling gloves
- A tight-fitting pair of sunglasses
- A comfortable helmet

There is more you may want, of course, but these basics are your staples, the items you can't live without.

Always race with gloves. Crashing your bike and injuring any part of your body hurts, but until you braze or cut your hands you won't realize how much you depend on them.

The fit of your clothing is almost as important as the fit of your bike, and for the same reasons: if they don't fit well, you're going to have some painful physical problems. A jersey that is too big might seem fine in the shop, but after three hours of a banana causing your pockets to sink below the saddle, you'll be ready to turn that jersey into a cleaning rag. A helmet that is too tight will eventually give you a headache, and a helmet that is too loose will be useless in a crash as it slips off your head on impact.

Buy the tightest clothing you can that is comfortable and doesn't bind. This applies to shorts, jerseys, vests, jackets, shoes, gloves, and helmets. The repetitive movement of riding a bike makes skin very susceptible to chafing and discomfort, but well-fitted clothing minimizes that risk. Try it on, and if it feels like your normal clothing (or

Photo courtesy of Susan Yost

Always race with a light wool or synthetic short-sleeved undershirt to help keep your body temperature even and to protect your skin in the event of a crash.

hat or shoes), try on a smaller size. Just remember that while tight is fine, uncomfortably tight is not.

The secret of successful winter riding is simply to wear good clothing. Your winter clothing wardrobe doesn't require too much more than the basics already discussed. First, find a warm hat that fits easily under your helmet. Next, find a long-sleeved undershirt made of wool or a synthetic wicking material. Add a long-sleeved jersey that covers your neck and wrists even when you are in a riding position, a pair of thermal tights to go over your shorts, and thick full-fingered gloves and polypropylene covers for your shoes. Combine all of them with the basic jacket and vest, and you should be enough to ride in the most miserable conditions. Just *think* warm.

If the temperature outside is below 75 degrees Fahrenheit (24 Celsius), both legs and arms should be covered. Though it may seem convenient to wear shorts on the bottom and a jersey and arm warmers on top if it's slightly chilly, remember that you need to protect your knees; they take the brunt of the work on the bike. If it's cold enough for arm warmers, it's cold enough for leg warmers.

Chapter 3

Am I Ready to Race?

You've been riding a few months on a racing bike and you're asking yourself, *Am I ready to race?* The answer depends on your goals. If you just want to see what it would be like to enter a race, go for it—you are ready right now. If you're not so sure you are ready or if being competitive is one of your reasons for racing, this chapter will help you. It provides some tests to take and questions to answer to determine whether you're likely to have a good experience in your first race.

You don't have to be super-fit to enter your first race. However, you should be strong enough and skilled enough to participate in the race and not simply be left behind in the first miles. The fun of bike racing comes from riding with the other racers, so racing is much more enjoyable if you can keep up. After reading this chapter, if you feel that you and your bike are ready, you can test your strength and skills by entering a race. If you feel fit but are uncomfortable with pack riding, a local time trial is a good place to start.

Most racers have somewhat loftier goals than to simply *enter* and *finish* a race. They want to get top placings or win races. They want to earn prizes, adulation, and respect. They want to be on a winning team. Some, whether they admit it outwardly or not, want to be on the covers of newspapers and magazines. There is necessarily a long delay between doing your first novice race and becoming a famous and respected racer. Even if you have the natural ability, it takes between two and five years of racing to become a national-class racer. Becoming a successful racer means accepting that delay but also committing to moving forward along the path to your ultimate goals.

Determine Your Goals

To achieve a goal you must commit to it and to an outline of the steps that will get you there. Goals are typically divided into three categories: *long-term, progressive,* and *short-term.* We add a fourth category we call the *shoot-the-moon goals,* because everyone should dream.

So how do you figure out what your racing career goals should be? First, recognize that if you've not raced bikes before, becoming a professional cyclist is a shoot-the-moon goal. There are tens of thousands of licensed bike racers in the United States and hundreds of thousands in the world, most of whom would love to be paid to race bikes and a fair fraction of whom know how to train; and yet there are only a few dozen American riders making their living from road racing and less than several thousand in the entire world. The only way to find out whether you are going to be one of them is to start training and racing and see what happens.

Photo by Jim & Mary Whitmer

Keeping up with the main racing pack throughout a race is a common beginning goal.

Reaching one's potential in cycling typically takes 5 to 10 years of cumulative training. Male professional cyclists tend to peak in their late 20s and early 30s and retire a few years later. Male pros over 40 are a rarity. Women seem to peak a few years later, with some of the world's best riders in their early 30s. For older riders, these facts may provide a reality check on professional cycling aspirations. Fortunately, cyclists of all ages may aspire to national- and world-class amateur competitions.

Keep in mind as you form your goals to keep them positive. Rather than thinking in the negative (*I hope I don't get dropped this weekend*), phrase your goal in a way that motivates you to stay with the pack. For instance, for an entire month your goal might be to stay in the top 10 positions of the second chase group in a local race or training ride. Once you achieve this goal, you might upgrade to staying with the first chase group.

Shoot-the-Moon Goals

Many beginning racers have dreams of winning the Olympics, the Tour de France, or junior or master nationals. At the same time, most racers know that this not a realistic goal for their first season. Your shoot-the-moon goal is the dream goal that keeps you motivated. It's the most outlandishly wonderful outcome to your cycling career that you can imagine. You don't have to know that you are going to get there, only that it would be really cool if you did. The shoot-the-moon goal helps you identify with your heroes. It may or may not be realistic, but the only way to find out is to try. You will find that the obstacles and successes that you experience while trying is part of the satisfaction of bike racing.

Long-Term Goals

Long-term goals are achievements that you want to reach within one to five years and that you are pretty sure you can achieve. They may be part of the progression toward your shoot-the-moon goal, or they may be completely independent. These are goals you share with your coach and your cycling buddies, goals they can help you work toward.

Your long-term goals might be as simple as *I want to upgrade to category 2;* as optimistic as *I want to win a medal in my age group at some point;* as specific as *I want to win the master 40 to 45 national road race championships in the year I turn 40;* as egocentric as *I want to be the strongest rider in my club;* or as hopeful as *I want to be riding when I'm 90 years old.* Your goals should mean something to *you,* and they should be both specific and measurable.

Your long-term goals will probably change many times in your first years of racing. As you get stronger and learn more about riding you'll have a better sense of what your realistic possibilities are. The important thing is to have a goal you are working toward that guides you in determining short-term goals. If you don't have long-term goals, it's very difficult to stay motivated and to know whether your training is having the desired effect.

Progressive Milestones

Once you know your long-term goals, you can start to figure out the intermediate milestones that you have to pass in training and racing to get there. These are your progressive goals. When you have progressive goals and a timetable for reaching them, you can test your training plan. Are you making the progress you expect? Common progressive goals for a rider who wants to win the master 40 to 45 national road racing championships, for instance, might be completing a series of extensive training periods, hanging with the front group of the training ride consistently, or being able to squat a certain amount of weight.

Within a few years of starting racing, you will have a sense of how successful you can be on your local scene. For most riders, the first few years of racing are a constant challenge with few extrinsic rewards. However, if you have the right attitude, facing and overcoming those challenges can be extremely satisfying. Each race is an opportunity to test yourself. Each race provides you with a new sequence of progressive goals.

If you expect to win all your races, you're likely to be disappointed. Many riders have this as their only goal because they don't know what else they could aspire to. However, the following checklist provides some other possible progressive goals for a novice road racer who wishes to become an experienced bike racer.

1. Enter a race.
2. Finish a race.
3. Finish a race with the main pack.
4. Finish a race with the leaders.
5. Participate in the sprint or breakaway.
6. Place in the sprint or stay away in a breakaway.

7. Place top three in the sprint or win solo.
8. Upgrade to cat 4 (men) or cat 3 (women).
9. Go back to step 2 and repeat through to step 7.
10. Upgrade to cat 3 (men) or cat 2 (women).

Some people, perhaps because of natural talent or because of a background in other sports, will move through this whole list in a year or less, while others will find it takes several years of work. Others may find that due to a lack of available time, lack of a good plan, or just plain bad luck, this novice racer's checklist is impossible to complete.

Short-Term Stepping-Stones

What do you intend to do each day and week to get to your progressive goals? These daily steps constitute your short-term goals. For example, if you are preparing to race your first race, your short-term goals may include getting a racing license, subscribing to a cycling paper that has a calendar of events, finding the local event calendar on the Internet, getting your bike-fit checked by an expert, finding a mentor or coach, making a training plan, and increasing training volume.

All coaches emphasize the importance of having a goal or goals for each day's training. A training plan (which we explain further in chapters 5 through 7) is just a list of goals for each day or week for the coming months. When you have a goal for the day's training, you can stay on track toward your progressive and long-term goals. When you don't have short-term goals, you just ride. Sometimes "just riding" makes you stronger, and sometimes it makes you weaker. Often "just riding" results in doing a lot of what you are already good at and not doing much to improve what needs improvement.

Identify Your Strengths
and Areas for Improvement

To make the most rapid progress as a bike racer, you need to learn the basics and make efficient use of your training time. What don't you know? What aspects of your cycling do you most need to improve? What are your strengths, and, just as important, what are your weaknesses? Do you need to improve some things to allow you to safely enjoy your first race, or can addressing these weaknesses wait? What kind of terrain do you enjoy riding? Are there plenty of races available to you on that kind of terrain, or do you need to broaden your repertoire to find races that suit you?

It's possible to learn a lot about your weaknesses by entering bike races or doing weekend group training rides. Then have a more experienced rider or a coach validate your responses to the following assessment questions.

- Do you always move backward compared to other riders in a sprint? Maybe you need to improve your acceleration or top speed.
- Do you get dropped late in long rides and races? Maybe you need to build your endurance.
- Do you get dropped on straight descents? Maybe you need to improve your tuck or get faster wheels.
- Do you have trouble accelerating out of corners to stay with the pack in criteriums? Maybe you need to improve your short-term power. Or maybe not. Maybe you need to do less work

© Sport The Library

One of the best ways to identify your strengths and weaknesses is to simply try a few races. A time trial is a non-intimidating way to start racing.

Find a Mentor or a Coach

To accelerate your progress through the ranks of bike racing, find a mentor racer and hire a coach. A mentor is someone who has been racing a few years more than you and can give you most of the advice you'll need to get through your first races.

A coach is someone who has studied bike racing and can listen to you, watch you, and deliver the advice you need when you need it saving you the trouble, time, and frustration of figuring things out on your own. Unlike your mentor, who knows what worked for him, an experienced coach can bring together the experiences of dozens or even hundreds of racers and extract the information that will be most valuable to you.

USA Cycling licenses coaches in the United States. Unfortunately, the level of experience and knowledge required to get the various levels of coaching licenses is minimal, so we recommend that you don't choose a coach based only on the level of the coaching license.

We recommend finding a coach by word of mouth and interviewing several candidates. Different coaches have different styles and approaches, some of which may work better for you than others. Don't be awed by the coach of a successful racer. You want to know that the potential coach will take the time to get to know and support you as well as provide you with a proven training program.

early so you'll be stronger for the sprint, or eat and drink more, or draft better to conserve energy in long races. Or maybe you need to practice cornering until you can put the brakes on less than other racers instead of more.

Are You Ready to Race?

Certain minimal levels of fitness, technical preparation, and skill are needed to make your first racing experience safe and enjoyable. Here are some questions and tests to use to find out whether you are ready.

❑ **Is my bike up to it?** As you learned in chapter 2, you don't need an expensive or fancy bike, but it does need to be safe. Do the brakes work well? Are the wheels true? Do the tires hold air? Does it stay in gear? Is it race legal (no aerobars, no forward-directed bar ends)? Is it free of rattles and loose parts?

❑ **Is my basic endurance adequate?** To enjoy a bike race, you need to be able to hold a decent pace for the length of the race. Since you'll want to do some warm-up and not finish the event completely exhausted, you should be able to easily ride one hour longer than the time you expect to spend racing. The length of many criteriums is given in minutes; for road races you can assume that men's cat 5s will average around 15 to 22 miles per hour (24 to 36 kilometers per hour). Women's 4s, beginning masters, and beginning juniors are just a couple of miles per hour slower.

❑ **Is my high-end endurance adequate?** To really be a participant in a bike race, you need not only to be able to do the distance, you need to be able to respond to changes in the speed of the pack. Can you go really hard for a few minutes, rest, and then go just as fast again? When you can go hard for a total of about 20 minutes in short segments during one ride, you've got adequate high-end endurance for your first race.

❑ **Am I fit enough?** That is, can you ride fast enough without going hard to keep up with the pack? There are so many variables that the only way to answer this question is to do a race. You can do your own time trial test to get some hints. We're not saying that if you can pass this test, you can keep up in a race; but if you can't pass this test, you're very unlikely to be able to keep up. Of course, you don't have to keep up to enjoy racing, but it helps.

Time trial test instructions: Find a 2-mile relatively flat stretch of two-way road with no stoplights or stop signs. Ride out and back (you have to go both ways to cancel the effects of the wind). Males ages 18 to 45 should be able to do the 4-mile ride in under 15 minutes without breathing hard before their first race. Males over 45 and females 18 to 45 should be able to do it under 18 minutes. It's rare that older women get age category races, so they pretty much need to be able to match the younger women. Riders under age 18 should not worry about this test.

❑ **Am I comfortable on the bike and a good enough bike handler?** Here are some riding skills checks. Passing these checks doesn't mean that you can ride safely in a group, but failing them means that you can't.

- *Can I ride in a straight line?* Try to ride on the white stripe at the side of the road. When you can keep your front tire in a 6-inch- (25-centimeter-) wide band for a few hundred yards or meters while looking ahead, you can ride straight enough.

- *Can I look over my shoulder without swerving?* Try checking behind you while riding on the white stripe. After a moment, turn to face forward again. Are you still within a handlebar's width of the white stripe?

- *Can I take a flat 90-degree corner at 20 MPH (32 KPH) without braking?* (See chapter 13 for information on cornering.)

- *Can I pedal through a flat corner at 18 MPH (29 KPH)?*

- *Can I negotiate an entire race course, riding alone without anxiety about crashing?* If you are worried about crashing you can't enjoy the riding or ride safely in a group.

❑ **Am I comfortable enough moving around in a pack?** In a race, you may be in front of other riders, behind them, next to them, or even between them. You need to be comfortable in all these situations at race pace. The best way to test this is to go riding with a club ride. Many club rides are essentially little races with no entry fee and no prizes, so they're actually a great way to experience the feel of racing without the pressure of formal competition. When you are comfortable on group rides with riders in your race category, you are ready to try a training race.

❑ **Am I emotionally prepared for whatever happens?** Thinking positively, it's possible that you may win your first race. That, of course, would make you happy and proud. However, even athletes who have been successful in other sports are often humbled by their first bike race. You might finish far back in the pack or even off the back. Will you still be a tolerable companion to your friends and family? Will you avoid moping and snapping at the people around you, and instead regroup to prepare yourself for a better performance next time around?

When you can answer *yes* to all these questions, you are ready to try your first race. If you are answering *yes* to some and *no* to others, or all *nos*, the *no* questions are your progressive goals to get to your goal of entering your first race. Make a plan to meet them. Once they are met, race. Good luck!

Chapter 4

Choosing Your First Race

You have the bike, the racing license is on its way, and you are beginning to shape your goals. Now what? It's time to find a bike race.

Over the past 10 years, the number of resources for finding cycling events all over the world has grown tremendously. While racers once had to find race flyers on the local bike shop bulletin board, now a simple search on the Internet can turn up several regional race options for a single weekend. Many races offer their own Web site, where everything from course directions to online registration may be included. For those who do their fact-finding away from the Internet, most races post their race flyer in the window of the local shops, and many regions in North America have monthly printed newsletters that advertise races, offer advice, and include classified advertisements to buy and sell racing equipment. (See page 215 for racing resources.)

In looking over any race flyer, take into account several pieces of information to determine whether a race is right for you. Consider the following questions.

What type of race is it? Most races are road races, time trials, or criteriums. Often racers attempt a time trial first so that they won't have to ride in the immediate vicinity of other racers or worry about tactics other than choosing a pace. However, don't limit yourself if you aspire to get in the mix with other riders and test your legs in a pack. Review the self-assessment checklist in chapter 3 (pages 34 to 36) to see whether you are ready to race with a pack.

Is your category offered? If you've found a race type that appeals to you, check that the event offers a race for your category. As mentioned in chapter 1, many races may combine categories. As a beginning racer, you will most likely prefer racing only with other beginning category 4 or category 5 racers. (This isn't as important if you are doing a time trial.)

Is it close to home? Driving three hours to arrive in time for an 8 A.M. race start, especially without knowing what to expect at your first race, can be an exercise in frustration. If possible, choose a first race that is within an hour of your home. Sitting in a car for hours can deaden even the best-trained muscles. Your legs will thank you for the shorter drive once the starting gun fires.

Is the race distance appropriate for your fitness? Choose a race that is a length you've ridden recently. For instance, if you have been training consistently for an hour or so most days during the week and manage a two- to three-hour ride on the weekend, a 35-mile (57-kilometer) race will probably fit into your plan. If you haven't been able to fit in longer rides, start with a shorter race. Remember, however, that the shorter the race, the faster the field of riders will cover the distance!

What is the terrain of the race? Choose a first race that suits your strengths and preferences as a rider. You have probably noticed during group rides that you are better at some aspects of riding than others. Perhaps you beat others climbing hills but get left behind in the sprints. Or maybe you are towing the ride for miles at a time during the flat, windy sections and are competitive in the sprints but begging for mercy on the climbs. Choosing a first race that favors your strengths, whether they are climbing, sprinting, or extended high-end riding (like that used in time trialing), can help you find a first race experience that is going to be the most gratifying and encouraging.

What do others think of the course? Ask around to find out what other riders have to say about the course (if it has been used in previous years) as well as what they think about the promotion of the race itself. Is the event well organized? Is the course free of unusually dangerous obstacles, rough pavement, or sharp corners? How many years has the race existed?

Your choice of race may be nearly limitless or restricted, depending on the number of racers in your area and the amount of racing going on. In some areas, you may have no choice but to drive that three hours to your first race simply because there are no other races offering the kind of race you want. Take the chance anyway—it won't be your last three-hour drive for a race!

Registering

Once you choose your race, you need to register for it. The registration process is usually fairly self-explanatory. The race organizer has you fill out a form with your racing license number, category, address, and club name (at minimum), and you have to sign a liability release. Registration can usually be done in advance or on the day of the race. If you wait until race-day, however, you risk that the field may already have reached its limit, leaving you at the race venue with nothing to do but go train as usual.

Waiting to register until the day of the race often costs more because most promoters tack on a race-day registration fee of $5 to $10 to encourage riders to register in advance. Preregistering lets the promoter know ahead of time how many racers are interested in the race and may keep beginner fields from being combined with other categories due to lack of numbers. Preregistering may also save you from standing in a long line at the registration table on race day— your name will already be on the start list, and all the promoter needs to do is hand you your race number.

Preparing for the Race

The following chapters cover the preparation for race day that begins long before the start line—training, skills, and race tactics. For now, we cover the immediate preparation for a race the night before as well as what you can expect on a typical race day.

Cycling absolutely requires advanced planning for every race. Training is only half of the race preparation you need. All the best training in the world will do little to save you if your chain is skipping gears or your race shoes are sitting at home in the garage.

Packing

The night before any race, pack all race clothing, warm-up clothing, cool-down clothing, and postrace clothing into an organized race bag so that you can find clothes the next day as you need them and aren't rushing around in the morning, potentially delaying your departure

Why Racers Shave Their Legs

If you have been doing group rides, you've probably noticed that the majority of bike racers have smooth legs. This goes for the men as well as the women. Most people in the Western world are accustomed to seeing women with shaved legs. However, if you are a man, you've probably never considered shaving your legs before. Should you start now?

Leg shaving is not required by any racing rule. It is completely your choice. Most bike racers shave their legs for two reasons. First, they believe that having smooth legs makes cleaning wounds easier after a crash. Second, having shaved legs makes massage more efficient. While both of these reasons are valid, neither concern is usually enough to make most riders shave.

Not many riders will admit it, but most shave to fit in. Road bike racing is a tightly knit community, and leg shaving is just part of its culture. After several years of racing, many riders can identify other cyclists outside of their cycling clothing just by seeing them in regular walking shorts because their shaved legs and "biker tan" give them away. At best, riders who don't shave their legs are the recipients of frequent good-natured teasing. At worst, riders who don't shave may be automatically labeled as not being committed to the sport by those who take it a little too seriously.

The final reason that a man may continue shaving his legs is that once his girlfriend or wife gets used to the sight of his hairless legs, she will often encourage him to keep shaving! Muscles honed over many miles on the bike can be an intimidating and impressive sight. As more than one American male has remarked, "Chicks dig shaved legs."

from home. Remember, too, to pack more than you think you may need; it's always better to have that extra pair of leg warmers or long-fingered gloves if you need them. Set prepared food and drinks in the refrigerator and leave a note to yourself where you'll see it, or place the cooler in front of the door so that you won't forget these items in the morning. Your night-before and prerace meal and drinks should be thought out in advance. (See chapter 8 for complete information on eating during and around races.) Your bike should be waiting in the garage, cleaned, checked over, and ready to go. Table 4.1 provides a sample race-day gear checklist of the essentials you'll want to be sure you've packed.

Table 4.1 Gear Checklist

Clothing (head to toe)

- helmet and headband
- glasses (dark and clear lenses)
- jerseys: 2 short-sleeved, 1 long-sleeved
- undervest or -shirt
- jackets: warm-up, rain, and wind
- arm warmers and leg warmers
- fingerless gloves
- shorts: 2 pair
- skinsuit (if time trial or criterium)
- socks: 2 pair
- riding shoes

Additionally for cold weather

- warm headband or hat for under helmet
- cap with brim for under helmet (if rain)
- neck warmer or bandana
- long-sleeved undershirt
- knee warmers, knickers, or tights
- booties
- long-fingered gloves

Equipment

- bike
- wheels: race set and spare set
- pumps: floor and frame (or CO_2 cartridges to use if you flat during warm-up or cool-down away from the race start)
- rollers or a trainer
- tool kit, chain lube, and rags
- Spare inner-tube or pre-glued tubular tire (with long stem if you have deep-section rims)

Miscellaneous

- racing license and release form (pre-signed by parent if junior racer)
- money and cell phone
- race flyer, directions, and map
- race number and safety pins
- sticky labels or tape for spare wheels
- paper and permanent pen

Pre- and postrace prep kit

- towels: 1 for face, 1 for clean-up
- soap, chamois cream, sunscreen, lip balm
- embrocation for cold or rain
- petroleum jelly or baby oil for rain
- water/alcohol mix in spray dispenser for clean-up
- jug of water for clean-up
- plastic trash bags for wet clothing
- roll of paper towels
- toilet paper

First aid kit with usual supplies plus

- inhaler or other personal medication
- surgical scrub brushes
- gauze wrap and pads
- Tegaderm or other wet dressing
- fishnet dressing retainer
- antibiotic ointment
- cotton swabs
- triangular bandage for potential sling
- saline eye solution

Postrace clothing

- dry shirt, underwear, socks, and pants
- extra (nonriding) jacket or sweatshirt for keeping warm. Even if it's hot out, air-conditioned restaurants may be too cold.
- hat (cap or warm hat for cold weather)
- shoes or sandals

Fuel

- prerace drink mix
- race food: more bars, gels, bananas, or other food than you think you will need
- water bottles: 2 per bike plus at least 1 for prerace, 1 for postrace drink. Carry extra in pockets if you don't have a feeder.
- large water container for drinking

No matter where or how you travel for a race, make sure that your racing license and shoes are the first things you pack. Before you leave for a race, double-check that they're with you. It's a good idea to keep a photocopy of your racing license in the glove compartment of your car at all times. There is nothing as frustrating as traveling to the start of a race to find that you can't race because you left your license at home! Likewise, you can usually get away with borrowing a bike, a helmet, and clothing at a race, but it is nearly impossible to find another rider who wears the same shoe as you and has her cleats positioned the same way. Borrowing another rider's shoes is a bad idea, risking injury to your ankles or knees.

Knowing How to Get There

Find out how long it will take to drive to the race start, and tack on an extra half-hour in case you get lost. Have a map in the car even if you think you are sure of where you are headed.

Knowing the approximate travel distance and the time it will take you to get to the start, time your departure from home to arrive at the race location at least an hour and a half before the start of your race (see table 4.2 for what you will need to do during that hour and a half). Better-organized races have signs and volunteers leading you to the start, while for smaller races you may just have to watch for riders warming up, barricades, and other telltale signs that a race is in progress. Try to park as close to the registration and start areas as possible because it helps to be close to your vehicle to drop off clothing before the race start or retrieve last-minute items. Look to

Table 4.2 Prerace Checklist

☐ Register

☐ Last-hour nutrition

☐ Warm up and stretch

☐ Final preparation: shed or add clothing, top off bottles, touch up sunscreen

☐ Use the restroom as many times as necessary

☐ Get to the start staging area in good time for a first-row starting position, if possible see where other racers are parked, and keep a lookout for shaded or sheltered parking for hot or rainy days.

Checking In

Once you arrive at the start, locate the registration desk (even if you have preregistered for the race), find the appropriate registration line for your category, and get officially registered or checked in as quickly as possible. Bring your racing license, even if you have preregistered.

When you leave the registration table, you will have your race number(s) and possibly race swag (such as a T-shirt) and information. The race may have each rider wearing between one and four numbers, including a number for the bike frame. Be sure to ask at the registration table on which side of your body and in what position the race numbers are required to be pinned.

Pinning Race Numbers

The actual pinning of the number is an art form, passed through the years from racer to racer, that can spark debate between even the most senior riders. In general, racing numbers are pinned on with safety pins in either of two positions—Euro or American style (figure 4.1, a and b).

© Human Kinetics

a   b

Figure 4.1   Check with race officials to find out the required number positioning. Standard European *(a)* and American *(b)* style pinning are shown here.

You'll want to pin on your race number as aerodynamically as possible in the position designated by the race. One way to ensure that a number that doesn't flap in the wind is to ignore the four corner holes. Instead, pin through the number at the side of one corner and work the pin through the fabric of your race jersey and then back through the number about a centimeter apart so that the number is held tight to the fabric once you close the pin. It may take up to eight pins in a single number to make it as form fitting as possible. Make sure your undershirt or bib shorts aren't pinned along with the jersey. It's stressful—and kind of funny—to wait in line at the bathroom only to discover minutes before your race that your number is pinned through your undershirt to your bib shorts!

The best idea is to have an experienced racer pin your jersey for you while you lean forward in the position you hold on your bike. Some riders prefer to crush the number in the palm of their hand and then flatten it out again before pinning it. Others feel that leaving the number smooth is more aerodynamic. Race officials usually prefer that your number is uncrunched, making it easier to read from a finish line video camera, so be sure to ask around before you crunch your number. Officials will also want your number to be completely visible, with no folding that obscures the number. This may be a problem for some women or smaller riders who simply don't have enough back or shoulder space to display the whole of the number. In that case, some overlapping or folding may be permitted.

> If you don't have anyone to pin your number on you, spread your jersey on the hood of your vehicle and try to pin your number as flat as possible. If you are able to register the night before the race and you have your number at home or in a hotel room, stuff a pillow into your jersey and then pin your number on.

Bigger, better-organized races may also require a frame number fastened to the frame with zip ties through holes in the number plate and around the bike's top tube and head tube. Once the number is tight on the frame, clip the ends of the zip ties to lessen the chance of scratching your legs. Small riders (usually those with 52-centimeter or smaller frames) may need to attach the number underneath the rear of the seat using the seat rails and seat post.

Fueling Up

About an hour before the race starts, top off your food and water tanks. Have your race bottles for your bike in place and your race food (if you will be using any) in the pockets of your jersey. Slightly unwrap any hard-to-open energy bars and be sure you can reach into your pockets without being obstructed by the number pins. Depending on when you had breakfast or other prerace food, you may want to eat something small, drink an energy drink, or consume race food within an hour of your race. In general, if the race is longer than an hour, you will need to carry race food with you (see chapter 8).

Warming Up

Once you have your food taken care of, move on to your race warm-up and stretching routine. In general, the shorter the race, the more warm-up you need, and vice versa. The shorter a race, the harder the riders go from the start—thus the more warmed-up your muscles need to be to avoid injury. A longer ride, on the other hand, allows you more time to get warmed up as the race moves along. Your warm-up also depends on the terrain you will face early in the race.

For a beginning racer, a good warm-up is usually between 20 and 60 minutes and includes a gradual building of intensity along with efforts at race pace and then a short cool-down. Warm-ups for shorter races include additional intensive efforts. While a warm-up on the road gives you a truer sense of how you are feeling before the race starts, allowing you to help plan your race strategy accordingly, you can do this warm-up on a trainer or rollers if the traffic, terrain, or weather is not conducive to an effective warm-up. Stretch either before or after your warm-up. Most riders do some stretching before and then do a more extensive stretching routine when their main warm-up is complete.

Once you are feeling warmed up, return to your vehicle or other preparation area to shed warm-up clothing, top off your bottles, touch up sunscreen, add or subtract layers of race clothing, and mentally prepare for the start. Go over your race plan in your head and psych yourself up for the start of your race, but also relax so that you don't become overly nervous.

Many riders make sure that visiting the restroom is the final thing they do before heading to the staging area. Nerves may have you standing in the restroom line as many as five times before the start of a race. Don't ever assume that it can wait until after the race. Nine times out of ten, you'll find out in the middle of the race that it won't wait.

What if you have to go to the bathroom during the race? This can be simple or complicated, based on how fast the race is going, where you are racing, and how urgently you have to go. First, if the race is moving slowly enough in the opening miles where you think you can stop on the side of the road, ask around to see whether anyone else needs to go. You never know—there may be 20 other riders dying to go, too, but afraid to suggest it. It is always better to have others to help chase back to the pack. Make sure that any follow vehicle understands that you are just stopping to relieve yourself so that no one comes dashing out of the car carrying wheels to you as you are dropping your shorts! Find a place in a ditch or near a tree, if possible, and away from homes or businesses. During races in populated areas, you may just be out of luck when it comes to "going" on the bike. There are a few male riders who are able to pee on the bike off the back of the pack while another rider pushes them. Some riders can even talk themselves into peeing through their shorts on the bike. However, we don't really recommend it unless you are in the winning break of a championship road race and absolutely don't have a choice.

Getting to the Start Line

Most races call riders to the line a few minutes before the start of a race. Riders begin to collect around the entrances to the course closest to the start line even before the previous race is finished. Hang out near enough to the starting area or staging area that you have a good shot at being one of the riders right on the start line. While it's not imperative that you be right in the first row, it does help to get good position in the race once the gun goes off. The riders who look to be only a few meters ahead of you on the line may have a half-block advantage on you after several turns slow down the rear of the pack.

On the line, the main race official gives last-minute instructions before sending the race on its way. Pay attention because last-minute course changes or hazards are announced at that time. Other than the specialized start of a time trial (covered in chapter 16), most mass start races have you starting with one foot on the ground and one foot clipped into your pedal. You'll need to master the skill of taking off quickly, clipping into your pedal, and getting under way smoothly— all with other riders immediately around you doing the same thing.

Photo courtesy of Susan Yost

Staying relaxed during your first races will help you remain focused on the task of keeping up.

As you stand at the start line, there will always be someone in the race who looks faster and fitter, who is wearing nicer clothing and riding a nicer bike than you. Don't be intimidated. Looks can be deceiving. What counts is how you make the pedals go around when you arrive at the hardest parts of the course—or, in racing lingo, "when the hammer goes down."

After the Race

What happens inside the race is covered extensively in chapters 10 through 18. For now, we'll skip directly to the end of the race. Once you cross the finish line and catch your breath, get to your vehicle or race base to gather immediate postrace fuel and water and put on or remove clothing. On cold days, get out of wet clothing immediately and bundle on warm, dry clothing. On hot days, get out of sweaty, salty clothing and into something cool. Once your clothing is squared away, proceed to your cool-down. A proper race cool-down is just as important as a warm-up. Usually an easy ride of 10 to 30 minutes where you are just spinning the pedals lightly is a sufficient cool-down.

While you are cooling down, keep an eye and an ear out for the announcement or posting of the race results. Once the official race results are posted, a 15-minute period follows in which riders may protest a disputed race result. If you think you may have placed in the race, be sure to stay near the start/finish area during your cool-down or even cool down on a trainer or rollers as you await the posting of the race results.

Finally, once the race results are finalized and you've collected any prizes you've won, you may want to watch other races. In that case, be sure to bring a lawn chair with you so that you can stay off your feet and maximize your recovery. Remember that the moment your race ends, your recovery begins in preparation for your next race.

Once you pack up to head home, make sure you clear the area around your vehicle or race base of litter. There's nothing more disappointing than losing a race venue due to the carelessness of racers littering energy bar wrappers on the side of the road.

Part II
Training for Performance

Training to race means having a program that conditions your body for the specific endurance, speed, and power aspects of bike racing. Your plan should build your fitness gradually over the course of the season to ensure that you are in peak form for your most important races. The next few chapters describe how to plan this training; they include workouts as well as ways to fuel the workouts with proper nutrition and balance them with rest.

Chapter 5

Training Basics

Many racers go to their first race with dreams of riding away from the pack but instead find themselves off the back of the group, or at least not up front where they expected to be. Some decide at this point that they were never meant to be racers, that maybe it's not in their genes. They end up thinking that they're not as fast as they had previously imagined—and they are right, at least at that moment.

What these racers who get discouraged and quit after just a few races don't realize is that while there are genetically faster people and slower people, the difference between being trained and being untrained is much bigger than the difference between being talented and untalented. You won't know how good a bike racer you can be until you have trained for several years. This chapter and chapters 6 and 7 focus on ways to specifically train the body for bike racing performance, while chapters 8 and 9 focus on caring for the body so it can go on training.

Benefits of Training

Physiologists measure two quantities when guessing an athlete's potential as a cyclist. The first is $\dot{V}O_2max$, the maximal amount of oxygen the working muscles can use during hard exercise. Think of it as the size of the athlete's aerobic engine. $\dot{V}O_2max$ is determined primarily by the heart's size and ability to pump blood, not by the lungs or the legs. The upper limit of $\dot{V}O_2max$ is genetically determined for each athlete. $\dot{V}O_2max$ increases rapidly when you begin training regularly and levels off within a few months as you near your genetic limit. After that it can continue to rise gradually for several years, but the bulk of improvement relates to other physiological and tactical variables that improve more quickly with training.

Typically the difference in $\dot{V}O_2$max between sedentary and trained individuals is about 25 percent. This huge difference is why anyone who becomes a little bit active can ride away from just about anyone who has never ridden.

Exercising muscles produce and consume lactic acid constantly. At low exercise intensity, the muscles can use that lactic acid as fuel. As intensity increases, the muscles produce lactic acid more rapidly than they can use it up; the concentration of lactic acid in the muscles increases, and lactic acid leaks into the bloodstream.

This leads to the second variable that physiologists measure: the power an athlete produces at the *lactate threshold* (sometimes also called the *anaerobic* or *ventilatory threshold*), the intensity of exercise above which lactic acid begins to accumulate in the blood. The lactate threshold represents the highest power you can generate steadily for long-duration exercise. This is also the best laboratory predictor of racing success. The power you produce at your lactate threshold determines how fast you can ride on level ground for a long distance. The ratio of this power to your body weight determines how fast you can ride uphill. While $\dot{V}O_2$max can be improved only a little beyond a point that is reached after a few months of serious training, the power you are able to produce at lactate threshold can continue to increase dramatically for several years with good training. This is why it is so important for potential racers not to get discouraged if they are not immediately successful. We've seen many athletes go from routinely falling off the back to routinely getting top 10 finishes after a couple of years of good training.

Even after your power produced at threshold has plateaued, efficiency and good use of tactics can continue to improve your results. Only after several years of riding and racing will you know how good a racer you're going to be.

Make a Periodized Plan

The most important thing about any training plan is simply to *have one*. The chances of achieving your potential as a cyclist are greatly enhanced if you take the time to plan out how to reach your potential.

Chapter 3 guided you in setting your cycling goals. But how are you going to get there? How much do you have to ride this month, this year, or in the next few years to reach your chosen goals? Will

Photo © Tony Halford

The type of training you do on group rides depends on the training phase you are in.

you do the same training every month, or will you do certain kinds of training at certain times of the year? What races do you need to attend? What body weight do you need to achieve? If you don't think these things out and plan for them, they probably won't happen.

There is no one-size-fits-all training plan. The perfect plan for your buddy or your hero could be a disaster for you. Your plan needs to be individualized to your available time, your goals, your heart rate limits, and your current condition. A beginning racer who tries to do a professional-level training plan will burn out within a few weeks and could get injured. A rider who increases training gradually may someday be able to handle that same professional plan and may even become a pro racer.

Even if you have infinite time available for training, you can maximize your progress by making good use of that time. The best way to optimize your training time is to *periodize* your training—that is, break your training within a year into phases or periods. A yearly training plan is typically divided into four general phases:

Base phase: This consists of 8 to 12 weeks of endurance work (see chapter 6).

Transition to intensity phase: After the base phase, the transition to intensity phase involves 8 weeks of gradual buildup to race-pace intensity (see chapter 7).

Racing phase: Following the transition to high-intensity intervals, the next 26 to 33 weeks make up the racing phase. Beginning racers should expect to ride and race well for 12 to 16 weeks once they commence racing. The racing phase includes a series of racing periods interspersed with rest weeks and rebuilding weeks.

Rest phase: Following the racing phase, the rest phase includes 3 to 6 weeks of very easy training or no training at all.

The phase you start with when you organize your training depends on the time of year relative to your racing season, your current fitness, and your goals. You've probably picked up this book because the racing season is near (or here) and you want to give it a try. If that's the case, you may want to jump straight into the period of the year that contains the racing itself. If you've been doing a lot of riding, this may work for you. If not, go back to the beginning of base development, or at least to the transition phase.

Base Training Phase

The base period is two to three months of endurance riding, cross-training, and perhaps some weightlifting. You'll gradually build up your fitness by adding one hour or 10 percent per week to your training time until you hit your maximum weekly hours near the end of this period. You may spend a few days per week cross-training with some aerobic activity other than cycling, but beginning riders especially benefit most from getting on the bike, whether indoors or out.

Endurance training makes you faster at any given level of exertion and lays a foundation for later higher levels of exertion. Going harder than endurance pace during this phase prevents you from developing aerobic power, which is the goal of the base phase. One of the most valuable training tactics for long-term development is to use a heart monitor during this period and set a strict upper limit of 80 percent of your maximum heart rate for all rides for two or three months.

Transition to Intensity Phase

The transition to intensity phase is only two months long and includes a variety of interval training sessions, starting with longer moderate intervals in the first month and continuing with shorter high-intensity intervals in the final weeks before racing starts (see chapter 7 for interval instructions). Do intervals one or two days per week (and not more) for a maximum of two months. Devote the other days to continuing endurance and strength training.

Racing Phase

A beginning racer might do 5 to 20 races in a single racing season in alternating periods of racing and training. In time, a top amateur racer may race as many as 100 times per year. The primary training focus during this period is riding at race-pace intensity and recovering from that intensity to progress in your racing. During the racing season, aim for one or two very hard or race days per week and one longer endurance ride to maintain your base endurance. If you are not racing in a given week, substitute a personal time trial or a session of high-intensity intervals for a race. Devote the other days in the racing season to recovering from the last race and resting up for the next one. When you have several weeks together in which you are not racing, devote some extra energy to adding a longer endurance ride each week.

Reserve one of the lower-intensity days for developing a skill such as cornering, sprinting, or descending. There's not a lot of sitting on the couch during racing season, but most of the rides between weekend races are short and in the endurance and recovery intensity zones. If you have weaknesses to work on that require high-intensity training, such as climbing or time trialing, the best time to work on them is on race day after the race so you have a full week to recover before your next race.

A common error among beginning racers is doing too much hard training in the form of intervals or group rides mixed in with racing. The result is never being fresh on race day and never racing up to one's potential. An ideal racing season schedule has no more than two days per week at harder than endurance pace. If you won't be racing every week, do at least one hard club ride weekly to continue getting used to speed and to riding in the pack.

Rest Phase

After a race season comes a period of rest. The rest phase is just that: a period of three to six weeks during which you don't think about training. This rest is just as much for refreshing your mental state as it is for resting your body. Many riders suffer from a Puritan work ethic and a deadly fear of losing fitness. Our riders perform much better later into the season when they take a full rest period before the season starts. By the end of the season, many riders have become so accustomed to being a little tired all the time that they have forgotten what it means to feel good. They have become so used to little aches and pains that they don't know that another couple of weeks of rest might actually let them clear up.

What should you do during a rest period? As little as you like, but no more than one exercise session every other day, nothing over a couple of hours, no exercise above the endurance level of effort, and nothing that feels like training. You can play other sports and hike. In other words, have fun being active, but stay off the bike. You'll be back on the bike once you start your base phase again.

Understand Training Intensities

The goal of training is to cause certain physiological adaptations to occur in your muscles, blood, blood vessels, heart, and brain that enable your body to ride faster for longer while using less energy—that is, more efficiently. You achieve certain adaptations by training at specific intensities to bring about these changes.

Two common and effective ways of determining the intensity of training are by feel (perceived exertion) and by heart rate. Recently, tracking intensity by power has also been gaining popularity. The effect of training on the body depends on the intensity and duration of the effort, but not on how that effort is measured.

You can glean some interesting and potentially useful information from power meters, but since the price of dependable power meters puts them out of reach for most racers, we don't advocate using them in the first year of racing. We do strongly recommend using a heart rate monitor to help you gauge intensity, along with constantly monitoring perceived exertion—judging intensity by how the effort feels. Even the most scientific training programs don't ignore a rider's perceived exertion.

To create a scientific, heart rate-based training plan, you'll need to know your maximum heart rate and anaerobic threshold heart rate. Identifying each of these isn't a magical process reserved only for elite racers. Most large universities (health sciences or exercise physiology departments) and some health clubs administer fitness tests and help with training prescriptions for all levels of athletes.

Call around to find one that will administer bicycle-based maximum heart rate and anaerobic threshold tests. The typical cost for a testing session is $100 to $200 for both tests. The tests are hard training sessions in themselves, so schedule them to work with the rest of your training plan and vice versa. A good test must allow you to make a maximal effort. Some tests designed for sedentary individuals try to predict maximum and anaerobic threshold heart rates from a small effort, so be sure you are getting the right test before you sign up.

The common formula for determining maximum heart rate, subtracting your age from 220, is often off by as much as 20 beats per minute in either direction, so it's best to have your maximum heart rate tested before you use a heart rate monitor in training. Anaerobic threshold also varies from person to person and changes with training as well.

Using percentages of your maximum heart rate (HRmax) and perceived exertion, we group training intensities into six specific zones.

Active rest (< 60% HRmax): Gentle riding, swimming, or walking with little or no resistance

Recovery (60-70% HRmax): Easy cruising with very mild resistance; singing is possible (this zone and the next provide great aerobic benefit with little fatigue)

Endurance (70-80% HRmax): Some effort, cruising at a speed that allows you to comfortably finish a long session; talking is possible (this zone and previous zones are used all year)

Moderate intensity (75-85% HRmax but at least eight beats below anaerobic threshold, no heavy breathing): A pace that you can maintain for a long time; hurts only a little and breathing is only slightly raised (used mostly one to two months before the start of racing)

High intensity (anaerobic threshold HR ± five beats): Breathing is deep but controlled; the hardest pace you can maintain for more than a few minutes (used mostly in the last month before the start of racing)

All-out (HR may be high or low, depending on the length of the effort): A pace you can sustain for only a few seconds or minutes (used only during racing season)

Training in each zone has specific effects on the body. For example, training in the endurance zone (see chapter 6) makes you more efficient aerobically, helping you go faster at any given heart rate and any perceived level of exertion. Endurance training, also called base training, is the foundation of all cycling fitness. The benefits of endurance training continue to accrue for years and you can benefit from this training throughout the year.

Unlike endurance training, which continually makes you stronger and faster for as long as you do it, training in the higher intensity zones causes rapid improvement that soon plateaus and results in deep fatigue if overdone. Therefore, train in the harder zones only in the final months before the beginning of the racing season. The same training that is appropriate in the middle of the racing season is not appropriate at the end of the season or in the middle of the off-season.

Set a Realistic Schedule

Your training plan needs to be something that you can stick to for the long haul. An unrealistic program is as useless as no program. So the first thing to consider is how much time you can allow for training and still take care of your other responsibilities. How much flexibility in your schedule do you need to allow for work, school, a job, or family? There's at least an hour of dressing, showering, changing, and eating with each training session. Trying to squeeze too much riding into a busy life will not make you as strong a rider as will an appropriate balance of rest and training.

Include in your training enough of the right kinds of work at the right times that if you stick to it you will reach your goals. How much must you to train to achieve your goals? You probably need to train about as much as other racers in your category. The minimum training to prepare for racing is 4 to 5 months of 8 to 12 hours of riding per week for masters, juniors, and beginning senior men and women. Even devoting this minimum time can allow you to make good progress if you follow a good training plan (Olympic- and professional-level athletes train closer to 20 to 30 hours per week). If you are already riding the appropriate amount for your category, good for you—keep it up! If not, build up gradually; add up to an hour or 10 percent per week to your current training time. Table 5.1 shows a typical goal-based season plan.

Table 5.1 Typical Goal-Based Season Plan

Goals

Shoot-the-moon goal: Win world championship medal

Long-term goal: Compete in national championship

First season's goals: Race full season; upgrade to category 4; good performance at state championship, June 22

Parameters

Racing starts: April 5

Last available race: September 15

Season overview

November: Base/endurance building and weight training. Potentially race cyclocross once every two to three weeks for fun and skill building.

December: Base/endurance building and weight training.

January: Base/endurance building and weight training, move toward more bike-specific training and less cross-training. Peak weekly volume of base training is reached.

February: Begin moderate-intensity training, continue base/endurance building and weight training.

March: Begin high-intensity training in preparation for racing. Continue base/endurance training. Move toward light maintenance weight training. Include some kind of warm weather training camp to top off base and get in some intensity outside of normal routine.

April: Begin racing, continue intensity training once per week outside of racing, depending on recovery and energy level. Continue endurance training once per week. Focus on race recovery and continuing to build intensity.

May: In-season racing. Focus on race recovery and preparation for each weekend's racing. Do some racing in both May and early June that matches the kind of racing found on the championship course.

June: In-season racing and peak for championship race. Train and race in early part of month and then taper for state championship.

July: Potential one week mid-season break. Potential base/endurance rebuilding. In-season racing, focusing on recovering and preparing for each weekend's racing.

August: In-season racing. Focus on recovering and preparing for each weekend's racing. Enjoy weekday twilight racing.

September: Wind down or end race season, depending on racing region and races available. Potentially begin end-of-season break.

October: End-of-season break. Easy exercise, rest, focus on other activities than cycling. End of month: begin weight-training adaptation and ease into winter training.

Be realistic not only about your available time but also your body's ability to recover and benefit from the training. Do not include too much work too soon while skimping on recovery. This leads to early burnout and may cause you not to stick to the plan. Consistency in training over many months or years determines your success—not the peak miles you can hit in any one month.

Stick to your training plan long enough to figure out what works for you. Then modify and improve it for later months and seasons. Don't change the plan every time a friend or favorite magazine tells you about a new exercise. There are new drills every year. You must do something consistently if you want to know whether it works for you.

A few lucky athletes have the natural talent to compete on fewer hours of training than most others. You'll have to experiment to find what works for you. If you can be satisfied with your racing results on three or five hours per week of training, there's no need to train more. Note that when we talk about hours needed we're referring to hours of aerobic activity, including riding, racing, and cross-training. Of course most of your training should be on the bike. Plan your available training time by breaking down your weekly schedule into half-hour blocks of time, figuring in everything from work to training to sleep. While this may strike you as overstructuring, finding an extra half-hour during the day or even just an extra hour over the week to contribute to training time can make a difference in your improvement.

Most everyone these days has a life that's already packed with work, school, family, or other commitments. If you have a busy life, you face extra challenges in making your training plan. To get racing fit, you need to consistently ride at least four days per week. Here are some tips that might help you get the hours you need.

- In the few months before the start of racing, at least one day per week ride as long as your longest race plus one hour.
- Break up your training time on the other days by doing a morning and an evening session.
- Commute by bike to get more training time; you'd have to be on the road anyway.
- Get an indoor trainer and ride at home when it's dark out. Or get a lighting system for your bike and train in the dark.

No matter how hectic your life is, you're going to be competing against folks who somehow found the time to train. The less time you have to train, the more important it is to make good use of that time.

Include Rest in Your Training Plan

Training does not make you stronger, it makes you weaker. Think about it. When was the last time you got home from a training session feeling stronger and faster than when you started? The recovery and rebuilding that occurs during rest after good training is what makes you stronger and faster.

Too much training without enough rest, or too much hard training, can make you slower. This is called *overreaching*. A little bit of overreaching can be corrected with a few days' rest. An extended slump of performance caused by many weeks of too much training or not enough rest is called *overtraining*. Recovery from overtraining can take months or years.

If it were true that "practice makes perfect," we could all just ride our bikes whenever and however we liked and we'd get better and better until we were perfect. In fact, practice makes *habits*. Good practice makes good habits, and bad practice makes bad habits. If you are training and you get tired enough that you are riding slowly even while you ride hard, you are practicing to ride slowly. Trying to build up distance too quickly or when you are not ready for it does not help you get faster. Bag a training session if you are so fatigued that you are no longer riding strongly.

If you feel tired or have trouble getting your heart rate up in training, take an easy day. If you are slower than usual or your legs are sore, take an easy day. If you feel you might be getting sick, take an easy day. If you've been training consistently and you suddenly have a bad day, you are not out of shape, but you may be tired or getting sick. The worst thing you can do when you're tired is more hard training. Just take a few easy days and return to the plan when your body is rested and ready.

Sudden weight loss or gain of more than a few pounds (more than a kilo), constant hunger, sore muscles, loss of enthusiasm, grumpiness, insomnia or constant fatigue, difficulty raising the heart rate in training, and raised resting heart rate are all signs of overreaching. If you have more than one of these symptoms for more than a few days, take a break.

How many consecutive training days and how much rest an athlete needs must be determined individually. A general rule is to take at least one day completely off every 10 days of training. It's common to take a day off once per week. Many books suggest you take one week easy every four or five weeks. If you pay attention to how you are feeling on a daily basis and take a rest day before you get really tired, you probably won't need that whole easy week each month. As a result, you can have more good training days and faster progress. While you are making your training plan, you don't know everything that's going to happen to you over the coming months and years. Don't be a slave to the piece of paper, no matter how much work you put into developing it. Pay attention to your body's needs, and be ready to change the program when you are unusually tired or energetic.

While sitting at a desk is not training, it's not always recovery, either. If your job or family life is stressful, you probably need more recovery time than another athlete with a simpler life. This may be another reason why older athletes seem to need more rest than younger ones. If your life tends to be nonstop, schedule your downtime and stick to it as religiously as you stick to your training plans. You may need as much as one day off for each three days of training. If you can't handle three consecutive days of training, you should probably examine your desire to race or make adjustments in your life to allow for better training and recovery.

Keep Track of Your Training

Maintain a training log or diary that records your daily workouts and other related information. If you have a diary, you can look back to see what you were doing and how you felt just before you overreached, and you can use this information to help you adjust your training plan for later months or seasons. (See table 5.2.) You can also look back to see what you did in the weeks before particularly good periods of training or racing so you can try to repeat those actions. The most important benefit of keeping a log is that while you are writing in it each day you may spot patterns that call for early attention before things go wrong. Write down everything that seems relevant about your training each day. Include the ride time,

Table 5.2 Information to Include in a Training Log

General info	Additional daily info
Goals	Weight
Annual training plan outline	Resting pulse
Training zones	Standing pulse
	Energy level
Daily info	Mood
Date	Nutrition level
General health	Stress level
Workout type (ride, race, weight training, cross training)	Weather
Workout time (also compiled weekly)	Workout rating
	Maximum heart rate
Ride mileage (also compiled weekly)	Average heart rate
	Average cadence
Workout intensity	Average wattage
Race (if race day) description and placing	Maximum wattage
	Wattage readings during interval

intensity, and how you felt. Also record any strength training or other cross-training that you do. Other information that might be useful includes weather conditions, route, partners, food and drink consumed, morning weight, morning heart rate, hours of sleep, and other stresses of the day. Each of these will be more relevant to some athletes than others.

Plan and record your training by *time*, not by mileage. The reason for this is simple: The benefit of riding 10 miles per hour for an hour into a headwind is about the same as or maybe greater than riding 25 miles per hour for an hour with a tailwind. Your body doesn't know the difference. In addition, 25 miles one day can be quite different from 25 miles another day on the same course but with different weather and wind conditions. It is important to plan and record not only the time but also the intensity of your training.

Check Your Progress

As you follow your training plan, you'll want to know whether it is working. Of course the ultimate test of your training is your racing results. You may not, however, want to wait through all the months of training to find out whether you are making progress. In the meantime, you can visit the test lab or test yourself by revisiting a standard course once a month. Checking your progress in this way does not all have to be done at maximal effort levels. Rather, find out how long it takes you to climb a certain hill or complete a certain loop at an endurance pace. What is your speed on the trainer or rollers at a given heart rate? If your training is going well, you should be getting faster at the same effort level. Improvement is fast at first and then more gradual, so don't test more frequently than once a month. And keep in mind that training well when you're fresh and resting when you're tired makes you stronger and faster; testing, no matter how fancy or expensive the battery of tests, won't make you any faster. Checking your progress every so often helps you adjust your training and may help you keep up your motivation as you see the progress you have made.

Ride With a Group

Training with other people is vital to your development of drafting and pack-riding skills. Without these skills, you can never be a skilled racer. With them, you can win races against other riders who are stronger but less skilled than you.

Group rides may also seem like a natural place to test yourself. Many group rides tend to degenerate into informal races, however. You will likely need to be careful about including group rides in your training plan. Judge the pace of group rides for yourself. One person's easy ride can be another person's race, depending on relative fitness. One or two days per week of high-intensity riding at the right time of year can help prepare you for your races. But riding at race-pace intensity at the wrong time of year or too frequently will hold you back at the times you want to perform at your best.

Chapter 6

Building Endurance and Strength

Many new racers who experience being dropped in a race think, *If I could have gone harder, I wouldn't have been dropped.* They then add interval after interval to their training, hoping for better legs at extreme intensities. While this may satisfy their desire to do *something,* it won't do much for their racing performance.

New racers may mistakenly think that going hard or suffering is what wins races. While these are important, the ability to go fast without going too hard is far more valuable. When you've done a few races, you'll notice that there are usually a few riders who are chatting about bike parts or the latest results from pro cycling as the pack cruises, even while other riders are already breathing hard and starting to suffer. When the pace picks up a little, those earlier sufferers are often off the back while the chatting folks are just beginning to make an effort. When the pace increases enough that the strong begin to suffer, the weak are long gone. Among the strong, the ones who can handle the most suffering survive to the end of the race. Yet it is not this ability to suffer that wins the race. Rather, it is the ability to go fast and steady without going hard that earns you the opportunity to outsuffer the competition.

How do you train your body to be able to go fast without going too hard and burning itself out? You get good at what you practice. If you practice going all out and hurting all the time, you make every ride a punishment and you get really good at suffering when you ride, whether riding 25 MPH (40 KPH) or 12 MPH (19 KPH). If you practice riding smoothly and efficiently without excessive effort, you get better at riding effortlessly at all speeds, including speeds that used to be hard. The scientific way to say this is that you will increase your ability to go long distances at an intensity just below your lactate threshold while increasing the speed you can ride without exceeding the lactate threshold until that speed is faster than the typical speed of the competition. Stated this way, it's obvious that riding below the lactate threshold is the optimal form of base training.

Coaches often say "Train slow to go fast," but this is only half the story. The complete line should be "Train slow to train a lot; train a lot to go fast." Training in the moderate- and high-intensity zones leads to fairly rapid fatigue, which means you either experience short or infrequent training sessions or ride while fatigued. In both cases you complete a low volume of high-quality training. *High-quality training* means riding fast for the effort level, with a good, smooth movement pattern; appropriate cadence; and a feeling of easy strength and power. A good volume of high-quality aerobic training (less than 80 percent of HRmax) enhances fitness.

Training at higher perceived exertion or at intensities above the endurance zone won't enhance the benefit of the training and may even reduce it if the training is overdone or done at the wrong time of the season. The payoff of training at an endurance pace is that you can do many more hours of quality aerobic training than you can at

Photo courtesy of Susan Yost

The ability to outlast others in the final, whittled-down group depends as much on your ability to ride hard without suffering as on your ability to withstand suffering.

Developing a Smoother, Faster Spin

You can develop a sustained higher cadence on your endurance rides. If you are not currently comfortable riding 90 to 110 RPM, choose one gear easier than your most comfortable gear and boost your cadence a little at all times on your cadence-building spin rides. The correct cadence for spin practice is the highest cadence you can maintain and still be smooth. If you start to bounce or rock on the saddle, you're probably trying a higher cadence than you are ready for. One of the tricks to keeping your pedaling smooth is to fully relax the back pedal as it rises. You don't need to actually pull up with your foot, just take the weight of your leg off the pedal.

If you have a cadence monitor on your cycle computer, you can do this systematically. If you usually roll around at 75 RPM, shoot for 78. If you're comfortable at 80, go for 85. If you don't have a cadence monitor, ride a comfortable speed in a certain gear, count the RPMs for 10 seconds, and multiply by 6. If you're not at the right RPMs, shift to one gear easier while maintaining the same speed.

After you've accustomed yourself to your new higher cadence for a few weeks, it will start to come naturally. Once you've achieved your first cadence goal, increase cadence again. Eventually you will be comfortably spinning 90 RPM or more for hours at a time. As your cadence increases, you may find that you are getting sore in odd spots such as your rear end or your knees. If you've been building up cadence and ride time gradually, this may be a sign that your bike or shoes do not fit properly. While there are many possible problems that can cause pain, handlebars that are too low or a seat that is too high or too low can make it impossible to spin smoothly without injury. If you are getting sore or just can't seem to get comfortable spinning, talk to a coach or bike fitter and get the bike better adjusted to you.

a higher pace. The strongest reason to do most of your training in the endurance zone is that athletes who do so improve their performance steadily for several years. They eventually become very strong and consistently place well in races.

In opposition to this are the racers who constantly train at high intensities. If an athlete starts racing or high-intensity training without first establishing a base of endurance fitness, performance will steadily decrease after a month or so. For best results, start each training year with basic aerobic fitness and strength training. If necessary, delay the start of racing to allow for this.

Endurance-Paced Riding

Endurance-paced riding is consistent riding done while keeping your heart rate between 70 and 80 percent of your maximum. If you don't have a heart rate monitor, endurance pace means maintaining steady pressure on the pedals but never feeling that you are struggling. If you are going fast but not working hard, you're likely doing an endurance-paced ride. The endurance pace is well below the anaerobic threshold. If your legs are burning or you are breathing quite hard, you are above the endurance zone.

Start each endurance ride with a 15-minute easy warm-up. Then settle into your endurance pace. If all is well, this is a comfortable heart rate range you can stay in without having to think much about it as you pedal. If you find it harder than usual to hit this zone or you

Freddie's Breakthrough Year

© Casey B. Gibson

In February 1998 American Fred Rodriguez scored a stunning three stage wins and top 10 overall place in the grueling Le Tour de Langkawi, beating out many top European road pros. This performance got him noticed and picked up by the strongest squad in the world at the time, the Mapei team. How did he prepare for this astonishing feat?

Freddie had already been riding for many years with his coach, René Wenzel. Wenzel knew Freddie could handle a tough program. He started out with one hour per day of endurance-paced riding in early October and continued to add 20 minutes per day each week until he was doing six hours per day, all at an endurance pace. By the time he left for the Malaysia event, he had only very briefly been above 80 percent of his maximum heart rate on one occasion during team training camp. At 80 percent of his MHR, Fred was averaging approximately 25 MPH (40 KPH) on flat sections of his training rides. The rest is history.

need to concentrate to keep up this effort, you are ready for some recovery. In that case, let your heart rate drop to 59 to 70 percent of maximum as you continue the ride. Training time in this zone is still effective for aerobic fitness development, so don't feel bad about riding this pace. If you are having trouble staying in the recovery zone, it's time to head home and rest immediately.

If you are a first-year racer, build up to at least one endurance ride each week in base development of two to three hours, or one hour longer than the longest race in which you will compete in the coming season. If you are very strong and can participate in group rides while keeping your heart rate below 80 percent maximum, do your endurance rides with a group. In fact, few riders can do this, so we recommend doing group rides only with others who are committed to monitored training or dropping out of a group ride when it becomes too intense during your base training period.

A typical two-week training period for a beginning racer during the base-building period might look like the following.

Typical Two-Week Base Training

Monday	Strength training (see pages 71-75)
Tuesday	Day off
Wednesday	Strength training
Thursday	Endurance ride or cross-training
Friday	Strength training
Saturday	Endurance ride (group ride)
Sunday	Endurance ride (group ride)
Monday	Strength training
Tuesday	Endurance ride
Wednesday	Strength training
Thursday	Endurance ride
Friday	Day off
Saturday	Endurance ride (group ride)
Sunday	Endurance ride (group ride)

Indoor Training

If you live in a part of the country where the roads are snowy in winter, or you have a job that allows you to train only before sunup or after sundown, you are not at a terrible disadvantage compared to folks who can train outdoors all year, but you will have to be tough and dedicated to make good use of indoor training.

Most outdoor exercises (except standing exercises) may be done indoors as well, using a trainer or rollers. On rollers, you can develop a very smooth pedaling style and the ability to ride a very straight line. The things you can't develop indoors are bike handling, pack skills, and gear use. So if you find that you have to do many of your rides indoors, find some time to go outdoors to work on these skills.

Because there are no descents or stoplights on indoor trainer rides, training indoors can be very efficient; you can work every minute of the ride. The legs don't know whether they are spinning a trainer or pushing you down the road, so you can conceivably get more endurance or power training in less time. Indoor intervals are very predictable. The hill is always long enough. The light never changes with a minute left in your interval. All this makes indoor training efficient for developing endurance and power.

When you ride outdoors, you change positions frequently: standing for short accelerations or climbs, leaning for turns, tucking to deal with headwinds, or sitting up when just cruising. When you ride indoors, if you're not deliberate about changing positions, you'll probably stay in the same position. This leads to a sore rear end and numb or sore hands and feet. To avoid this, shift about on the bike. Stand for a few seconds every few minutes. Change your hand positions. Change gears so you'll pedal differently, which makes you sit differently. If you're getting sore or numb despite moving around, take a break. Then get back on a few minutes later, or later the same day, and get in some more quality time. Don't push yourself to the point of using up all your enthusiasm in one session.

What Doesn't Bore You Makes You Stronger

Why do you have to be tough to make good use of indoor training? Because it can be boring—the scenery never changes. Because it can be painful to not change positions. Because it can be hot without a breeze. Because competition won't motivate you when there is no one to keep up with. Each of these challenges can be dealt with, but indoor training is psychologically harder than outdoor training.

There are many ways to minimize the boredom of indoor endurance training. Watch videos, listen to music, chat on a hands-free phone, or even work at a computer or read a book (both of these require a bookrack that attaches to your bike). To maintain motivation for longer sessions, get together with a friend or two who have training goals similar to your own. Always arrange a whole session's worth of entertainment before you start.

It's OK to break up long indoor sessions to maximize your ride. You could take a 5-minute food or drink or bathroom or stretch break every 45 minutes. You can make up exercises for yourself: Pedal one-legged, ride no hands, spin faster or slower, focus on full-circle pedaling, or invent your own drills. On rollers, put a strip of tape in the middle and practice riding on the tape by watching your reflection in a mirror. Drills that involve doing so many minutes of this and so many minutes of that are best. They won't make you stronger than just riding, but they will keep you on the bike longer.

Keep Cool

About 70 to 80 percent of the energy you expend in exercise becomes heat. When you ride outdoors, breezes and sweat evaporation carry heat away from your body. When you can't dissipate heat, body temperature rises and exercise becomes less efficient. Heart rate rises for a given power output as blood goes to the skin for cooling. Less blood goes to the working muscles. The brain tries to slow the production of heat by reducing the exercise rate. The apparent effort to maintain a certain power output increases. If you cannot cool yourself effectively, training becomes more difficult but simultaneously less effective.

To avoid this when training indoors, find a cool place with moving air, in front of a fan near an open window or air conditioner. When you drip sweat, you are not cooling effectively. As you gain fitness, the heat you can generate increases. Effective cooling becomes more important and more difficult. When you train indoors, you will probably sweat a lot, so drink plenty of fluids. If you were to weigh yourself before and after a session, your weight would be unchanged if you drank enough. Don't think that if you are losing weight during actual training you are training well. The opposite is true: If you lose weight as water, your training loses effectiveness.

Sweat is salty and acidic. It corrodes steel and aluminum bike frames and components. To protect your bike when you train indoors, drape a towel over the top tube where the sweat drips. Wipe down the bike and trainer afterward.

Aerobic Cross-Training

You can also build endurance by doing aerobic training besides riding at certain times of the training year. In the first two months of the base training period, it's OK to do several days per week of running, swimming, hiking, snowshoeing, cross-country skiing, skating, aerobics, or other activities that get your heart rate up to 70 to 80 percent of maximum and keep it up steadily for a half-hour or more at a time. Cross-training is not as effective as training in your chosen sport, but it is better than skipping training when the weather is bad and you've lost your enthusiasm for the indoor trainer.

Always do at least one day per week of pedaling so you don't lose your cycling form. Reduce cross-training to no more than one day per week two months before racing starts and eliminate all cross-training one month before racing. Always make your cross-training match your cycle-training goals for the time of year. Don't do races or hard training in your cross-training sport in the base-building time of the year. Racers who live in snowy climes who can't do enough months of outdoor riding to be satisfied with a cycling focus are the exception to this rule.

Strength Training

The ability to ride fast is closely related to the ability to pedal hard. Studies comparing national-class time trialists with other racers show that the elite riders simply push down harder on the pedals at a high cadence for a longer time. How can you improve your ability to push on the pedals? Certainly, you must do many hours of riding to develop the smooth, efficient pedal stroke of a champion, but you can gain further improvement from training specifically for strength on the bike or in the gym.

Why is strength training important for cyclists even though they are not always pushing with maximal force on the pedals when they ride? The rate of fatigue when exercising or riding depends in part on how hard you are pushing compared to how hard you *could* push. If you are making a tiny fraction of the force you could make, you fatigue more slowly than if you were pushing with a large fraction of your ability. By increasing strength, you decrease the fraction of your total strength that you need for any given effort.

Our experience suggests that riders who have not recently strength trained can add 25 to 50 percent to their strength in just the first 10 weeks of a recommended 22-week strength program. Compare this to $\dot{V}O_2$max, which is determined by heart volume and maximum heart rate and is close to its maximum value after just a few months of regular cycling (see chapter 5, page 51). While some riders are naturally stronger than others, the weakest are likely to enjoy strength training least but benefit from it most.

Studies show that strength training does not improve steady efforts but that increased strength allows you to make the short, hard efforts to match bursts of speed, accelerate out of corners, or crest hills in a bike race with less fatigue. While strength training does not increase endurance as defined by physiologists, it does improve the ability to be strong at the end of long races.

A good program of strength training done in the nonracing season improves power and fatigue resistance, but strength training itself is very fatiguing and will make it impossible to perform at your best *during* the training. The benefits of strength training come weeks or months after the training itself. Do not begin or continue heavy strength training in the racing season; if you lift regularly into the racing season your legs will feel heavy and slow. You may feel this way for several weeks even after you end your main weight-training program. Do your strength development along with base training and do only strength maintenance in the racing season.

Improved pedaling strength is not the only benefit of strength training. Strength-trained muscles also get fewer injuries from normal hard activities. An athlete without strength training who gets sore leg or lower-back muscles when riding hard can probably eliminate the problem with a good offseason strength program. Riders with weaker upper-body muscles have trouble controlling the bike in hard cornering, on bumpy roads, or when sprinting. Many women and some men have this experience. Many of these problems can be corrected by strength training.

Just as muscles can be made stronger through training, the tendons, ligaments, and cartilage around joints become tougher and more resilient if they are stressed repeatedly at a level below the stress that tears them. When they are strengthened through training, it takes larger forces to damage them. Since cyclists lose a lot of training time to shoulder, hip, knee, and ankle injuries, this is worth considering.

Building Your Strength Training Program

Performing strength training exercises incorrectly can cause serious injuries. If you are not familiar with the proper form for the exercises you choose, consult a trainer in the gym. Tell him that your goal is to race bikes and that you'd like to gain strength without bulk.

Select 8 to 10 exercises that specifically work cycling-related muscles, and do the same exercises throughout your lifting program. This number of exercises is enough to work all of the necessary muscle groups (quadriceps, gluteals, hamstrings, calves, abdominals, lower back, chest, and arms). Doing the same exercises consistently will help prevent the injuries that come from starting new exercises partway through a program. Don't waste your time doing lifts that strengthen muscles that don't add to bike handling or pedaling. Don't waste your time doing lots of different exercises for the same muscle group. If you have a choice and have been trained in how to perform the exercises, use free weights (barbells, dumbbells, and loose plates) rather than machines. Machines control your movement pattern and prevent you from using small support and control muscles.

Exercises for Power Muscles

Partial squat (no deeper than having the thigh at 30 degrees to the floor)	Shallow leg press (knee bend no sharper than 100 degrees)
Hamstring curl	Deadlift
Standing calf raise	Situps (for hip flexors)
Leg lifts	

Exercises for Bike Control and Support Muscles

Crunches	Bench press
Situps	Bicep curls
Back extensions	Bent-over rowing

Gym Strengthening Program

We suggest a 22-week program that starts at the beginning of the base phase with lifting once the first week and then two to three times per week. This program is designed to make you stronger with minimal injuries. You will get sore the first time, no matter how light you start. If you start very light, the soreness will be minimized and will pass quickly. On your first visit, make the weights light enough that they feel almost silly and focus on ensuring that your form is correct.

Our athletes typically don't get sore after the second week if they lift appropriate weights two or three times per week. But if they go a whole week without lifting, the rate of gaining strength decreases and soreness returns. After the first session of light lifting, you should still never lift to failure. Choose weights with which you can finish the sets and have enough strength for at least a few more repetitions.

Continue a once-weekly maintenance routine of light strength training into the racing season, but stop in the few weeks before an important event. Once you stop, do not start lifting again until you begin training for the following season.

To prevent injuries, increase strength, and enhance the enjoyment of strength training, begin and end every strength training session with 10 to 15 minutes of cycling. Stretch both before and after lifting.

On-the-Bike Strengthening

The cycling muscles get a strength workout when you ride. Some coaches are concerned with translating gym strength to the bike. We find that riding a program with a good balance of higher and lower intensities will take care of this, but if you want, you can do some big gear work to help apply your gym strength on the bike.

Training for any sport should be similar to the movement patterns of that sport. Cycling-specific leg strength can be improved by short intervals, say one minute of uphill riding in a very hard gear. Only do such big gear work when you are well warmed up, and only do it so long as you continue to feel strong. When you do big gear work, stay within the endurance or recovery intensity zones. Like strength training, big gear work is very hard on the body. Don't do it if it hurts. Start with one interval the first day. Add an interval or two per week. You can do big gear work as often as you would do strength training. Big gear work is very fatiguing, so don't do it in the week before an important race. Along with big gear work, we suggest that you also do a gym routine for the core muscles of the abdomen and back.

22-Week Strength Training Program

WEEK 1	**Getting Started**	1 to 2 sessions per week Weights so light they're almost silly 3 sets of 6-10 repetitions for all exercises
WEEKS 2-6	**Anatomic Adaptation**	2 to 3 sessions per week Weights heavy enough to offer some resistance but no struggle; you could do twice the required repetitions 3 sets of 6-10 repetitions for muscles that hold body over bike 6 sets of 10-12 repetitions for muscles that power the bike
WEEKS 7-12	**Basic Strength**	2 to 3 sessions per week Continue adding weight as you gain strength; keep the feeling about the same as in the previous phase; never lift to failure 3 sets of 6-10 repetitions for muscles that hold body over bike 6 sets of 10-12 repetitions for muscles that power the bike
WEEKS 13-20	**Muscular Endurance**	2 sessions per week, ending after the first month of racing (provided the first month of racing is introductory and not the most important of the season) Weights are about 75 percent of what you did in basic strength; if the weights are chosen correctly you get a little burn in the last two to three repetitions of each set, no sooner For first two weeks add 1 set per week to what you were lifting in basic strength phase, then add 30 percent each week to the number of repetitions of each exercise
WEEKS 21-22	**Maintenance**	Continue if desired: 1 session per week until you are preparing for an important event or one month before the end of the racing season Weights are heavy enough to offer some resistance but no struggle; you could do twice the required repetitions 3 sets of 6-10 repetitions for muscles that hold body over bike 3-6 sets of 10-12 repetitions for muscles that power the bike

Remainder of the Year: Taper, no strength training

Stretching

The base phase of training is a good time to develop a regular stretching habit that you carry out throughout the season, especially for the hamstrings. Stretch at least three days per week all year long. From the physiologist's perspective, it doesn't matter whether you stretch before or after training. The most effective stretches involve at least 10 to15 seconds on each muscle group. Enter the stretch very gradually, never with great force or bouncing. Move into a stretch until you feel just a little tension, and then relax and wait for it to pass. Then move deeper into the stretch until you feel a little tension again. Repeat this pattern until you reach a depth of stretch from which you can no longer eliminate the tension by relaxing.

Why stretch? Your ability to increase strength and power is limited. But if you can make your frontal area smaller on the bike, you can go faster with the same effort. Reducing your frontal area means getting narrow and low on the bike, which you can't do with tight hamstrings. If your bike fits properly, you can ride the drops all day. If this position hurts your hamstrings or lower back, you can benefit by stretching. Tight hamstrings interfere with smooth leg movement and rob you of power, so stretching can also increase your pedal power. Stretching enhances blood flow and speeds recovery. Finally, loose muscles are less likely to be strained during normal use, strenuous racing, or in violent crashes, so stretching correctly helps prevent injury.

Many athletes already know basic stretches for their major leg and arm muscles. Most just don't like to do them! Consult a coach or personal trainer to learn stretches to benefit muscles that you will use in cycling, including your back, neck, and smaller leg muscles.

Chapter 7

Increasing Speed and Power

The simplest component of being a good bike racer is your ability to ride in a fast-moving pack with ease. However, to be competitive, you also need to generate strong accelerations and short bursts of higher speed. Regular endurance training allows you to cruise steadily at a high pace, while speed wins races.

If you're having trouble keeping up with the pack when it is steadily cruising along, no amount of speed work will help you. In that case you need more aerobic fitness, better drafting, less braking, or less wind resistance. If you can keep up on the flats but not on longer climbs, you may need to work on your climbing form or lose body or bike weight. However, if you are able to ride steadily with a pack and have built up your aerobic fitness, it's time to add speed training to the mix.

When coaches talk about speed, they mean short bursts of high or maximal speed. Training for speed means training to go very fast for a very short time. Speed helps you jump out of corners, establish or join breakaways, and participate in final sprints. Being able to make these short bursts and maintain a high steady pace means finishing flatter races with the group.

The Importance of Speed

When you go around a corner in the middle or back of a pack, the front of the pack is accelerating down the straight while your section of the pack is still slowing for the corner. That means that after the corner you are farther from the front than you were before the corner. You'll have to go faster than the leaders on the next straight to maintain your position in the pack. Even if you'd like to just roll along steadily, the riders in front will jump to close the gaps that opened in the corner, and you'll have to jump to keep up with them or give up their draft. To establish a breakaway, you have to ride faster than the front of the field for long enough to get a gap.

Another obvious need for speed comes in final sprints. To win a sprint, you typically draft other riders until you are very close to the finish line and then come around them. Coming around them means riding faster than they can ride for the few remaining seconds of the race.

Clearly, there are times in bike racing when you need to be able to go fast for a short time. So how can you enhance your speed? There are two aspects to improving your bursts of speed: *acceleration* and *top speed*. To be a speedy rider, you need to be able to accelerate when you want to and you need to be able to hold a high top speed longer in relation to the other riders. Paradoxically, the secret to both of these is to learn to ride smaller gears.

Acceleration: Pedal Cadence Versus Gears

You can maintain the same speed by riding a low gear at a high cadence or a higher gear at a lower cadence. However, the lower the cadence, the harder you have to push on the pedals—that is, the greater force you must develop to maintain speed or accelerate. You can increase your ability to generate force on the pedals by increasing the strength of your muscles through weightlifting or on-the-bike strength training (see chapter 6). However, your ability to apply force to the pedals on any given day is set. This is where gears come in.

In endurance-paced (aerobic) training, we advocated spinning lower gears at a higher cadence because churning along in big gears at a lower cadence produces fatigue relatively quickly. When we discuss speed, spinning at a higher cadence becomes even more important. When you use much of your force for maintaining speed, you have little strength left for acceleration. By shifting to a smaller gear for cruising along, you have a bigger strength reserve for acceleration. You can easily test this. Pick a gear in which you can comfortably ride a good pace on a flat road. Check your speedometer and pedal hard until you've added five miles per hour to your speed. Repeat the test in two gears harder and two gears easier than the comfortable gear and see how long it takes to get up to speed in each gear as well as how much is taken out of your legs by the effort. Which gear would you rather do four times per lap in a 20-lap criterium?

Photo courtesy of Susan Yost

Successful racing means being able to pedal at a variety of high cadences.

As you accelerate using a smaller gear, you will of course be pedaling faster than if you were riding a bigger gear. To accelerate in a smaller gear effectively, you must be trained to ride routinely at high cadences and for short bursts at very high cadences. Review the instructions in chapter 6 for developing a high spin (page 66). Many cyclometers have a cadence readout. If yours doesn't, you can still check your cadence by counting full pedal revolutions for 6 seconds and multiplying this number by 10. Successful racers of all levels typically ride along at 90 to110 RPM and can easily hold the upper half of that range for a half-hour or more at a time. Road race and criterium sprints are typically contested at cadences up to 130 RPM for 20 seconds or a little longer. If you can't hit and hold these cadences, you'll be at a big disadvantage in races.

Unlike strength, which can increase only gradually, and $\dot{V}O_2$max, which increases slowly after the first few months of consistent training, you can develop fairly quickly the ability to apply force to the pedals at a higher cadence. It's more a matter of learning to pedal faster than of causing physiological changes in the muscles. That is, you are training your legs to get used to pedaling faster. Learning is generally faster and more permanent than physical training. For some people a smooth spin and comfort at high cadences come naturally, but with practice and a bike that fits well, anyone can become pretty good at it.

Top Speed: Bursts of Higher Cadence

Once you can hold 90 RPM or more for the length of a ride (as outlined in chapter 6), it's time to work on short bursts of higher cadence. While on an endurance ride, throw in some higher-cadence intervals of 30 seconds separated by 2-minute rests at 90 RPM. Your interval set could go 95 RPM (30 seconds), 90 RPM (2 minutes), 100 RPM (30 seconds), 90 RPM (2 minutes), 105 RPM (30 seconds), and so on. Keep increasing cadence until you find a cadence that you cannot maintain smoothly for 30 seconds. Then go back down in intervals of 5 RPM. Don't worry about your heart rate during these intervals. Choose a gear low enough that you are limited by your ability to spin rather than your ability to push. Don't practice spinning faster than you can smoothly spin. Unchecked spinning where you are bouncing around on your seat can strain tendons and is inefficient. Keep doing these drills weekly until you can maintain 130 RPM smoothly with pressure on the pedals for 30 seconds. It should take a few weeks or even a few months to get to this point.

Once you master high-cadence bursts in an easy gear, start working on high cadence with the resistance of a higher gear. This is *sprint training* or *jump training*. The technique and training drills for sprinting are discussed in greater detail in chapter 11. When you first begin doing sprint training, your legs will go weak after just a few seconds of sprinting. After you've been practicing for a few weeks, you'll be able to maintain a strong effort for longer. The first time you ride hard enough to drive up your blood lactic acid levels, your brain senses that higher level and thinks something is wrong. It follows up by slowing and weakening your muscles. After a few sessions of high-intensity training, however, your brain will adjust to being rinsed in lactic acid and will allow the muscles to keep working longer at high intensity.

Even after the brain adjusts to higher lactic acid levels, there is a limit to how long you can maintain an all-out effort because an acid-soaked, oxygen-deficient, hot muscle becomes very inefficient. To a minimal extent you can increase the muscle's ability to buffer lactic acid, allowing a longer anaerobic effort. That increase comes through racing more than any kind of training. The outer limit of all-out efforts is still just a minute or two. After that, the speed inevitably begins to drop.

The physical benefit of doing speed work is maximized after just a few weeks to a couple of months. If you are not satisfied with your speed at that point, focus on tactical and technical aspects of sprinting or go back to developing your endurance base, a higher comfortable cadence, and better aerobic fitness so that you can ride comfortably at a higher speed before you need to surge. The fitter you are and the more efficiently you ride and draft, the fresher you are when it comes time to sprint. These factors, rather than pure sprinting ability, often determine your success in races. A typical two-week training period for a beginning racer during a speed- and power-building period might look like the following. Note that this is a building period, rather than an inseason performance period. During the performance period, recovery and getting ready for the weekend's racing is the focus.

Typical Two-Week Speed and Power Building

Monday	Day off
Tuesday	Endurance-paced ride
Wednesday	Hard intervals in high-intensity zone
Thursday	Endurance-paced ride
Friday	Easy spin/tune up for weekend racing; mostly recovery zone/low-end endurance zone riding with several sprint jumps and short, high-intensity intervals of 2 minutes or less.
Saturday	Race, group ride race simulation, or hard intervals in high-intensity zone if no race or group ride is available
Sunday	Endurance-paced ride (longer than during the work week)
Monday	Day off
Tuesday	Endurance-paced ride
Wednesday	Sprints
Thursday	Endurance-paced ride
Friday	Easy spin/tune up for weekend racing
Saturday	Race, group ride race simulation, or hard intervals in high-intensity zone if no race or group ride is available
Sunday	Endurance-paced ride (longer than during the work week)

The Importance of Power

When you are talking about a near-maximal effort for up to 30 seconds, you are talking about speed. Besides speed, another vital capacity for bicycle racing is power (force multiplied by speed). While strength is the ability to push hard on the pedals once or a few times, power is the ability to push hard on the pedals repeatedly over an extended time. For instance, the ability to time trial or climb a long hill depends on sustained aerobic power, whereas going fast over a shorter rise requires short-term, anaerobic power.

Your body type and muscle fiber type determine what type of power is your forte. Muscles are made up of thousands of individual muscle fibers. When you exercise and a certain muscle contracts, only some of the fibers in that muscle actually generate force. Which ones contract depends on the speed, force, and duration of the exercise. Only the fibers used in training become stronger, more efficient, or able to contract more quickly or more often.

There are two basic types of muscle fibers: *slow-twitch* and *fast-twitch*. By the time you are a young adult, you have all the muscle fibers you will ever have and their type is determined. The basic type and number of fibers cannot be changed by any amount of weightlifting or other training. Most people have about a 1-to-1 ratio, 50 percent of each type. The slight differences between fiber-type ratios in different riders help determine whether they can be great time trialists (more slow-twitch), great sprinters (more fast-twitch), or great all-arounders (50-50).

Slow-twitch fibers are used during endurance training and steady-state race riding. These fibers are highly trainable. Even when they are trained, they do not generate the highest forces, but they do use oxygen very efficiently and recover quickly from each contraction so they can be ready to contract again and again many times. Fast-twitch fibers generate large forces (they are used in weightlifting or pushing a big gear, for example) but do not recover as well, so they are less useful for extended efforts like time trialing. The fast-twitch fibers are divided into two categories, sometimes called *fast-twitch A* and *fast-twitch B*. Fast-twitch B fibers are brute fibers; they generate large forces but are really bad at using oxygen. They can use up their stored fuel in just a few seconds and then require minutes or longer before they are ready to go again. They are used mostly in sprinting and other short, maximal efforts.

When fast-twitch fibers are recruited regularly in training, some become fast-twitch A fibers. These have the force capability of fast-twitch B fibers and some of the oxygen-using capacity of slow-twitch fibers. These fabulous fibers can generate high forces and recover relatively quickly to do it again. An abundance of fast-twitch A fibers characterizes the powerful rider who can go hard several times in a race. Only training that repeatedly calls on the fast-twitch fibers can cause the switch from type B to type A. The push, big gear / little gear, and surge rides (outlined later in this chapter, pages 85-86) call for large pedaling forces and so help initiate this switch. The high-intensity intervals (page 84), if done near 90 RPM, also call on fast-twitch fibers in some riders.

Time trials of over a few minutes must be ridden for the most part at an intensity below the lactate threshold because efforts above the lactate threshold lead to a rapid loss of power and a slowing down, even as effort and heart rate are maintained. Aerobic power is developed primarily through the accumulation of endurance-base miles in the months when you train exclusively and do not race. The finishing touches are applied to your aerobic power in the last couple of months before the start of racing.

Long-Term Power

A rider gets good at what she practices. Thus, to become good at making extended hard efforts, you must train with extended hard efforts. Typically this is done in the form of intervals. *Intervals* just means alternating periods of work and rest. The intensity of intervals can be anything from moderately paced to all-out effort. Doing moderate- and high-intensity intervals after your base is developed optimizes aerobic power.

Moderate-Intensity Intervals

Once you have done a couple of months of endurance training, it is time to begin your transition to intensity phase. In the first month of this phase, do moderate intervals two days per week—warm up for at least 20 minutes at a recovery pace, and then push up to a moderate intensity (75 to 85 percent of HRmax, but at least eight beats below the anaerobic threshold; see chapter 5, page 56, for a description of the intensity levels). The first week, do just one interval of 15 minutes at this pace on each interval day, then cool down and go home. In the second week, do two intervals each time and take a 5-minute rest in between. In the third and fourth weeks, do three intervals of 15 minutes each with 5-minute rests on each interval ride.

Put as much variety as possible in your moderate-intensity interval rides. Include flat rides and hilly ones. Include corners. If you will do time trials, do some intervals on your time trial bike or time trial position. The moderate intervals start to challenge your body with slightly higher lactic acid levels in the blood and, in this way, prepare you for harder work.

High-Intensity Intervals

Once you've done a month of moderate intervals, with some endurance riding on the other days, your body should be ready to handle the harder work of high-intensity intervals. These intervals are done near your anaerobic threshold (plus or minus five beats per minute of anaerobic threshold heart rate). We suggest doing two days per week of high-intensity intervals in the second month of the transition to intensity phase.

To do a session of high-intensity intervals, warm up with at least 30 minutes of riding in the recovery and endurance zones, and then jump hard to get your heart rate to the high-intensity zone. If you are not using a heart monitor, jump just until your breathing begins to accelerate. Settle in at a pace that keeps you in the high-intensity zone either by heart rate or by perceived exertion. The first session, make your intervals 3 minutes long. After each interval, rest by riding in the recovery zone for at least 5 minutes. After the rest, jump again and attempt another interval. Continue doing intervals until you can no longer reach the target heart rates, you are going slower than on earlier intervals, or you have done six intervals. Once you are tired or you've done the six intervals, it's time to cool down and go home. Spin in the recovery zone for at least 10 minutes to cool down the body.

On your next session of high-intensity intervals, if you were not able to do six in the previous session, just do the same length again. If you were able to do all six, make the intervals and rests longer. For example, do 5-minute intervals with 8-minute rests. When you are able to do six of these, again add 2 minutes to the work intervals and 3 minutes to the rests. As with the moderate intervals, put as much variety as you can into these high-intensity intervals. When you can do half an hour or more of hard work at the high-intensity level without too much fatigue, your aerobic fitness is optimized for this year. Further gains in long-term power will most likely come from more base riding, not more or harder intervals.

Short-Term Power

Usually when cyclists refer to power, they mean power for 20 seconds to a few minutes of intense effort, as when climbing a short hill, pushing over the crest of a longer hill, or bridging to a break. Since power is the product of strength and speed, short-term power can be improved by improving pedaling speed or increasing leg strength.

While all riders benefit from training both speed and strength, if you are a very skinny, light rider, you'll probably end up drawing mostly on leg speed as your way to improve power. Stockier, more muscular riders can choose between higher force and higher leg speed as ways to express power but will probably end up pushing harder on the pedals.

Since we've already addressed leg speed and strength training in this chapter and in chapter 6, we'll talk now about on-the-bike methods to improve leg strength for hard pedaling and developing power for short-term bursts.

We use several exercises for developing power on the bike. The following three are especially good for beginning racers. For all power exercises, most of the effort comes from the downward-pushing muscles of the rear, not from the forward-kicking muscles of the thighs or the pulling-up muscles of the hip. If you feel that much of your power during hard pedaling is coming from the quadriceps and going through the knees, your seat is probably too low or too far forward.

Be warned that pushing hard on the pedals means delivering large forces through your hips, knees, and ankles. You should not do these exercises—or ride hard, for that matter—unless you have a few years of cycling experience, a month or more of good endurance training at a spinning cadence this season, and no knee or other joint injuries or problems. You should also not do on-the-bike power work unless your bike has been properly fitted. The possibility of an annoying or even career-ending injury is very real. If you develop any knee pain or other joint pain when doing these exercises, back off. Return to spinning for several days at least. If you are under 16 years old, do not do the big gear/little gear exercises. It's still OK to do the push ride and the surge ride.

Push Ride

After a 15-minute easy warm-up, choose the gears that make your cadence come out to just over 70 RPM while staying in the endurance or recovery zones. Continue pedaling at 70 to 80 RPM until you have about 15 minutes left in your ride, and then switch to an easier, spinning gear. You'll probably find that your average speed on this ride is pretty high for an endurance ride but that you also come home more tired than usual.

This exercise is OK for any rider who does not currently have knee troubles and who has at least a month of spinning base. Every second or third endurance ride should be a push ride in the offseason. Push rides are fatiguing, so don't do them the week before an important race.

Big Gear/Little Gear Ride

After your 15-minute easy warm-up, shift back and forth every 5 minutes between a big gear that makes your cadence between 60 and 75 RPM and a little gear that makes your cadence between 90 and 110 RPM. Keep your heart rate or perceived effort in the endurance zone for the length of this ride. Choosing mostly rolling and flat terrain for this ride will help you stay in the zone. A few hours of this exercise makes a very hard training day. Do this exercise only when you have at least four months of at least once per week regular push ride training behind you. Never do more than one day per week of big gear/little gear, and don't do it in the week before an important race. Some coaches recommend short intervals of even harder pedaling than what you get with this exercise, but in general we don't believe the extra benefits, if any, outweigh the extra risks compared to the big gear/little gear exercise for first-year riders.

Surge Ride

This ride involves accelerations rather than steady effort. Warm up with at least 45 minutes of spinning in the endurance zone. Find a gradual hill. As you start to climb the hill, find the gear that makes your cadence about 70 RPM in the endurance intensity zone. Accelerate fairly hard but remain seated until your cadence is about 90 RPM. Hold that for 1 minute. After the minute is up, spin easily for about 5 minutes before doing another surge. Keep doing surges until you are not feeling as strong as you were at the beginning of the ride or until you've used up your training time. Spin easily for at least 10 minutes after the last surge.

Indoor Training for Speed and Power

Indoor training is at best a substitute for outdoor riding. Unless weather conditions such as black ice, slippery pavement, and minimal sunlight make outdoor riding dangerous, get on the bike and ride outdoors. Riding in the rain, cold, and wind makes you tough. You can still train for speed and power indoors using a trainer or rollers with resistance and performing the same speed and power exercises you would outdoors. (Rollers without resistance are not useful for developing strength or power.) Keep yourself cool with a fan and wet towels, and eat and drink as much as you would on an outdoor ride. It's also OK to get off periodically to stretch.

Offroad Racing for Road Racers

When you first start out racing bikes, you need not restrict yourself to one kind of race. The special talents needed for road racing and offroad racing overlap quite a bit. Mountain bike and cyclocross racing involve tight corners at high speed on loose ground, so they help you develop excellent bike-handling skills. Because there is such a big advantage to going a steady pace in these events rather than alternating between anaerobic and resting paces, they are great opportunities to learn to pace properly. For these reasons, we suggest that first- and second-year road racers do an occasional mountain bike or cyclocross race.

The downside of frequent offroad racing is that the pedal cadences don't match those of road racing. In addition, it is difficult to maintain endurance in offroad racing and training due to the longer recovery times that large amounts of anaerobic effort and offroad bouncing and bumping require. Don't do more than one offroad race per month when you are building an aerobic base or during the road racing season. The chances of crashes and injuries in offroad racing are significant, so also don't do them in the few weeks before more important events.

Chapter 8

Nutrition and Hydration

Endurance training is the foundation on which your training and racing stand. The bigger and stronger the foundation, the taller your house can be. To take the analogy further, lifestyle is the ground underneath your foundation. If it includes a healthy diet, plenty of water and sleep, low stress, good hygiene, and regular medical care, your foundation rests on solid bedrock. If your lifestyle includes stress, junk food, alcohol, late nights, and unwashed shorts, your foundation is sitting in a swamp. No matter how big the foundation, the house won't stand if it is sinking in a muck of sloppy lifestyle.

Training makes you weaker. You become stronger during recovery when you repair damaged tissue and actually change your body, replacing muscle, blood vessels, and nerve tissues that are adequate for sedentary people with new structures suitable for athletes. Repair and creation of these new structures requires certain nutrients, which must come from the foods you eat.

If your diet does not replace the fuels you use during each training session, you become weaker instead of stronger from session to session. Certain vitamins and minerals are necessary for efficient functioning of the athletic body. On the other hand, eating too much will make you gain weight. Even a small amount of excess body weight can make the difference between staying with the field and getting dropped in the hills. For these reasons, the right diet is part of the bedrock on which you build your training foundation.

Nutrition for Bike Racers

We recommend four basic eating plans for performing optimally on the bike throughout the training year as well as on race days. The main everyday diet promotes overall health and fitness and fuels your body for training. The prerace eating regimen includes adjustments you'll make to your everyday diet on the day or two before a race as well as what to eat on race day before you set your wheel on the starting line. You'll use the remaining two eating plans during and after a race or major training event.

Everyday Eating

The everyday eating plan is a balanced, healthy diet that is low in fats, especially the saturated fats found in butter, red meat, and deep-fried foods. It includes little or no alcohol and little or no processed sugar, including cakes, cookies, jams, and candies, even if the candies are labeled as athletic energy foods or drinks. It includes generous amounts of protein. The protein is distributed so that you get a little in every meal or snack, both to support muscle repair and to help regulate appetite. You'll fill up on fruits and vegetables rather than junk food or breads and pastas. Use whole-grain breads and pastas when possible. Eating a good everyday diet, with the volume of food intake adjusted to your activity level, will help make you lean no matter how much or how little you exercise.

How much should you eat? If you are eating enough, you maintain weight and are energetic for training. If you are eating too much, you gain weight. If you are eating too little, you lose weight or do not recover well from training sessions. Individual calorie needs vary so much that only tracking your own eating and your own weight changes can accurately measure your food needs.

Pre-Event Eating

Your everyday diet should change a bit starting the day before an event and as much as two days before a longer event. Add a serving of white starchy foods (pasta, rice, bread, or potatoes) in each meal at this time. Glycogen is the form in which your body stores carbohydrate, an important fuel for endurance exercise. Eating an extra serving of high-carbohydrate food in each meal the day or two before a race helps to ensure that your glycogen stores will be topped off before you race. Notice that we say an *extra serving,* and not as much

Twelve Rules for Healthy Daily Eating

The following are 12 rules for healthy daily eating (rules for prerace, race, and postrace eating are somewhat different). The first five rules are good for everyone. The remaining rules are particularly valuable to people who want to lose weight.

1. **Cut out all processed sugars.** Sugar is addictive, so you will probably feel tired, draggy, or ravenously hungry for two days to two weeks as you adjust to a sugar-free lifestyle. The worse you feel, the more addicted you are. Eat lots of fresh fruit instead.

2. **Seek balance in every meal.** Include some low-fat proteins (such as fish, poultry, tofu, tempeh, beans, yogurt, or cottage cheese), some complex carbohydrates (such as pasta, rice, potatoes, couscous, oats, or corn), a little bit of fat (it's OK to sauté, but not deep fry), and a lot of vegetables or fruit in every meal. The only calorie counting we advocate is to keep approximate count of how much protein you eat: one-quarter to one-half a gram per day per pound of weight you want to keep.

3. **Drink a lot of water before you eat.** Urine should ideally be clear and colorless all the time. Avoid sugar waters (sodas, lemonade, sport drinks) and fruit juices. Orange juice has about as many sugar calories as cola.

4. **Eat a lot of fruits and vegetables.** If you're still not full once you've had servings of protein and carbohydrate foods, complete the meal with a salad or vegetables (raw, steamed, or boiled). Don't overdo raw spinach, or anything else for that matter.

5. **Salt is OK.** Unless you have high blood pressure or have a family history of it, you don't have to go out of your way to avoid salt. Salt to taste, but don't go overboard. Consult your doctor if you have questions about your salt intake.

6. **You don't have to clean your plate.** Regardless of what your mother said or how many children are starving in Africa, never eat to the point where you are uncomfortably full. Always leave the table still able to eat more.

7. **Eat in courses.** Take a small amount of food on your plate at one time. After you finish, ask yourself whether you are still hungry. If you are, take another small serving. Don't take the whole package or pot of anything to the table or couch with you. Put whatever you eat in a bowl or on a plate so you'll have to be conscious about refilling it.

8. **Don't eat to be polite.** You don't need to try a little bit of everything that someone makes when you are a guest. Heap on praise for what you do eat, then declare yourself full. Don't eat the last bite to prevent having leftovers or to help the host not have to clean up.

9. **In restaurants, assemble a meal of salads and appetizers.** If you eat the bread that's put on the table, you can probably get enough nutrition from a salad or an appetizer-sized portion. In Mexican restaurants, pick one thing you like rather than the four-item combination. Order the smallest pizza that might satisfy you. You can always get another item to fill you up.

10. **Reduce slowly.** It's better to lose half a pound or a pound per week for long enough to get to your target weight than to lose two or three pounds a week for two or three weeks. If you lose more than one pound per week (half a pound for some people), you will lose strength and power.

11. **Identify your triggers.** Many people eat well until some emotional situation comes up, and then they look for comfort in food. Go for a walk or call a friend instead of pigging out. For many athletes, the fear of not getting the right nutrients is a trigger to eat too much. Plan your meals so that when you've eaten enough calories you've gotten your carbohydrates, protein, veggies, and so on.

12. **Weigh yourself daily and average the weight weekly.** Your weight fluctuates a few pounds from day to day, especially when heavy training affects your state of hydration. Therefore, rather than being concerned about your weight each morning, keep track of your average weight for each week. That will more accurately indicate whether you are really gaining or losing weight.

as you can eat. A day or two before the race, focus on eating easily digestible foods so you won't have to carry a load of partially digested food in your intestine during the event. This means fewer whole grains, fibrous veggies, and fatty meat than in your everyday diet.

In the night before an event, your body uses some glycogen during sleep. Be sure to have a good breakfast before the race to top off the fuel tank in the morning. Since you probably won't be comfortable racing on a full stomach, have that breakfast at least two to three hours before your event. Good prerace breakfasts include things like bagels, toast, scrambled eggs, oatmeal, cereal with milk, yogurt, and fruit. Include plenty of starchy foods and a protein source. We do not recommend fatty meats (ham, sausage, bacon) and fatty breads or cakes (muffins, donuts, and coffee cakes) unless you are doing a very long day because the fats are not available for energy until many hours after you eat them. Many riders find that orange juice causes stomach distress during races. Experiment to find what works for you.

In the final hour before your event, nibble another carbohydrate-rich snack, such as a bagel, roll, or energy bar. Around 100 to 200 mostly carbohydrate calories sitting in your belly as you begin to race will serve you well. Wash it down with a half-bottle of water. Research shows that for some individuals, eating or drinking high-sugar (sweet) items an hour before a race decreases endurance and interferes with performance. This problem does not occur when sweet foods and drinks are consumed after exercise has started. Once you've begun your warm-up, it's OK to start using sweet drinks and foods.

How much to eat for breakfast and in the prerace snack is an individual preference as well. If you feel bloated on the line, you ate too much. If you feel hungry on the line or just into the race, you didn't eat enough. If you feel bloated and hungry, experiment with different foods. Try potential race foods in training. Once you've discovered a race-day breakfast and prerace snack that seem to work for you, use them routinely before your hardest training rides as well. If you are not bloated and not hungry in the first half-hour of a race, you've got your prerace nutrition dialed in.

Eating During a Race

If you ate well the days and morning before your race, your glycogen stores are topped off, and you'll have enough carbohydrate on board for an hour or a little more of hard exercise. If the body runs out of glycogen, it can also use fat as exercise fuel, but a small amount of carbohydrate is required for rapid use of fat. So when the carbohydrates run out, the body can only continue working slowly by metabolizing fat alone. In cycling jargon this is called *bonking*—the body is switching over from glycogen plus fat for energy to fat only. Once you bonk, your speed drops and you may become lightheaded. If you bonk during a race, willpower will not keep you in the hunt. You'll be off the back in minutes. You can avoid this unpleasant situation by eating the right amounts of appropriate foods during the ride.

During hard riding, a medium-sized, well-trained rider can easily expend more than 1,000 calories per hour. An untrained person uses almost exclusively stored carbohydrate as fuel for exercise of any

© Casey B. Gibson

In long road races, it's impractical to carry all the food necessary to fuel your efforts; you'll require a food hand up from the side of the road.

intensity. A well-trained person can derive a significant portion of the needed energy from fat when exercising at lower intensities. As exercise intensity increases, the fraction of energy derived from fat decreases while that derived from carbohydrate in the form of glycogen increases. During an event, you want to preserve your glycogen stores for as long as possible so as to avoid bonking. If you are doing a 45-minute criterium, you probably don't need to eat during the race. Sipping a bottle of sport drink is enough. For longer events, you need to eat high-carbohydrate foods with a little protein and almost no fat, in addition to drinking water or an energy drink.

No matter how much you eat and swallow, your bloodstream can absorb only 200 to 450 calories per hour of carbohydrate. Since you can expend 1,000 calories or more of carbohydrates and fats per hour while riding hard, the goal of eating during an event is to slow the rate of carbohydrate depletion. Once the supply is depleted, you can't absorb enough to catch up. Therefore, you must eat early and often while you race. Eating a big bite of something every 15 to 20 minutes from the beginning of the race works for most racers. There are many normal foods that work well as race foods: boiled potatoes, jam and cheese sandwiches (that's jam, not ham), bagels, fig bars, bananas, and toaster pastries are common choices. Many racers also survive on energy bars. Bars containing less fiber are probably better for racing because they don't fill your belly with fiber, which draws in water and keeps you from using that water other places (such as the working muscles) where it is needed.

If you are eating too much, you'll feel bloated on the bike. The discomfort may interfere with hard effort. Up to the level where you begin to have a full belly, more eating while riding is better. The goal is to eat as much as you can absorb—no more, no less. If you arrive home famished after a training ride, you did not eat enough. In a race, it may not be possible to eat and absorb enough. Get down as much as you can without feeling full. Practice chewing and swallowing small bites even while riding hard, because the pack is not likely to slow down when you need to eat.

Also determine whether your chosen foods are realistic for eating while riding. Can you get them out of the jersey pocket and unwrap or peel them one-handed while pedaling? Many racers will pre-tear energy bar wrappers. Some will even break the energy bars into small pieces beforehand.

Some racers prefer an energy gel product. If you plan to use gels, think about how many you are going to need. They typically come in 100- to 125-calorie packages. To get 300 or more calories per hour, you need two to three packets an hour; that's six to nine packets in a three-hour road race. Some gel-type energy foods contain only simple sugars and no complex carbohydrates. They tend to give you a big rush and a big crash, perhaps even bringing on a bonk while glycogen stores are still full. If you use these gels, carry enough for the whole event or start using them later in the event.

Whatever you choose to eat during your races, carry at least one bottle of an exercise drink. If you are not comfortable eating on the bike, exercise drinks may be your only calorie source. Most racers find that they can tolerate and enjoy certain drinks more than others. If you can't stomach the first drink you try, try another. Or try diluting it with water.

In hot races, you will probably want one extra bottle of water with you so you can rinse sweat out of your eyes. (Never put sunscreen on your forehead on a day when you are likely to sweat profusely. Ouch!)

In longer or hotter races, you often cannot carry enough food and water to perform at your best for the full event. Promoters of these races usually designate a *feed zone,* where supporters are allowed to hand food to the moving racers. Feed zones are 100- to 200-meter stretches, typically near the top of steep hills, where the riders are moving relatively slowly. In flatter races, "relatively slowly" might still be over 20 MPH (32 KPH)! You'll need to recruit the help of a willing soul to sit patiently on the side of a race course for hours on end, only so you can come by once in a while and scream for water or food. If you're lucky enough to have such a person, avoid cursing at him in the heat of the moment and learn the proper technique for snatching a bottle on the move. In amateur races, it is generally illegal to take a feed outside of the feed zone or from a moving vehicle, so connecting with your feed in the feed zone is important.

Taking a Feed

Feeders in a feed zone generally must stand to the right side of the road. If you're not sure of the feed zone location or rules in a particular race, ask an official. To receive a feed, you have to move over to the side of the road where your feeder is. If you are doing well in the race, you will come by with a group and not want to slow down or risk having to stop. This means that the feed has to take place quickly and efficiently. You can receive only one item from each feeder you have at each feed zone, such as one water bottle. If you plan to receive both food and water, have your feeder put them together in a *musette bag,* a fabric purse with a long strap.

The feeder stands on the side of the road, facing the direction you are coming from. She sticks the outside arm into the road, holding a bottle loosely at the top with a few fingers. As you pass, hold your arm out and grab the bottle. The feeder should let her arm swing back in the direction you are riding, letting go of the bottle as soon as the smack of your hand is felt against it. At the same time as you grab the bottle, allow your arm to bend to help absorb the impact and gain control of the bottle.

When you receive a feed in a musette bag, have your feeder hold the bag out so that you can grab the straps as you pass. As soon as you have it, put the strap over your shoulder and head so that it hangs across your body. You can then continue riding hard while you take things out of the bag and stash them in your pockets. Musette bags are available at some better bike shops, or you can make your own from any tough, light fabric.

Some racers don't want to go to the trouble to find a feeder, preferring to tough it out without a feed in a long race. In races over two hours in which other riders will get feeds, this is a mistake. If you don't have enough to eat or drink, weaker but better-supported riders will beat you. You can often get a feed from some friendly person who is there to support someone else if you ask around before the start of a race. If you really can't get a feed, carry a third bottle of energy drink in your jersey pocket from the start of the race.

Eating After the Event

After a race or long training ride, your body is drained. You are dehydrated, glycogen depleted, and electrolyte imbalanced. The sooner you can correct these imbalances, the sooner you can train and race again. Immediately after racing, drink a full 16-ounce bottle of recovery drink, whether that is a laboratory-based mix or a fruit and yogurt smoothie. Drink a bottle of water, as well—two if it was a hot day. Then get some carbohydrates and proteins right away. Including your recovery drink, aim for taking in about 300 to 400 calories in the first hour after the race. This could be one bottle of drink and one energy bar, but it's better to start eating real food again as soon as possible. Energy bars are expensive calories, and it's pretty likely that you will eventually lose your taste for them, so save energy bars for times when you really need them, like in races.

Once you've had your postrace food and drink, go out for at least half an hour of easy spinning. This will help the blood flow through your muscles and will speed recovery by delivering water, calories, and electrolytes and washing out the waste products of exercise.

After you cool down and change, eat some food you crave. Unless you have a race the next day, this is the only time of the week (and year) to eat a double-bacon cheeseburger with fries and a malt. If you've stuck to the everyday, prerace, and during-the-race eating plans and to your training plan, you've earned it!

Dietary Supplements and Performance-Enhancing Substances

Most athletes can achieve the U.S. government recommended intakes of nutrients in their daily diet. However, these levels weren't worked out with the serious athlete in mind. Bike racing, as an extremely demanding sport, makes any rider who races regularly a serious athlete. For that reason, we recommend that you supplement your daily diet with a quality multivitamin. Female athletes in particular can benefit from supplementation of calcium, believed to be beneficial in maintaining regular menstrual cycles even when training increases substantially. Iron-rich foods are the preferred source of iron for most athletes, but a small iron supplement may be in order for those prone to low energy due to low iron levels. Consult your doctor if you think you may be low in iron.

In addition to supplementation, many athletes wonder about ergogenic aids—supplements that are supposed to increase performance. The use of illegal or banned performance-enhancing drugs in any sporting event, called *doping,* is considered cheating and is also potentially dangerous. Hundreds of products exist that tout increased performance in strength or endurance. However, many products advertised as legal ergogenic aids have not been proven to actually improve performance. While there are a few legal products available that may positively affect your racing performance, they aren't likely to be needed for beginning racers.

The main thing most legal ergogenic aids have in common is that they are expensive and not worth the money. Use of some ergogenic aids, such as creatine, may actually decrease performance for some riders even if taken as directed. The list of substances banned in cycling, both in the United States and internationally, is extensive, so be sure to check any supplement or medication that you are considering using. Even some over-the-counter cold medicines contain banned substances. If you are still inclined to seek ergogenic aids, read their labels and learn to use them properly, and make sure that you try them in training before you use them in racing.

Hydration

Water is vital to the function of your athletic body. The blood, which is mostly water, carries oxygen and nutrients to your working muscles and carries waste products away from them. Water is also expelled through sweat as your body seeks to cool itself during hard exercise. The problem for athletes is that as water is sweated away the blood becomes gradually thicker. Thick blood is harder for your heart to pump and is therefore a less efficient carrier of oxygen, nutrients, and wastes. Reduced blood volume also leads to inefficient filling of the heart between beats. When you lose water equal to as little as 1 percent of your body weight, which can occur without your feeling thirsty, performance begins to decrease. Drink regularly before, during, and after exercise, even when you are not thirsty. It is not uncommon to see professional cyclists and other athletes sipping bottled water all the time. Finishing one small water bottle during a one-hour time trial will make you about two minutes faster than toughing it out with no water, even on a day that is not very hot.

Most serious road racers do not use hydration packs unless they are riding in extremely hot areas. This may be as much a matter of tradition as good judgment. Hydration packs do increase the weight on the hands and buttocks, which are taking enough abuse already during a long ride. The main advantages of a hydration pack are that you don't have to bend down to pull a bottle from its cage and that you can carry and consume 70 or even 100 ounces of water between refills. By the time you are a skilled racer, however, you will have no trouble reaching for a bottle, even in the middle of a dense pack of riders, and you will know where the good water stops are on your training rides. Meanwhile, if you are not comfortable reaching for the bottle, the hydration pack may help you drink more easily and therefore more often.

Photo courtesy of Susan Yost

Drink before you are thirsty and eat before you are hungry to keep hydration and fuel levels optimal.

What to Drink

The next question most riders ask is "What is the best thing to drink?" There are several dozen forms of sugar water on the market competing to be your sport drink. Some advertise "magic" energy ingredients. Some have more sodium, some less. Some promise balanced electrolytes. Some taste good; some don't. Fortunately, scientists have settled this issue pretty clearly: if a drink contains carbohydrate and salt and you enjoy it enough to drink it, it will work for you. The differences among brands are trivial compared to the difference between getting some calories and water while you ride and not drinking at all. Both the calories and the water in sport drinks are important. You can even use diluted fruit juice if you enjoy that. When no sport drink is available, water will keep you hydrated. On very hot days or rides over three hours, carry plain water as well as sport drink—do not try to survive on plain water alone. On hot days you may not need all the sugar that would come with the amount of water you need to replace sweat. Carry and use an electrolyte-laden sport drink or electrolyte tablets. As many athletes are hospitalized for *hyponatremia* (sodium depletion from sweating salt water and replacing only the water) as from dehydration. For rides up to an hour, plain water is adequate.

How Much to Drink

You can tell whether you are consuming enough liquid if you need to urinate at least every few hours and the urine is close to colorless. On warmer days and days on which you train longer or harder, drink more than on cool days or rest days. Water needs vary greatly from person to person and from season to season, but in general a rider can go through a 21-ounce water bottle in 35 to 45 minutes in moderate weather or as little as 20 minutes in hot weather.

Water bottles, especially if they are used for sports drinks, tend to get funky pretty quickly. Drain, clean, and rinse them well after each use and replace them often. A teaspoon of bleach with a little water shaken around in a bottle will kill most of what grows in bottles. Some bottles are dishwasher safe, but others melt and warp in the heat. Don't put a beloved bottle in the dishwasher. When bleach no longer cleans the inside of the bottle, throw the bottle away.

Chapter 9

Rest and Recovery

Preventing and recuperating from illness and injury are necessary skills for any bike racer. Knowing how to best take care of yourself will keep you healthy and will get you back on the bike sooner after being injured or sick.

Getting Enough Rest

The changes in your body that support the improvements in performance happen only when you take time to rest. In fact, certain growth-, repair-, and health-related hormones are released into your bloodstream only when you are deeply asleep. This means that if you do not sleep enough, you do not get the full benefit of your training. How much is enough? Many professional athletes sleep 9 or 10 hours per night. If you're not sure how much sleep you need, we recommend a minimum of 8 hours per night, combined with sleeping in at least one day per week. If you are sleeping enough, you can lie down to relax in a dark quiet space at midafternoon and not be asleep after 20 minutes. If you drift off shortly after lying down in the middle of the day, you are definitely sleep deprived. Research shows that people who sleep enough are healthier overall. Still, losing sleep one night before a race won't impair your performance much if you sleep enough in general.

It may be difficult to fall asleep the night before a race, especially if you are in strange and noisy surroundings. When you travel to races, carry earplugs and eyeshades so you can fall asleep in hotel rooms. Get your stuff organized the afternoon before the race so you don't have to review your to-do list as you are falling asleep. Develop a falling-asleep routine—read, count slowly backward from 100, take your pulse, meditate, or do anything else that you find relaxing. Avoid caffeinated beverages and exciting activities in the evening. Some people can't sleep shortly after exercise. If this describes you, avoid exercising just before bed.

Cutting Back on Stress

If you are having emotional stress from work or family life, you will not recover as well as if you were more relaxed. When you exercise or experience emotional stress, the levels of adrenaline and nora-drenaline in your blood go up. When the levels of these hormones are high, your body is ready for action. Blood is directed to your brain and your muscles, and away from your gut. When you relax, the levels of these hormones drop, and blood picks up more nutrients from your gut for delivery to the muscles. When you relax, your level of growth hormone also rises. Growth hormone is thought to drive many of the processes that are essential to recovery and growth.

Stress, whether it comes from emotional or physical sources, prevents you from recovering and benefiting from training. We have several times seen moderately talented athletes become successful racers after quitting jobs or resolving difficult family or job situations. While quitting your job to become a better bike racer is probably not realistic for you, you can probably adjust the way you approach your job and other aspects of your life to better support your racing.

Many racers have busy lives. They have to find time to train in there somewhere. If you cut back on sleep to allow time for training, you're making a bargain with the Devil. Just when you demand the payoff in improved performance, you'll learn the truth. As a result, racers tend to lead fairly ascetic lives: no late nights, few nights out, no partying, and a lot of early mornings. To reduce stress and improve training, you may have to not train when your life is particularly busy. If your life is too busy to allow good training too often, you need to adjust your life or give up your cycling dream.

Studies show that interrupting a stressful day with a few minutes of relaxation now and then has its benefits. Even if you are working hard, take a deep, relaxing breath every few minutes. Get up and walk or stretch every half-hour. Rather than working yourself into complete exhaustion, go home a little earlier and start again fresher the next day.

Recovering From Illness

It is normal for bike racers to get sick with a cold or flu once or twice per year, just like anybody else. How you deal with being sick determines whether it keeps you off the bike for a few days or ruins your season. When you are ill, the highest priority is getting well again quickly, not sticking to your training plan. Returning to training too soon can cause a relapse. It is better to miss a few days of training voluntarily than a few weeks due to a more serious illness that you acquired from training while sick. But how much should you back off? For how long? How can you come back to full training? The answers to all these questions depend on how sick you are.

Illnesses divide into two categories as far as training is concerned. Do you have a little sniffle, or something worse? If you have a little sniffle, continue to do recovery-pace rides up to half the length of your longest recent training rides. You can continue to lift weights provided that you quit if you start to feel worse. Continue these lighter workouts (as well as continuing to get plenty of rest and eating right) until you feel well, and then for one more day. Then return to your full training.

If you have more than a sniffle—chest congestion, fever, body aches, deep fatigue, or nausea—you are too sick to train. Do not ride or lift while you have these symptoms. Start to train again when you feel close to fully recovered. If you feel sick for a day or two, take a day or two off. If you feel sick for a week, take a week off. If you are are not recovering after a full week, it is time to consult a doctor.

After you've been ill, do you just return to your training plan, or race the first day you feel good? Not if you want to have a long and healthy season!

If you miss one to three days of training, just take one easy day and rejoin your plan. An easy day is done low in your endurance zone for not more than half of the time of your longest recent ride. If you feel weak on the easy day, take another easy day. Continue taking easy days or days off until you have a good day. You should always have four symptom-free days between an illness and any hard training or racing. If your schedule calls for hard training or racing in the first four days after you return from an illness, just do long endurance rides instead. Don't try to make up the missing days.

If you miss four to seven days, you will need six days to return to full training. The first two days of training, ride or lift, whichever is on your schedule. If you ride, do one-quarter the length of your longest recent ride, and do it at a recovery pace. If you lift, do one-half your normal sets and one-half your normal weights. On days three and four of your return, if you ride, do one-half your long ride at an endurance pace. Drop to recovery pace if you get tired. If you lift, do your normal weights but only half the normal sets. On days five and six, you can do three-quarters your normal long ride at an endurance pace or your full normal lifting routine.

If you miss more than seven days of training, it may be best to delay the remainder of your schedule or do some testing to see how much you have really lost. You may need a few weeks to build up your training again.

How long after an illness should you expect to be strong again? It is our experience that after even a mild cold, riders are not able to race or train at their best for at least two weeks, and often as long as three. Don't be discouraged if you cannot race well immediately after your symptoms clear up. Gradually return to your normal training routine, and you will recover your strength and fitness. We had a rider win a nationals medal just six weeks after taking a week off for illness.

Dealing With Injuries

An overuse injury is a sore muscle, tendon, or joint that you get from extended normal riding as opposed to an injury from a crash. Overuse injury is actually a misnomer. Some professionals can ride 20,000 miles per year without getting an overuse injury. If you get a sore knee on a 3,000-mile-per-year program, it's clearly not because you rode too much. We prefer to think of overuse injuries as *extended misuse injuries*. Most extended misuse injuries are the result of improperly sized or adjusted equipment, inadequate clothing, bad pedaling form, or improper training. Most of these injuries can be avoided by having your bike and cleats fitted by a professional coach, by wearing warm clothing over your knees when the temperature drops below 75 degrees F (24 C), and by building up training gradually, both in miles and intensity. Sore knees that don't result from badly adjusted bikes often result from pushing hard gears instead of spinning and from riding hard without establishing a base of easier training first.

Knee Troubles

Many cyclists develop painful knees at one time or another in the their cycling careers. Here are some ways to avoid, survive, and correct sore knees.

Avoiding and Preventing Recurrence of Sore Knees

1. If the temperature is below 75 degrees F at the start of a ride, wear leg or knee warmers or tights to keep your knees covered while you ride. You can take them off as the temperature rises and put them back on if it gets chilly. When racing, use protective warming gel.

2. Get your bike properly fitted to you by a professional fitter. Most frontal knee pain is caused by having the saddle too low or too far forward. Pain in the back of the knee is often caused by the saddle being too high or too far back. A skilled coach can get you correctly positioned before you have knee trouble. Once you get your bike fitted, mark the seat post with tape so you can return it to the correct position if it ever gets moved. Experienced and serious cyclists who have found a riding position that works record those measurements and their cleat angle. If the cleat holds your foot in a position other than its natural one, it may cause your knees to become sore.

3. Use good-quality, supportive, stiff-soled cycling shoes. Most riders do best with pedals that have some "float" in the angle, though others need the support of a floatless pedal.

4. If you have flat feet or you tend to roll your foot inward (pronate), an expensive orthotic or even a cheap, drugstore arch support will help keep your foot and knee aligned.

5. Learn to spin. Pushing hard against big gears can make your knees sore. As you get stronger and fitter you deliver more force through your feet and knees to the pedals, so bad habits that were OK when you were starting out may become injurious when you are well trained.

6. Train consistently. Going for a hard ride once a week or taking a few weeks off and then doing your full normal training the first day back on is a good way to injure your knees. If you are forced to take time off the bike, take a few easy days when you first get back on. If you take time off to travel, get in at least half an hour every second day on a spin bike or exercise bike while you are away.

Dealing With Sore Knees

1. Sore knees caused by position problems generally clear up within a few days once you get the position corrected. If you let sore knees go for weeks or months, it may take much longer for the pain to clear when you correct the position. You may even develop permanent problems. Bottom line: If you have sore knees, deal with them right away.

2. Ice the problem area soon after each ride. Use a bag of frozen vegetables or crushed ice. Press it to the painful area for about 10 minutes at a time. You can repeat this once an hour if you like. Many sources recommend putting a thin towel between the ice and the skin to prevent burning. The ice reduces the inflammation and pain but does not correct a position problem.

3. Use nonsteroidal anti-inflammatory drugs (NSAIDs) only to help you sleep and only as a last resort. Ibuprofen and similar drugs reduce the pain and swelling but do not correct the underlying problem. Never use anti-inflammatory medication to make it possible to ride.

4. Some sore knees respond well to stretching of the quadriceps or sartorius. Talk to your coach, chiropractor, or physical therapist about suitable stretches.

If you take good care of your knees, following all the guidelines given here, you should be able to enjoy a lifetime of cycling with no knee pain.

If you get an extended misuse injury, the first and most important thing to do is to stop making it worse. Take a break or at least back off the time and intensity of training for a few days as soon as you realize you have a problem. Apply ice to the injured area for a few minutes after each training session or when the area hurts to reduce swelling. Many injuries will resolve themselves quickly if you let them. Never ride through an extended misuse injury. If you make the injury worse, you may lose a whole season or even become permanently disabled.

If the injury is not resolving itself in a day or two, figure out what caused it and get it repaired or adjusted. This may take some sleuthing. Did you recently get some new shoes or pedals? Did your cleat move? Did you change saddles? Did your seat post sink in the frame? Sometimes you can ride for months in a certain position with no problems, but as you get stronger and put bigger forces on your joints a problem arises. Don't be in too big a hurry to make big adjustments. Experienced cyclists often need their saddles adjusted within one or two millimeters to be comfortable and injury free. Typically, if you don't ride long on a sore joint, the soreness will fade in a few minutes when you correct the position.

Cyclists often have trouble in the lower back. The muscles of the legs attach to the pelvis. When they contract to move the pedals, the forces applied to the pelvis are huge and the muscles and bones of the lower back take a lot of abuse. We recommend a regimen of year-round situps or crunches to help protect your back. If you have back pain associated with riding, see a chiropractor or physical therapist. They can usually recommend stretches or exercises to get you pain free again quickly. As with other injuries, don't ignore a sore back. Deal with it as soon as possible.

Saddle Sores

Another common and unpleasant cycling injury that can keep a rider off the bike is the *saddle sore.* Saddle sores are inflamed pimples or boils on the part of your rear end that presses on the saddle. They can be very painful. They can be as small as a pea or as large as a golf ball. They typically start with an infected hair follicle or a small cut. You can avoid them almost completely by always wearing clean shorts with a chamois in good condition. Don't wear underwear with your cycling shorts because sores will start at the chafing from the seams. Do use a chamois lubricant in your shorts every time you ride. There are many lubricants available at bike shops. Men can even use cold cream. We don't recommend pure petroleum jelly, because it keeps the skin moist enough to support fungal infections.

If you get a saddle sore, keep pressure off it and apply a drawing salve (available at drug stores). A saddle sore that refuses to clear up may need to be surgically drained. Consult your physician if a saddle sore sticks around for more than a few days or continues to grow.

Part III

Racing Skills

Racing your bike involves honing your bike-handling skills for surviving in tight pack riding, explosive sprinting, masterful hill climbing, and smart cornering as well as executing smooth, fast descents. The next four chapters provide drills to sharpen these skills and tactical tips for using these skills in the heat of the race.

Chapter 10

Group Riding and Racing

Riding comfortably within touching distance of other riders on all sides of you, just inches from another rider's wheel, and knowing how to hide in a group when you need to rest your legs are important skills you must learn to race effectively. Gaining good pack skills means constantly evaluating where you are in the group, where you need to be, and how to take advantage of the group dynamic. It means always thinking about the wind, the terrain, the riders in front of you, and the riders behind you as well as anticipating what those riders will do.

Experience eventually allows you to make decisions based solely on instinct and firsthand knowledge. In the meantime, learn the basics of group riding and racing etiquette, drafting, and riding in pacelines and echelons.

Group Riding Etiquette

Cyclists form groups to ride with for social reasons, training benefits, and racing strategy. The kind of groups you may ride in from time to time will depend on whether you are training with just a few friends, getting in some large-group rides, or doing some actual racing. Regardless of the kind of group you ride with, some universal etiquette applies.

Above all, keep in mind that you have to remain constantly aware of those around you and that your movements in a group affect everyone in that group. If you stand on your bike and allow your rear wheel to drop back six inches, everyone behind has to make room for the wheels coming back. If you are inattentive and slam on your brakes, you risk causing a chain reaction of braking and potentially a crash. This may sound nerve-racking, but it's not once you get the hang of it.

A few simple rules can help you be an effective and considerate group rider. Knowing them can also save energy and help you win races.

- Stay smooth. Pedal continuously in a cadence and speed that is consistent with the riders in front of you. If the pace slows ahead of you, try to soak up the distance between you and the rider in front of you by pedaling softer rather than braking.

- Look ahead. Keep your eyes on the road ahead of the riders in front of you rather than the riders themselves, and anticipate. Be alert, but stay loose.

- Be polite. Point out and call out turns coming up, obstacles, traffic, dogs—anything you would want to know about. Don't yell. Don't complain. Do stay calm. Road rage is just as silly on a bike as it is in a car.

- Don't half-wheel. If you're riding next to someone and easily maintaining the same pace, be aware of your relationship to his or her front wheel. Constantly upping the pace whenever the rider draws equal to you, *half-wheeling,* is rude and controllable.

- Ride the consensus pace. If the ride is too slow or too fast for you, leave and ride on your own. Riding with a group means riding the group's pace.

The same etiquette that applies to group training rides applies generally to racing as well—and the group tactics you use in racing should be drilled in training.

Drafting

Group riding smarts begin with a comprehensive understanding of drafting. When a single rider slices through the air, he creates a slipstream in the space behind the rear wheel where another can ride, effectively cutting down on the amount of wind resistance the rider behind encounters. This spot of protection in the slipstream is called the *draft* and is most efficient when the wheel of the rider seeking the draft is approximately a meter or less behind the rider in front. If the wind comes from the right, the draft will actually be slightly to the left of and behind the rider in front. The opposite will be true if the wind comes from the left (see figure 10.1, a and b).

a

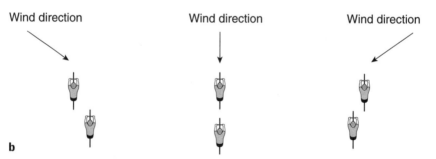

Wind direction   Wind direction   Wind direction

b

Photo © Tony Halford

Figure 10.1 Finding the sweet spot behind another rider where you are most protected from the wind takes practice in various wind conditions.

The basic premise of drafting another rider is simple: If you stay in the sweet spot of a draft, you potentially use 25 to 35 percent less energy than the rider in front is using—a substantial energy savings over even a short distance. The effect of the draft is so strong that you can actually *feel* the protection from the wind. This is precisely why riders form packs in races.

The power of drafting is very apparent when a stronger rider breaks away from the pack with a weaker rider. If the weaker rider manages to sit in the draft of the stronger rider for the majority of the breakaway, she can potentially equalize the opponent; this gives the weaker rider a much greater chance of winning than if, for instance, both competitors were to line up next to each other and drag race down the road. Of course, truly managing to just "sit on" is more difficult to carry out than it is to suggest doing so—part of the reason that road racing is so fascinating!

The tough part is that the quality of every draft is affected by terrain, speed, and even a slight side wind, meaning that a drafting rider may need to ride slightly to one side of another rider's wheel even when the rider in front or the space on the road isn't conducive to doing so. The wind shifts direction and changes intensity, just like a cycling pack. A subtle shift in the speed of a pack or the direction of a gentle breeze can change a mellow ride to a gutbuster. The faster the pack is going, the more the impact of a side wind will be felt. As you ride in a pack, you constantly evaluate the draft and attempt to position yourself in the most advantageous spot behind the rider in front of you.

Drafting properly also means riding close. Riding with your front wheel two feet behind someone's rear wheel *feels* close, until you realize that "close" means narrowing that distance to less than six inches. The increased quality of the draft at this distance can be amazing. The secret to getting your wheel closer and closer to the rider in front of you is to have a feel for the exact length of your bike and for how far in front of your body the tip of your front wheel sticks out. You need to be able to judge where your front wheel is without looking down. At the same time, your elbows should remain slightly bent and your shoulders should be loose to soak up any bumps or fend off anyone who bumps into you. As you learn to be comfortable moving closer and closer, remember to keep a distance with which you feel stable, relaxed, and able to react in a split second. Inefficient drafting will lose a race, but so will crashing after getting taken out by someone else's rear wheel. Crashing hurts more. By the time you are an experienced rider, you'll get used to having a brake lever brush against your leg occasionally, your bars gently bump the person next to you at least once a race, and your front wheel sporadically tap another's rear. You can practice these situations in close riding drills with teammates or attend a riding skills clinic. (See also Drills for Skills on page 119.)

Never stick your front wheel in the space next to a competitor in front of you such that it overlaps his rear wheel. If that rider shifts positions in your direction, crossing your front wheel with his rear, it will disrupt your steering stability and possibly cause a crash. Nothing will likely happen to the rider in front, other than feeling your wheel rub as you fight to gain control, but you will be lucky if you get by with nothing more than the panic of struggling to regain control and a tongue-lashing from the riders behind you who also have to react due to your negligence.

Riding in Pacelines

A paceline occurs whenever a group of cyclists draft each other in a deliberate line to organize the group's effort for an increase in speed. Pacelines make it easier for all the riders in a group to maintain a faster pace than they could on their own.

To create a single-file paceline, riders ride close together, taking turns at being at the front of the line to lead the pace, and then returning to the back of the line to reap the benefits of the draft and "rest" until their next turn at the front (see figure 10.2a). By keeping your front wheel closer to the rider in front of you, your nose out of the wind, your turns at the front smoother, and your reattachment to the back more efficient, you can save enormous energy for the finish of a race or for an acceleration during a group ride.

How long each rider pulls at the front depends on the pace, the relative strengths of the riders, and your goal. In general it can be anywhere from 10 seconds to several minutes. In a race, a paceline means hard effort at the front and that the riders sitting behind the front rider will need to make an effort just to stay with the group. The trick is to work hard enough to contribute to your group's success but not so hard that you use all of the energy you will need later in the race. Use your computer to time each of the pulls before yours, and when it is your turn, stay at the front about that long, or slightly less.

When it's your turn to pull, maintain the same speed as the riders before you. A jump in speed wastes your energy, makes it difficult for the person who has just pulled off to latch on to the back, and potentially splits the paceline as other riders deal with the sharp increase in speed. Increases in speed also disrupt the rhythm; so if you feel like the group needs to ride faster, pick up the speed gradually.

When your pull is over, let the person behind you know that you are ready to pull off. The most common ways are by flicking your elbow out or waving your fingers as they rest on the bars. If the paceline is stretched behind to your left, pull off to your right where you can easily let the group pass as well as shield the working riders momentarily from the wind as they go by. If the paceline is stretched behind to your right, pull off to your left. As you pull off, ease your speed so the rider behind you simply has to maintain your previous speed to pass you.

One sure way to make people dislike you is to peel off the front and *not* slow down. It disrupts the pace and rhythm of the group and forces the rider behind you to almost sprint in an effort to get past you. If you've finished your pull, it's over—ease up, let the group pass, and latch on to the back as quickly as possible so you can begin your recovery. On the other hand, if the rider in front of you fails to slow down when she pulls off, just pull in behind that rider again. Don't take your pull until that rider slows down.

Fixed Pacelines

The single-file paceline we just explained and the similar double-file paceline are the formations riders encounter most often in training and are the easiest to master. They are formed simply by a line of riders in single or double file allowing the rider or riders on the front to create the draft; after the front riders have led long enough, they pull off, slip to the back, and allow the next person or pair to ride at the front.

Double-file pacelines, in which there are two equal lines of cyclists and the riders dropping off move back on either one side or both sides of the pack, are good for long, steady rides where the pace is not high. They are compact enough so that traffic can ease by, and they regulate the group's effort and make conversation easy.

When the pace needs to be higher, however, single-file pacelines work better because it is easier to maximize the available draft by using more of the road and to use the strength of riders one by one. One rider may be weaker than another, but the weaker rider usually still takes a pull at the front when it is his turn as long as the pace can be held for a minimal time that makes it worth taking a pull rather than just sitting on the back of the line.

Rotating Pacelines

When a group of riders (usually five or more) wants to keep the speed high, the efficiency of a single-file paceline can be improved by transforming into a *rotating paceline* (see figure 10.2b). When the pace is higher, the weakness of one or two riders becomes more noticeable in a single-file paceline, causing lulls in the speed that the stronger riders will continually have to regain, making for surges that tire everyone.

However, if the pulls are reduced to just a few seconds, the weaker riders don't have time to slow down before they move over and allow someone else to come through. Rotating pacelines are faster and smoother, and are the most effective way to raise the speed of the group. In a group ride or race when someone yells *Rotate!* they mean that the group should form into a rotating paceline.

Each rider pulls through to the front, then shifts to the side and eases up slightly—just enough to head to the back gradually and

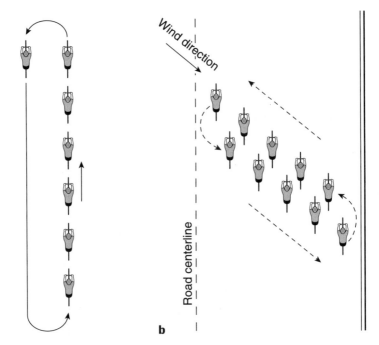

Figure 10.2 At left *(a)*, the single fixed paceline. At right *(b)*, the rotating paceline (in this case, an echelon).

connect to the more forward-moving line again. As the next rider pulls in front of the rider who has just pulled off, the rider now in front gives the previous rider a draft. Each rider moves back down the line until she reaches the end, shifting back into the fast-moving line, working her way up to the front again.

The most difficult part of a rotating paceline is keeping it smooth and figuring out which direction to rotate. The wind affects the rotation direction, as we discuss in the echelon section on page 115. Staying smooth means maintaining a consistent speed: don't speed up as you take your turn around the front, don't drop back too quickly from that lead position, and be sure to hug the wheel in front of you while also staying close to the other line so the paceline stays compact and efficient for everyone.

You will likely find yourself in a rotating paceline any time you're off the front of a race pack or in a small group. When you're in one of these breaks, remember that the goal is not only to stay away from the pack, but also to have enough energy to beat the other riders in your group.

Here are some additional rotating paceline tips:

- Save energy by positioning yourself in the paceline so that you follow the smoothest rider up the fast line.
- Occasionally sit out a turn to eat, drink, and rest. Sit at the back of the group in the sweet spot of the draft behind the riders continually coming to the back before moving forward again.
- Memorize who is in front of and behind you in the paceline so that you can anticipate when you need to start moving over from the slower line to the faster line. Don't wait for the rider to completely pass you, forcing you to jump on his wheel. Instead, as the passing rider's rear wheel pulls even with your front, accelerate slightly and move over onto the passing rider's wheel just as the space opens.

Echelons

When a string of riders are all drafting in a diagonal line in a strong side wind, you get an *echelon*. Another way to see an echelon is just as a single or rotating paceline turned sideways by the wind.

In an echelon, the riders who are moving back from a pull should "protect" the riders who are moving up to take a pull. This keeps the paceline moving fast. For example, if the wind is blowing from the right, the leaders will be on the right with the rest of the paceline stretched to the left, with riders moving in a clockwise direction. If the wind is blowing from the left, the riders will be stretched to the right and move counterclockwise (see figure 10.3).

Understanding the wind is a matter of awareness. In a race, good riders are always thinking, *Where is the wind blowing from? How hard is it blowing? When will it change direction? How much longer will we have this hedge next to us to block the wind? Are there turns coming up? Where will I need to be? Can I use the wind to my advantage?* This last question is one far too few riders ask. The wind can be both an incredible advantage and disadvantage, at the same time in the same race. Smart riders know that simply being at the front makes all the difference.

The key to taking advantage of an echelon is to work into the rotation rather than to sit on someone. When conditions are windy enough for an echelon or a series of echelons to form, there will always be riders who don't feel strong enough to work. With the riders who are working using up the entire available road, the nonworking riders will sit on the tail, being stung by the side wind even if they are only one or two riders away from the echelon.

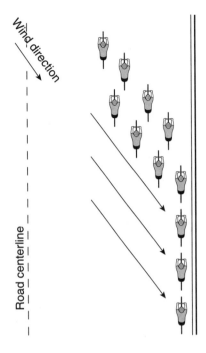

Figure 10.3 Sitting at the tail end of an echelon in strong wind conditions costs more energy than working in the echelon.

However, the riders who are working in the echelon are actually getting an easier ride. The draft is better because it is more consistent—they always have a wheel to follow. Other than a quick turn at the front, they are able to ride smoothly and consistently.

After a while, the riders in the tail along the gutter feel pretty ragged. If the wind direction doesn't shift, the tail falls apart as gaps open and riders give up on holding the pace in the gutter. The solution if you are caught in the tail is to swing over and form a second echelon. Unfortunately, this rarely happens in North American amateur racing—but try it, and keep trying, and eventually people in your local race will catch on.

Echelons are a fantastic tactical tool for strong side winds. If you have a team (or ad hoc affiliation of likeminded riders) and know a crosswind section is coming up, mass at the front. As you make the turn into the wind, form an echelon with one rider at the back not working. This rider, often called the *ticket taker,* directs the echelon, telling riders how far over they can go so there is only room for the riders who are working. When this is done correctly, five or six riders can squeeze off an entire field, leaving them behind to suffer in the wind, wishing they knew how to form an echelon of their own.

Racing Smarts

Races don't always break up; as often as not, you'll be racing in a large group, fighting to hold your position along with dozens of other riders. When a race pack is rolling, you need to be aware of your position in it at all times. You also need to keep tabs on where the edges of the road are, where the centerline is, how far back you are in the pack, which side of the riders in front you need to be on to protect yourself from the wind, and what is going on at the very front of the pack.

If you lose concentration for even a moment, a hard-won position at the front can slip away as 50 riders swarm around you. You need to continually exercise your general pack skills, such as looking ahead up the road instead of at the rider directly in front of you. Pay particular attention to avoiding swerving. Coast and soak up the distance between you and the rider in front of you when there are slowdowns, rather than tapping your brakes. This can be a tough thing to do when you are nervous, but a slowdown caused by even a little braking will be felt by the riders behind you who have to react to avoid running into you; be careful to avoid braking unless it is absolutely necessary.

Photo courtesy of Susan Yost

The pack will continually adjust for hills, wind, and turns. Here the pack makes a left turn, snakes down a hill, and immediately sets up for a right turn.

Of course, the closer you are to the front of the pack, the better you can see what is going on and react as well as participate. The trick of riding in a race pack is to ride as near the front as possible without actually being on the very front of it. This is the difference in being "at the front" versus being "on the front." If you are "at the front," you are in the first 10 riders or so (unless your pack has only 10 riders), keeping an eye on what is going on. When you are "on the front," you are the first rider in line, taking the wind and working harder than everyone else.

When a mass pack is rolling along without any particular chase or other hard riding going on, any time you are forced to roll to the very front, you will want to take only a short turn and then pull off, encouraging the rider behind you to take a turn. Riding strongly and visibly on the front wastes valuable energy and alerts the other riders to just how strong you might be. Never allow yourself to be boxed in so far that you can't ease out to the side with a few quick moves.

Hold a poker face at all times, biding your time in the pack and waiting to either make your own move or react to the moves of another rider.

While riding in a pack can be confusing, there are a few guidelines that can direct the way you behave in a group of riders.

- Your position in a group is crucial. In your first few races, it's enough to be "in" the pack; soon you'll want to be near enough to the front to easily jump into the action but far enough back to use the draft to maximum effect.

- Stay in the first third of the group (or in the front 15) at all times.

- Learn to recognize the wind direction. Study the route of your ride or race, and etch in your mind that day's prevailing wind direction. Glance at the grass or trees along the course and feel the wind on your skin to judge its direction and intensity. When the group turns right or left, you should know how that will change your relation to the wind, and thus where you need to be.

- Move around. The draft shifts, and so should you. Move right, left, up, and back when sitting on a wheel or in a group—always look for the perfect draft.

- Move to the front of the pack when encountering technical turns, pavement, or hills.

Drills for Skills

The Three-Rider Hole Shot

Two cyclists ride slowly, side by side, with about a foot between them. The third cyclist rides behind and eases her front wheel between the leading cyclists. Without taking her hands off the bars, the third cyclist "forces" her way through the gap.

Two-Rider Bumping

Ride side by side at a slow pace. Bump shoulders, elbows, knees, and hips—all while continuing to ride. Try a head-butt or two. But always keep your hands on the bars and your feet on the pedals.

Bunny Hops

Find a board or stick and lay it on the ground. Ride with your hands in the drops, pedaling toward the obstacle, relaxing your arms and legs. About 7 to 10 feet (2 or 3 meters) from the obstacle, lift your rear off the saddle and coast. When you're less than a foot away, "hop" the bike by lifting with your arms and legs and use your momentum to carry you over. The goal isn't to jump high but to jump high enough to get over.

Ring of Fire

This drill is a blast with eight or nine riders, although it can be done with just two. Use eight water bottles to set up a circle on a grassy field. The circle should be about 10 to 12 feet in diameter. Once riders enter the circle, anything goes. The goal is to be the last rider "standing." Riders must leave the circle if they fall, clip out of a pedal, or take a hand off the bars. Otherwise anything goes, including ramming, elbowing, bumping, head-butting, severe teasing, and taunting.

Bumping Wheels

Bumping wheels is a common occurrence in every race or group ride, but it causes a surprising number of crashes. On a grassy field, have a friend ride slowly in front of you while you ride with your front wheel overlapping his rear wheel by an inch or two. Then bump. Let it rub for a few seconds; you won't hurt the wheel or tire. Keep practicing and in one afternoon, you can overcome a lot of anxiety about riding in a group or paceline.

Learning to Crash

If you race bikes, you will crash, and it will hurt. It's just part of bike racing. The crash itself will be mercifully quick—you'll slide and crash within the blink of an eye. Crash wrong, and you may spend painful weeks or months off the bike. Crash right, and you may jump back on and continue in the same race. Here is how to be prepared.

Don't brace your arms—keep them bent and flexible so your wrists or shoulders don't break on impact. Go loose, and relax your body so the joints absorb impact rather than the bones. Maintain momentum, and try to roll with the crash. (Many small scabs and scrapes are much better than one or two big ones.) Always try to roll or slide rather than attempting to stop yourself with force. Last, don't be a hero. Many riders hurt themselves far worse when they attempt something crazy to keep themselves up in a crash. You may think you can bunny-hop over a nine-rider pileup and avoid going down, but it's better not to find out.

When you crash, begin your internal assessment as soon as you come to a stop. Can you move your arms and legs without sharp pain? Is anything broken? Flex your fingers, your wrists, your shoulders, and your knees. Everything work? Good. Pick up your bike and check it out as you prepare to mount it; if nothing's wrong, jump on and get moving. If something is wrong with it, you'll know soon enough. Unless you are in a criterium where free laps are allowed (see chapter 17), pace yourself back to the field, without panic, as quickly and smoothly as you can.

As soon as the race is over, find the medical tent or EMT on duty, and let the pros help you clean your wounds. Your two best tools will be clean rags and plenty of pure water. Use the water to irrigate your wounds, and the rags to scrub hard enough to make the wound clean. Asphalt is filthy and will penetrate deep into your skin. Sometimes getting that skin clean is as painful as the crash itself, but it has to be done or you'll end up with a dirt tattoo or, worse, an infection.

Once your wound is bright pink and quite clean, cover it thoroughly with antibiotic ointment and cover it with a bandage. Repeat the steps for each injured area. When you get home, take the bandages off and scrub each area again in the shower, making sure there is nothing left that can cause infection. Often this first shower hurts even more than the initial scrubbing. Use more ointment and rebandage, repeating this last step often over the next few days.

Chapter 11

Sprinting

Fitness? Competition? Camaraderie? No way. The real reason most of us race bikes is for the speed. There's nothing like an all-out, gutbusting blast to the finish line to top off a ride. Not all races have to end in a sprint, but when they do, you will almost always find someone who sprints as fast as or faster than you. The need for greater speed means a need to increase your top end—to push yourself farther and harder at a higher cadence that right now you can only imagine—and to avoid the basic mistakes in form and timing that can slow you down.

Unfortunately for those whose parents were not Olympic sprinters, the final limiter of raw speed is genetics. Or so we like to think. When we're looking for an excuse after being dropped out of a corner or being destroyed in a competitive sprint, the genetics argument is handy: *Oh, I couldn't beat him in the sprint because I just don't have it. I'm not really a good sprinter.*

Well, maybe you're not. Not yet.

Sprinting isn't about the maximum speed of top pros such as Mario Cipollini or Petra Rossner—it's about *enough* speed. The goal of sprinting isn't to be the fastest. The goal is to be faster than the people you are with, faster than the dog chasing you, and faster than the speed of the paceline behind you. If you *like* to sprint and seem good at it, being fast enough means climbing better than all the other sprinters so that you are left to sprint for the win against other riders who aren't quite as good at sprinting. If you leave other riders behind on climbs and love to climb, being fast in a sprint means sprinting better than all the other climbers. It means molding and honing your own natural speed and making the most of it when it counts.

One famous example of classic sprinting is the 1984 Olympic road race in Los Angeles. American Alexi Grewal clawed his way to the back wheel of Canadian Steve Bauer as Bauer stormed from the field, and the two left the pack to duke it out for the gold medal. Only Grewal wasn't really duking; he appeared to be barely hanging on, hoping Bauer wouldn't deliver a knockout blow.

Grewal, a skinny American best known for his climbing ability, was a contrast to the thick Bauer, a fearsome international star who sharpened his sprinting skills on the U.S. criterium circuit. So, as the two approached the final corner, cycling fans assumed Grewal was fried and Bauer had it won with a kilometer to go.

Unfortunately for Bauer, the medal was awarded at the finish line. Rather than leading the sprint from 500 meters out and using his superior power to ensure that Grewal could not come around, Bauer slowed over the final kilometer. Grewal stayed on his wheel. Bauer waited to sprint until the final 200 meters, and Grewal had just enough to come around, timing his greatest race to perfection and winning the Olympic gold medal.

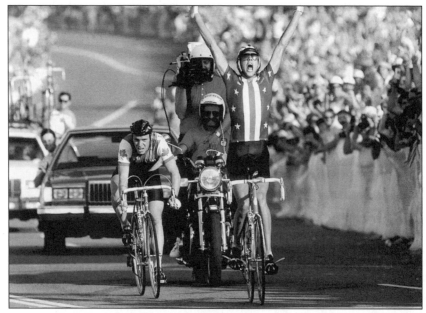

© Sport The Library

Winner Alexi Grewal used both drafting and a shorter path to the finish line to best sprinter Steve Bauer by half a bike length.

It wasn't much, but it was enough—and that's all you need to sprint.

Riders tend to be in one of two groups of sprinters: *power sprinters* or *speed sprinters*. Power sprinters rely more on being able to punch larger gears, powering the cranks over and using the whole body throughout much of the sprint to muscle the bike to the finish line. Speed sprinters, or *spinning sprinters*, rely on spinning smaller gears at higher and higher cadences. The reasons behind favoring one style over the other are most often linked to genetics and body type. More muscular riders usually favor bigger gears and using power to apply great force to the pedals at once. Smaller, slighter riders may find that relying on spinning produces more speed. Some riders find that they are lucky enough to have been born with the ability to handle both styles. As you experiment with the sprint styles and techniques in this chapter, figure out which category you fit into and then keep that in mind when it comes time to sprint during a race; don't be a rider more suited to a quick cadence caught trying to mash a huge gear, or a powerful rider trying to spin up to max speed in the saddle.

Sprint Technique and Timing

Training well, achieving new levels of fitness, planning a race to perfection, making the move, and being in the final selection are all worthy accomplishments. But without the speed to finish on the podium, even the strongest day is bittersweet.

The mistake is to think of good sprinters as burly Neanderthals with oversized thighs, or as crazy people who are willing to make any move to win and don't care if they crash. The truth is, anyone can learn to sprint better, for any situation. Remember, it's not just physiology; it's how you *use* your physiology. It takes patience and practice. Just as with any other part of cycling, sprinting is as much a skill as a physiological phenomenon. That's why it's best to break a good sprint into three core parts: the *jump*, the *acceleration*, and the *finish*.

The Jump

The most technically difficult part of sprinting is in the first 10 or so pedal strokes called the *jump*. The jump is the beginning of the acceleration. The explosiveness of a good jump (combining both speed and force) can mean an extra foot over someone doing it just a tiny bit slower. And usually, that one foot gained is more than enough when a tire's width is all you need to win at the line.

When you are jumping in a race, you are either initiating your own jump or following someone else who has just jumped. A good jump begins with good position in the pack or breakaway, whether you are initiating or following. Being in the right place at the right time is a large part of bike racing success, and this is especially applicable for jumps.

Standing Jump

The standing jump is the core of the sprint. Standing jumps are used in sprinting starting from both low speeds and high speeds. The power of getting up out of the saddle and driving one knee forward while driving back the other pedal with your strength and your body weight is unmatched in any other position. To do it right, start with your head up, eyes looking forward to where you want to sprint. Keeping your head up from the start helps keep your body in alignment and your energy focused for moving forward. Put your hands in the drops, where they have maximum leverage. (Sprint with your hands on the brake hoods only when you are on steep hills; on flat terrain being up higher doesn't call into use as many muscle groups from the back, and the leverage disadvantage is substantial.) Bend your elbows aggressively, and as you rise out of the saddle you will naturally go forward (figure 11.1). Place your hands in the lower part of the drops so that the angle of your arm is not too severe. Grip firmly and securely enough that you can pull forcefully, but not so tight that it restricts the movement of your wrists.

This initial jump requires coordination. As your first leg drives forward and downward, pull with all your might against the bars, both backward and upward. Pulling back and up keeps you from going too far forward over the bars. If you do pull yourself too far forward over the bars, you compromise the traction of the back wheel, where all of your power is being transferred to the ground, and make your balance unstable. After the first two pedal strokes, the pulling on the bars transfers more into a side-to-side yet still upward and backward pull so that you continue pulling yourself through the top part of the stroke, not just the bottom part. Slightly bend your arms throughout.

That first pedal stroke is explosive, and each of the next nine pedal strokes should be the same. Remember, the point is to move the bike forward, which means no thrashing the bike back and forth. Thrash-

Photo courtesy of Susan Yost

Figure 11.1 Remember to keep your head up during a sprint, even when you are tired and giving it everything you have.

ing may feel like you are really working, but it isn't efficient. The bike should move back and forth only enough for you to gain sufficient momentum from the sway of the bike to catch it with the extension of your arm. At the same time, concentrate on driving your knees forward over the pedals, as though you were pitching a baseball from the top of your foot. This will have you focusing more on speed than on mashing the pedals.

As you punch out your first pedal strokes, concentrate on breathing forcefully. Many bike racers actually hold their breath when sprinting. (Check yourself—you might be doing this, too!) It's a natural reaction to a significant change in effort, but sprinting is primarily an aerobic effort, meaning you need oxygen to carry it out. The easiest way to overcome this is to breathe out forcefully on the very first pedal stroke of your jump. Blow air out, and from there you'll likely breathe normally.

You can practice the standing jump in slow motion by putting your bike in a very big gear and then exaggerating the motions methodically and gracefully. Then practice it faster and faster to get the motion down. Watch the form of winning sprinters in other races and videos, and then try to emulate it.

Seated Jump

When the speed leading into a sprint finish is extremely high, such as that heading into a downhill finish, it's possible that you are already going and spinning so fast that it is impossible to get out of the saddle and jump into a higher gear. Or, it may be that you are heading down a road or descent where it is be dangerous to rise out of the saddle. In that case, you need to jump while in the saddle. Jumping while in the saddle means sending a burst of speed to your already spinning legs. Speed, not power, drives a seated jump. Seated jumps are best practiced in small gears because they are so reliant on speed.

Performing a seated jump is similar to normal riding but you must relax even more and concentrate on *pedaling faster* rather than riding harder. You should still make a marked "JUMP!" in your head and send the gas to the pedals.

The Right Gear Choice

Achieving an explosive first pedal stroke—whether from a standing or seated jump—cannot be done without being in exactly the right gear. The choice of this gear depends on your speed as you head into the jump. A coach can't just say, "Always jump in your 53 × 14," because various sprint finishes have different character and speeds. Most sprint finishes *will* take place in the big chain ring unless you are on a steep hill. If you do start sprinting in the small chain ring, make sure that you won't run out of cogs, leaving you stuck in too small of a gear—or, worse yet, forcing you to shift to the big chain ring in the middle of the sprint.

Too often, sprint finishes are lost because the person jumping is bogged down in too big of a gear. If you haven't seen it already, you will soon: someone tries to jump away, but the entire field latches directly onto his wheel or passes easily because the rider is "sprint-ing" in a huge gear. Remember, sprinting is about both power and speed. A rider who is very strong but lacks speed cannot make up for that deficiency by simply putting the bike in a bigger gear to sprint. So don't automatically shift down three gears bigger before you jump. Instead, shift down to the gear that you think you can hold until the finish. Choose on the easier side rather than the harder side when in doubt. Most good jumps won't be more than one or two gears bigger than the one you are riding before you jump. If you need one more, you will be able to tell right away and can quickly shift.

Never forget that the entire sprint is an all-out effort from initiation to finish. Fill your soul with all the energy and power you can muster, and give it everything you have.

The Acceleration

Once you've taken those first 10 or so strokes of the jump, you transition to the acceleration phase, picking up more and more speed. The acceleration is the "easiest" part of the sprint, as your momentum almost carries you to the higher speeds through higher cadence. Unless you're battling a fierce headwind, the initial jump is the most difficult part of sprinting.

The acceleration is a matter of continuing to spin faster and harder until you reach what you perceive to be your top speed in a gear you can stand on, then settling into the saddle to ideally continue accelerating through the finish line. The transition from standing to sitting should be a smooth one. Avoid "plopping" down hard on the saddle and potentially disrupting both the power and cadence of your pedal stroke. A common mistake is to stay out of the saddle too long, shifting to progressively larger gears until your speed actually begins to drop off. At that point, you may think it's time to sit down, but you'll realize once you do that the gear is huge and you can't turn it effectively while sitting down. This means either standing back up or shifting to an easier gear, both of which waste precious speed. In your training, practice finding the "sweet spot"—knowing when to stop shifting. There is no magic moment; it depends on the terrain, the wind, the speed, and your fitness.

The reverse of the rider who waits to sit down too late is the one who sits too early. Make sure you have maximally used the leverage and body weight available through standing before settling into the saddle. During a set of sprints, practice sprinting out of the saddle to where it seems most comfortable to sit down. In the next sprint, try sprinting out of the saddle for an additional five pedal strokes and compare your sprint time. If your longer out-of-the-saddle time is faster, you may need to concentrate on staying out of the saddle a bit longer during your sprints.

After you sit down, hold your speed or even continue your acceleration to the line. Tuck in your elbows and knees, drop your head low enough so that you can still see the line but so that your back is flat, and make yourself as aerodynamic as possible. Keep your cadence high, and breathe deeply. Above all, you don't want your speed to drop off. We'll discuss further the strategy of jump timing in races in the road racing and criterium chapters.

The Finish

The last 150 meters of any race are the simplest and most straight-forward in bike racing. This section is actually just an extension of the acceleration. Tactics are over. The last 150 meters are even more a "race of truth" than time trialing. There is no fancy equipment—just whoever can go faster and win the race. It's raw horsepower but for a few simple rules.

First, keep your eyes forward, no matter how much the effort robs you of your senses. Look to the line (figure 11.2), not to the side or the ground. Winning the race isn't worth it if you run into a car parked just past the finish line. Never look sideways to the riders you are passing or to those who seem to be coming up on you. Looking at other riders is a distraction and will not help you increase your speed. In fact, looking at an encroaching rider will often cause panic and more restricted breathing rather than an increase in speed. You can't control the other riders' speeds. You can only control your own by keeping your eyes targeted on the goal of the finish line.

Second, choose the most direct path to the finish line. Don't follow the slight curve of the road simply because the paint on the road curves. Make a beeline for the finish, and hold that line regardless of what the other riders around you do unless they are moving in on you in such a way that you will have to make an evasive maneuver. Do not suddenly shift from the line you've chosen or drift over the path of another rider. Drifting over to close another rider's path is called *not holding your line* and is grounds for relegation. Swerving suddenly to block or intimidate another rider is called *hooking* and is grounds for relegation or, in extreme cases, disqualification.

Third, don't stop sprinting until you are on the finish line itself. Sprint not *for* the finish line but *through* it. When you feel like you're right before the line, put everything you have into one punch of the

No matter how much you think you may be winning, never celebrate until you cross the finish line. Even the best pros have been nipped at the line with their arms up celebrating a win they didn't get.

Figure 11.2 Although the two riders at left look nearly even, it's easy to tell by the rider's hands coming off the bars at far left that he's won the race.

rounding pedal, and as you do, thrust the bike forward until your arms are straight. This is called *throwing* the bike, and is the equivalent of a runner leaning or a short-track speed skater thrusting a skate to the finish line. As you throw your bike, continue looking at the line. Photos of riders throwing their bikes usually show the losing riders watching the winner, who is looking at the line. It's the last little bit, and it pays to practice this move during your sprint training because losing by one tire width will haunt you more than any other race finish. But a win, even by a millimeter, is still a win.

Finally, know the rules and know the officials. Many officials will actually disqualify winners who take their hands off the bars to celebrate a victory, so be cautious. Of course, you'll want to keep a firm grip on the bars anyway for those last 150 meters, in case your wheel skips out or you have to maneuver to avoid road obstructions or the unexpected swerves of another rider.

Sprinting Drills

Sprint training outside of racing is often best accomplished through sprint intervals. Warm up for a minimum of a half-hour in the endurance zone, making sure that your muscles are warm and limber. Then choose a landmark approximately 200 meters down the road. From the starting point of the 200-meter stretch, sprint full speed to the designated landmark. Choose gears that allow you to pick up speed quickly, and then hold it. Sprint as forcefully and as efficiently as possible all the way through the imaginary finish line. After you cross the line, continue pedaling with some force as you switch to easier gears. Keep the lactic acid from building up in your legs as you rest by riding at recovery pace for 10 minutes before attempting another sprint of the same distance.

After your final sprint, cool down by spinning home for at least 15 minutes in easy gears. Start your first sprint session with two to three sprints, building up by adding two more sprint intervals each week until you reach six or more total sprints in one session. If you find that you are too tired to do the sprints properly, stop the exercise and head home for the day. Shake up this exercise by varying it: try uphill and downhill sprints, use bigger and smaller gears, and alternate between rolling into the sprint at race speed or sprinting from a near standstill. You can also vary the course, choosing curving roads or sprinting out of a turn. Whatever you choose, make sure that the course is safe from traffic, pedestrians, and pets.

Sprint intervals are often more fun if you do them with a partner or group. Having a little competition motivates most riders to try even harder than they do when alone. A group can do sprint intervals by rolling to the start all together, drag race style, then sprinting to be first across the line. Additional exercises include sprinting for the designated finish in a bunch to replicate racing situations, or arranging for one or two riders to "lead out" the sprint by breaking the wind at the front of the group while the other riders sit in the draft behind and then jump around, charging to the line. If people of varying abilities make up the group, certain riders can be given a handicap. The faster riders can be made to delay the start of their sprint against the group, or they can be the lead-out riders who still sprint for the line even though they have been pulling into the wind. Throw corners and hills into the mix to learn the variations of sprinting against a group in those situations.

Sprint Training

Sprint training is best done after you have mastered the technique of sprinting. The dangers of practicing bad habits, like sprinting in too large a gear, are just too great. To develop speed outside of predefined drills, designate sprint finish lines at various places along your route on your group rides. One traditional way to do this is to sprint for city limit signs. You can also sprint for hilltops, bushes, or whatever else is convenient. Remember that your goal is to develop speed that can be used in races. The need for speed in races often comes right after a corner, so rather than doing all your sprint drills on long, straight, flat roads, practice sprinting in places that simulate a real race course: include uphill and downhill, left turns and right turns as well as long straight roads. Of course, in real races you don't get to tell your competitors when or how to sprint. Keep the sprint practice real by keeping it free form.

Sprints in a group to real finish lines are hard, tiring exercise. Include them in your program only when you are well recovered and during the times of year when higher-intensity training is appropriate, starting no more than one month before the beginning of racing and stopping when racing stops for the year. Sprint training, although made up of short bursts of effort, is extremely intense and should be done only once a week as training outside of weekend racing. Only continue sprinting in any given practice session as long as you are strong and fast (for you). Don't practice sprinting slowly and tiredly. You don't want to get good at that!

Chapter 12

Climbing

Most bike racers consider an inability to climb their greatest weakness. Climbing is, in many ways, harder than a time trial, a sprint finish, or a windy road race. While it is the other riders in a race who make a race hard or easy, a course with major hills can sometimes defeat a rider before the race even begins.

Riders tend to fit into one of four categories when it comes to climbing:

1. The skinny climber type
2. The naturally talented rider who climbs well, regardless of shape
3. The average rider who enjoys several good climbing weeks a year
4. The rider who simply can't climb well

While the *best* climbers are usually thin, lanky, or tiny, *good* climbers come in all shapes and sizes and from all different backgrounds. While the bad news is that genes *do* play a part in the ability to climb well, the good news is that with training any rider can become a better climber. However, keep in mind that no technique or trick can overcome deficiencies in fitness.

Climbing Technique and Tactics

Just as there is technique for riding well in a criterium, for hiding yourself from the wind inside a pack, or for time trialing faster, there is proper technique for climbing, and it starts, surprisingly, with slowing down.

An endurance-based approach to training is difficult for many athletes because they don't like slowing down. Most of the cyclists we coach have a hard time keeping their heart rates low during the first few weeks of preseason training, especially on hills. An endurance heart rate ceiling of 155, for example, can make climbing excruciatingly boring. The speedometer reads 5 MPH, and even in the easiest gear, your cadence feels sluggish and slow. But cyclists who maintain discipline and continue to climb with their heart rates low find that they begin to climb better. After a few weeks, their cadence is not so bogged down, their speed has gone up a bit, and they feel much smoother than ever before.

The reason is that by slowing down they are able to focus on their technique. During a session of intensive hill intervals, there is often no time to concentrate on technique because an interval demands total concentration on the effort of going up the hill as fast as possible. But climb that same hill at half the intensity and many faults come out, such as how much rougher your pedal stroke is on a hill as opposed to on the flats, how you grab the bars tightly when you climb, and how your shoulders rock side to side when you climb even though they are hunched forward.

Proper Breathing

Good climbers' cadence and rhythm are predictable and smooth: tick, tick, tick, tick, 90 times or more a minute. Clockwork. That rhythm is one of the keys to successful climbing; it keeps the bike rolling through the steep sections, through the pain, and through the mental barriers that go with staying at the front in a hilly race.

Perfecting that rhythm takes time but not as much effort as you might think. Put down the book for a moment and take five rhythmic, deep breaths, each with an equally rhythmic exhalation. Feel more relaxed? Try it on your next ride by coordinating your breaths with the rhythm you're trying to maintain; open your lungs by spreading your shoulders and straightening your back. Breathe from your belly forcefully.

At the heart of a good climbing rhythm is relaxation. Deep, consistent breaths lower your heart rate, focus your mind and body, and help keep your cadence ticking along.

Seated Versus Standing

Your position on the bike and your comfort level should be well established before you tackle proper climbing form. As you're seated, keep your back straight, particularly where it meets your waist. Don't curve or hunch it. A straight back and slightly bent arms allow your head to remain high and your legs to draw power from the muscles of your abdomen and torso. Many cyclists hunch farther and farther forward as they tire on a climb, pressing their body weight over the front wheel. No position could be worse for allowing your bike to move smoothly and for riding with your most powerful muscle groups.

Simply put, the most efficient way to ascend a long, steady climb is in the saddle. Sure, every year at the Tour de France there is a phenomenal climber who ticks off each kilometer bobbing over the pedals without his rear hitting the saddle even once. Those riders' climbing prowess aside, out-of-the-saddle isn't the most efficient way to climb for most riders. Without the bike to support your body weight, riding out of the saddle for more than a minute or two causes higher heart rates and more muscle fatigue.

While being seated is most efficient for most climbing, you will inevitably stand. When the gear you are spinning up a hill while seated becomes too small or too large to stay with those around you, you need to either shift to a bigger gear and stand or simply stand in the gear you are in (see figure 12.1). Responding to surges in speed, stepping up to chase other riders, launching your own breakaway attempt, changing your body position for comfort, and powering up a short increase in grade all *feel* better and are usually more efficient when done out of the saddle.

The rules for standing climbing are the same as they are for seated. Keep your back straight (no humps), leave your elbows slightly bent, and carry your head high. Rock the bike gently underneath you, no more than four inches on either side. As your right leg drives the pedal down, use your right arm to pull gently on the bars. At the same time, the bike will sway to the left and your left arm will mostly straighten. Just at the point where your left arm is mostly straight, begin the downward pedal stroke with your left foot and pull against your left arm. The best climbers look as if they are actually dancing on the pedals. Keep that picture of grace in mind as you stand for any amount of time.

When you stand, be aware of pulling your bike up underneath you as you lift off the saddle. Too many riders simply stand up, allowing

Photo courtesy of Susan Yost

Figure 12.1 Climbing position can be an individual preference. In the short climb shown here, riders exhibit seated and standing techniques.

their bikes to move back two or three inches. Not only does this cost you precious forward momentum, but your rear wheel may drive into someone else's front, potentially causing a crash. So as you stand, take your bike with you.

Standing Hand Placement

The best place for your hands for standing climbing is on your brake hoods, gripping them firmly but not in a way that restricts movement or blood flow in your fingers and hands. Most riders prefer to keep the thumb hooked on the inside of the brake hood with the index finger resting over the top of the brake and the middle and ring fingers holding onto the outside underpart of the hood. The middle and ring fingers are strong enough to do the pulling even in a racing climb, and having the index finger over the brake allows you control over the brakes in case someone else brakes in front of you unexpectedly.

Climbing with your hands on the hoods allows you to move in and out of the saddle as necessary as well as to respond quickly to sharp surges in speed. Climbing out of the saddle with your hands in the drops of the bars may make you look like pro riders Jan Ullrich or Jeanne Longo, but it isn't the most efficient way to climb (except for

Standing Form Intervals

Some riders aren't comfortable rising out of the saddle in the middle of a hill, and some feel unnerved any time they need to stand. Standing intervals help you practice climbing in the standing position. Being able to stand for periods of time in your riding also helps you to literally "save your butt" by giving it a break every once in a while.

Always warm up for at least 20 minutes before starting your first interval. Start with a 2-minute interval, rising out of the saddle at endurance pace. Continue standing for the duration of the interval. Maintain good standing form—hips bent enough to get the seat near the back of the thighs, hands on the hoods (or in drops on the flat), your bike rocking while the body stays fairly still, powering the pedals around rather than just dropping your weight on them. These aren't meant to be hard intervals but rather exercises to help you become accustomed to riding out of the saddle in good form for extended periods of time.

Set a starting time for the first interval and just do it, regardless of the terrain. If you end up standing on the flats, that's OK too. But avoid doing a standing interval for too long on a downhill. If you do these intervals on a stationary trainer, make sure your hands are in the drops instead of on top of the hoods. After each interval, continue riding in your endurance zone for at least 10 minutes before attempting the next interval. Start your first session with two intervals of 3 minutes. Then add an additional interval and an additional minute to each interval each week until you reach five intervals of 5 minutes each in length. After the final interval, ride for 10 more minutes in your endurance zone, dropping to your recovery zone to complete the last 10 minutes of the ride.

extremely fast climbing on a very gradual hill). The lower position of the drops and the angle of the hill force your torso to be bent at an awkward angle, good only for people with the power output of a Tour de France winner.

Seated Hand Placement

During a straightforward climb with relatively wide turns and good pavement, rest your hands lightly on the tops of your bars, far enough apart to keep your chest open and elbows comfortable. There are variations on this—grabbing near the stem or resting them just above the brake hoods—but a neutral placement on the tops of the bars gives you the best control. This hand position also forces you to react more gradually to surges in speed caused by other riders choosing a more moderate pace to catch up rather than panicking and going too hard, risking going anaerobic and quickly falling off the pace.

When climbing on a technical climb full of tight turns or undulating terrain (variations of steep and gradual or even short downhill portions), keep your hands on the hoods to be able to stand quickly, steer tightly, or change gears without having to move your hands first. Keeping your hands on the hoods when you are climbing in a tight pack during a race also helps you protect the space around you from anyone bumping you out of position because you are able to move your elbows out or stand for a second, swaying your bike back and forth to let other riders know not to crowd you.

Whichever method of climbing you choose for a given hill, always keep your hands loose. Former Giro d'Italia winner and renowned climber Andy Hampsten used to say he knew he was holding the bars with just the right amount of force if he felt as though his fingers were loose enough to play the piano. It's a good analogy. Your grip should be firm, but your fingers should stay loose and comfortable.

Climbing Cadence and Gearing

When climbing, it is natural to feel that if you push a big gear you are gaining more ground than if you spin a smaller gear. For most people, it's easier to stomp, push, or mash those pedals at whatever cadence gets them up the hill. Often this is because cyclists aren't using their gearing effectively. Let's say the race approaches a hill along a flat road at a pace that keeps you in your big ring. At the base of the hill, as the road goes up, good climbers cruising along inside of a pack of riders will immediately shift into their small front chain ring and into gears easy enough for them to spin up the first part of the hill at 100 RPM or higher.

This serves two purposes. First, the high spinning gives your legs a quick break—even if only a 10-second recovery spin—before the serious climbing begins. Second, good climbers know that the surest way to disrupt forward momentum is to shift to an easier gear in the middle of a hill. As with sprinting for the finish, when you can see the top of a small hill, try to start the hill in the gear you think you will use all the way up. While steeper pitches may necessitate a shift to a smaller gear, shifting to a smaller gear on a hill that hasn't changed pitch means you are getting tired and going slower. It's possible that if you had started out in the smaller gear to begin with, you might not be as tired at the same point. So by maintaining a higher cadence at the bottom of the hill, you're giving yourself a better chance to ride that hill faster.

Before shifting to your small chain ring from your big chain ring, shift into a midsized or harder gear on the back cogs. This takes some tension off the chain, allows a smoother shift of the front chain rings, and prevents the chain dropping off the rings into the frame. If you have brake lever shifters, try shifting to a harder gear in the back while shifting from the larger ring to the smaller ring in the front so that the opposite forces on the chain make for an efficient shift.

What happens if you drop your chain on a climb? It doesn't have to be a disaster. First, don't panic. There's a chance that if you keep pedaling in a relaxed fashion and move the front shifter toward the big ring position that you may catch the chain back on the little ring and be able to continue with the momentum you have going. Even if you lose momentum quickly, there's always the chance that if the pack isn't going too fast, a considerate soul will give you a short push just long enough for you to get the chain hooked again by shifting. In the event that you can't get the chain hooked and you've run out of momentum, hold the line you are traveling and come to a stop. Riders will probably already be aware of your slowdown and will be going around you on both sides, so be sure not to swerve. Once you are stopped, get off the bike and reach down to hook the chain back on. Then just climb back on and get going again as quickly as you can. If the race has support vehicles, it's likely that a mechanic will be there to help get you going with a push once you are back on your bike. Remain calm throughout, and the whole process will go much faster.

Choosing Your Line

When climbing, choose the most *efficient* line, not necessarily the *shortest* line. Cornering on a climb is different from attacking that climb as a descent. On a descent, the line may be clear—arc your turn wide, cut it close at the apex, and exit smoothly to the opposite side of the lane or road—but it's not nearly as clear going uphill. (See chapter 13 for more on cornering.)

A steady, highway-style grade is simple to climb—this is the one kind of climb where you take the shortest route possible from corner to corner. However, even slightly steep or narrow roads require a more thoughtful approach. For example, if the road is steep going into a hairpin corner, the apex of that corner will be the steepest part of the road. It may be a shorter line, but it's taking an enormous amount of energy to boost your effort to keep your speed up. Instead, approach the corner on the outside, and imagine the apex in the middle of the road rather than the far inside of the turn. The road is far less steep there, and while you might be riding a few feet more than if you took the shorter line, the shallower grade will allow you to maintain a steadier and speedier cadence and better rhythm, and therefore higher speed.

Riding Your Own Pace

When you reach the bottom of an extended climb with another rider or group of riders, you face a choice about the pace you will tackle. Of course, to try to win the race, you need to be at the top of any given hill ahead of the leaders (figure 12.2), with them, or close enough to catch them immediately on the flats or downhill following the climb. To do this, you need to match the pace set by other climbers leading the climb, set the lead pace yourself, or eventually drop back to maintain your own steady pace in the hopes that others who go out too fast will fade later and you will catch them.

The art of mastering the pace on hills is learned over many races. Your chosen pace depends on your relative strength as a climber, your current fitness, and your experiences on recent similar climbs. Riders who already know that their strength is climbing want to be at the front setting the pace or hiding just far enough in the pack behind the front that they can up the pace at any time. Riders who typically have trouble on the hills may prefer to start the climb at a pace they know they can sustain up the entire climb. This is not to say that the rider choosing to climb her own pace isn't going hard. Choosing to drop off the first pack of riders *before* you blow up (go anaerobic and are forced to slow down) is a tough thing to do mentally when you are competitive. What often happens when you choose to climb your own pace from the start on a longer climb, though, is that you eventually catch many of the riders who attempt to stay with the front group as long as possible.

Try this sometime in a group ride, using your heart rate monitor (or a wattage meter) to help you judge your pace. As the group heads up an extended climb, notice when you are approaching your anaerobic threshold level (or maximum sustainable watt level at threshold). Once you reach it, refrain from pushing any harder to stay with the group. If you can stay with the group, great; if you can't, just drop off and continue going your own pace. You'll likely find that you reach

Photo courtesy of David Beede

Figure 12.2 Setting up successfully for a climb means being near the front of the pack at the start of the rise.

the top at the same time as usual, behind the leaders or faster, but much fresher.

Surging on a Climb

One of the toughest components of climbing is handling the bursts of speed that good climbers inject into a climb. If you are a good climber, upping the pace in unexpected surges can disrupt the rhythm of other climbers and potentially destroy both the morale and legs of riders who are barely hanging on your wheel. If you are a rider who has a difficult time handling surges, you may have to attempt to take charge of the climb by moving to the front and setting the pace steadily at what you can handle, hoping that you are moving along fast enough that no climber will up the speed around you. If you are already on the bubble, ready to pop, and the climbers continue upping the speed, you will have to get extremely focused. One technique is to plant yourself on the wheel of a good climber in front of you and refrain from looking up the hill. You know that more of the hill is coming and that it will hurt. Focus only on staying with that rider, no matter how much you suffer. Finally, if you know you are going to blow up if you stay with the climber any longer, drop back and minimize your losses by continuing at a pace you can maintain. Try to stay with the next rider or group that catches you so that you have someone to work with immediately as you crest the hill and reach flat terrain or a descent.

Pushing Yourself

Don't be afraid to go hard. The mental block that so many bike racers have about hill climbing keeps them from riding as hard as they could. The hill begins, and they shift into easier gears and allow the hill to ride them rather than riding the hill.

Attack it! Ride smooth, using your strength, speed, power, and endurance to roll up the hill as though it were your favorite thing to do. And give yourself every opportunity to do well on the hill by beginning it at the front. Remember, no matter how well you climb, if you begin a hill 20 or 30 riders back in the field, you automatically have that much ground to make up if you hope to go over the top with the leaders. The secret truth about climbing is that even when riders are excellent climbers, it still hurts. It's just that a good climber suffers the hurt at the front of the pack while a developing climber suffers the same off the back of the pack.

Finally, enjoy what you're doing. No commentator or racer waxes philosophical about the beauty of a frontage road loop race or the majesty of a downtown criterium course. Hills are what make our sport spectacular, and the more you learn to love them, the better you'll ride them. Follow the tips on page 142 for racing hills to help you master this skill.

Climbing Training

Training to climb can be carried out at various intensities and distances, which makes it an easy component to insert in your training throughout the year. In the season outside of racing, start including climbing in the endurance-building zone (see chapter 5, page 56). Ride hills on your normal training routes smoothly and steadily, paying attention to form and breathing. As the season nears, include specific hill interval training at increased intensities.

Hill climbing intervals can be as short as 30 seconds at high intensity to simulate short, powerful bursts during races, or 10 minutes or more for extended mountain climbing. The climbing intervals should simulate the kinds of climbing you encounter in your racing. If you race in an area where there are climbs lasting 5

Tips for Racing Hills

- Conserve energy. Push a small gear when you can get away with it, even if riders around you are pushing larger gears. In a circuit race with a hill you encounter many times, the more energy you can save early on with small gears, the more prepared you will be to push larger gears over the same hill when you are forced to with a higher pace.
- Draft. Sure, you're only riding 10 to 15 MPH, but that's enough for a drafting effect. Every bit of energy saved is energy you can use later to try to drop others. If you don't like to ride other people's pace, you can always surge to try to drop them from your wheel.
- Bluff. This is one of the great gambits in bike racing—when you aren't sure how well you're climbing, go to the front and set your own pace. If you can do it with authority, most people in the race will be happy to let you ride at the front. Odds are that your pace is comfortable for them, so they won't be inclined to come around and ride harder. If your climbing legs are unsure, act as though they are the best in the world and you just might bluff your way to the summit.

minutes or more, you will need to be proficient at that kind of climbing. If you live where there are more rolling hills, master short repeated efforts where you push through the top of the hill and then rest momentarily on the descent before rolling smoothly and powerfully into the next climb. These kinds of rolling hill efforts can also be interspersed with efforts over multiple hills where no rest is allowed between each climb.

Here are some other exercises you can do that focus on climbing.

Climbing intervals. This exercise trains you to ride race pace on hills of various lengths. Warm up with 25 to 45 minutes of endurance-pace riding. For your first session of intervals, ride three 4-minute intervals broken up with 5-minute periods of rest. Ride for 4 minutes at a pace five beats below to five beats above your anaerobic threshold. Rest by riding at recovery pace for 5 minutes, then ride another interval of 4 minutes. Ride the first interval near the bottom of the zone, settling into the pace at a cadence of 80-plus RPM. Ride the next interval near the top of the zone, if possible. For the final interval, ride in whichever zone your heart rate seems to want to settle. Cool down at recovery pace for a minimum of 20 minutes. Add one minute per interval each session and work up to as many as six intervals of 8 minutes per session, depending on available time and ability. When you can no longer ride in the suggested intervals zone, end your session and head home. This exercise is best done up to twice per week in the month leading into your first races of the year and up to once per week during the racing season.

Surges. This exercise trains you to adapt to surges in pace on a climb. Warm up 45 minutes, then find a gradual hill. Pick a gear in which you can do 70 RPM cadence with your heart rate at about 75 percent of maximum. Accelerate hard but seated to a 95 RPM cadence, and hold it for 1 minute. Rest for 5 minutes between each surge. Keep doing surges until you are not as strong as at the beginning, whether this is 3 surges or 20. Spin home at an easy pace.

Killer hill sprints. This exercise trains you to power up short, steep hills. These sprints are just like regular flat sprints, except that they take more time and are to be done on a certain type of hill. The perfect hill for these sprints is about 300-400 meters long with a gradual climb in the beginning that gets steeper as the hill goes on and then flattens at the top. The middle of the hill should be quite steep—nearly 9 to 12 percent grade. The finish line should be right at the top, where the grade levels to flat. Start by sprinting from the bottom of the hill. Pick your gear from the big chain ring, potentially starting with a 53 $\times$ 21 and working up to a 53 $\times$ 16; resist shifting during the sprint. The gear should feel easy at first and almost spun out, then get harder and harder as the hill and time wear on. By the time you near the top, you will struggle just to continue pedaling to keep sprinting for the line. Pedal through the finish line, not letting up until the hill has flattened out for a minimum of 20 meters (66 feet). Rest for a minimum of 10 minutes at recovery pace between each hill sprint. If you do these correctly, you will find that you have energy to do a maximum of only five sprints.

If you live where there are no real hills, train to climb by doing out-of-the-saddle intervals (see the standing intervals sidebar on page 136) and hill repeats on smaller hills available to you (even if it's just a freeway overpass). If you plan to race on major hills during your season, consider traveling to train on that kind of terrain in the months before your competition.

Chapter 13

Cornering and Descending

As with most other cycling elements, blasting through corners without touching your brakes or flying down a curving descent at full speed are skills that some do well naturally but others must learn. However, unlike pushing the pedals faster or harder to go in a straight line, cornering and descending depend on confidence in addition to balance and control. Building your confidence and challenging your fears fuel the synergy between body and bike as you negotiate corners and descents.

Building Your Confidence

The easiest way to boost your bike-handling confidence is to ensure that you and your bike are well prepared before you ride. A 50 MPH (80 KPH) descent is no place to discover stretched brake cables or any other problem with your bike. Inspect your bike often, especially the brakes and tires.

The fit of your bike determines your ability to corner and descend. Have it checked by a professional. For an ultimate cornering setup, sit a good distance behind the bottom bracket with the stem high enough to be comfortable but low enough to steer easily, thus balancing your weight evenly between the front and rear wheels.

If you wear glasses or contacts, make sure your prescription is current. If you don't wear glasses or contacts but may need them, don't delay. Most cornering mistakes stem from misjudging the severity of a corner. Finally, wear a helmet, even in training. It's cheap insurance and gives that added bit of self-assuredness while riding—

especially against the things you can't control when sharing roads with traffic.

Once you have prepared your bike and body for speed it's time to build your confidence on the bike. Cornering and descending skills are not body specific, so whether you are naturally a climber or a sprinter, it's physically possible that you can master cornering and descending like a pro. At the same time, top riders know how to adjust their speed based on the safety and conditions of a course. On a dry pavement race course closed to traffic, a pro will corner much faster than on the same road during a training ride. Unless you are training or racing on a closed and swept course with good pavement, keep your speed down. Allow time to react safely and decisively to unexpected traffic or road conditions. Ride with confidence, not cockiness.

Regaining Confidence After a Crash

Crashing once or twice doesn't cause you to lose cornering and descending ability. However, crashing can cause even experienced riders to question their own judgment and skills. Some of this questioning is appropriate, but too much can interfere with your enjoyment of riding. Just as you would rehabilitate physically after a serious crash injury, you may need to accept that you need some time and assistance to regain confidence. Ask for help from a certified sports psychologist if pep talks from cycling buddies aren't effective.

If you keep working at it, the normal feel and confidence will return. In fact, the difference from one day to the next will be so slight that you may not even realize you've gained your confidence back until one weekend you look at a tricky corner or descent no differently than any other part of a course. To get your confidence back, avoid negative visualizations. Riders who've had trouble building confidence and getting past fear of descending have "crash videos" that they review in their minds, essentially justifying and practicing fear. Instead, push the envelope from the inside. The part of the brain that learns and improves performance is pretty much shut down in times of fear. If you practice cornering fast enough to be in fear, learning becomes very gradual or stops altogether, meaning that you are practicing fear more than cornering. If you practice cornering slowly enough to feel completely in control, you are practicing control, and speed comes soon enough. If you have crashed on a corner or descent near your home, return to it during similar conditions and ride it over and over again at slower speeds until you see only the corner and not the previous crash.

Keep your head up and listen as well as look. In races, you often hear a crash coming long before you see it—as is the case with oncoming cars, dogs, or children playing. Look to where you want to go, not to what you are trying to avoid. Focus on making beautiful, smooth, and deliberate movements rather than fearing making a mistake. Predict and anticipate. Don't wait and react.

Fear is not entirely a negative thing. It is your way of noting that you're not certain you know how to deal with a situation. Unreasonable fear can hold you back from actions on your bike that other riders do every day. The balance comes with gradually building up your confidence so that the increased speed through a corner does not *feel* like a risk. Only when you corner or descend slowly enough to feel safe do you learn how to control the bike and go fast. To conquer fear in cornering and descending, you must learn and work with the physical limitations of your bicycle.

If you stand next to your bike and place the cranks perpendicular to the pavement and lean the bike toward the low crank, eventually the pedal touches the pavement. This is one limit to cornering on flat pavement, but chances are this is more leaned over than you would ever actually ride. Develop a feel for that limit when you lean your bike through a turn that may or may not allow you to continue to pedal. You need to instinctively know where to stop pedaling and when you can start again.

Another limit is the *traction limit*—that is, how far you can lean the bike without pedaling before the tires lose traction and slide out. Traction depends on the type of pavement: its smoothness or roughness, how old or new it is, how dry or wet it is, and whether it has oil, sand, or other debris. It also depends on the tires and air pressure. Contrary to tire manufacturers' claims, the tire tread pattern and stickiness are not very important as long as tires are in good condition. Your head should be a library of guesses of your bike's limits in all varieties of pavement and conditions. At some point, you will experience exactly where some of these limits are. Instead of fearing the same conditions again, learn from them and move on.

Components of Cornering

Good cornering is built on the same foundation as descending with speed. We'll cover cornering first and then add the descent. Any corner can be broken into three segments—the *approach*, the *apex*, and the *exit*— though collectively they feel like one movement. Most times you want to head into a corner as effortlessly as possible and with as much speed as appropriate for the situation. Remember, the quickest, easiest path anywhere is a straight line. For that reason, it's advantageous to shave off as much turning as possible. The path you choose through a corner is called your line. The faster you are going, the wider and straighter your line needs to be.

A rider cornering alone on a closed course would cut from the center of the road toward the curb, then return to the center of the road after completing the turn (figure 13.1a). In pack conditions, the lead rider chooses the fastest line and remains at the front; a rider turning from the inside must alter her line; and a rider coming from the rear will need to slow as he enters the turn (figure 13.1b). On a closed course with multiple corners, a rider should shave the turns rather than following the curve of the road (figure 13.1c). Table 13.1 provides an overview of good cornering skills.

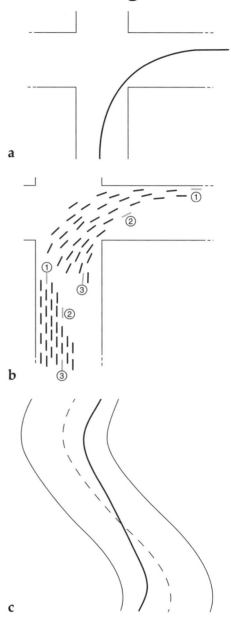

Figure 13.1   Cornering on a flat course (a), the positioning of three riders before and after a turn (b), and shaving the turns on a curved course (c).

Table 13.1 Steps to Successful Cornering

1. Keep your hands in the drops and your shoulders low.

2. Regulate your speed before entering the turn.

3. Start as wide as necessary for the speed: higher speed means wider.

4. Be smooth.

5. Your outside pedal should be down.

6. Lean the bike.

7. Keep your head straight up and down.

8. Plan the exit, and look where you want to go.

The Approach

The first step in rounding a corner is the approach, including everything from scanning the scene to committing to a line. The approach begins as soon as you can see and evaluate the corner: the width of the road, the tightness and angle of the curve, and at least some of what lies past the corner. Once you've done a quick scan, your eyes should focus on the apex, the pivot point at the center of the turn, resting there just long enough to identify your path from your current position through the apex and out the other side. At this point, simultaneously judge the speed you can maintain through the turn and scan the roadway for gravel, potholes, or grates that could throw you off your line.

Using a typical 90-degree turn around a city block as an example, position your approach so you can go through the apex of the turn as close to the inside curb as possible while maintaining your speed. Figure according to your speed how close to the curb or how far out into the road you must be to start your turn to cut the apex at the desired position. Ideally, if you have the whole road, it's better to travel down the center as you come toward the corner and move toward the outside only if necessary to be able to carry your speed through the turn. Otherwise, making a swerve to the outside before cutting into the corner means that you travel extra distance, and it increases your chance of crashing into another rider.

Maintain control and a low center of gravity by keeping your hands in the drops whenever you corner at speed. As you begin to commit to your line, straighten your outside leg and place most of your weight on it, leaning the bike into the turn while you keep your body upright. Think of it as standing on the edge of the bike to press the tires against the pavement. Lift slightly off the seat but lean lightly against it with the inside of your leg for added control. At the same time, straighten— but do not lock—the arm closer to the inside of the turn while pressing it down and forward into the drops to keep the front wheel in line with the bike. Meanwhile, relax your outside arm and inside leg. Continue looking forward to where you want to go. Hold your head straight; resist leaning it into the corner. This method of cornering is called *countersteering* and is the most common used in cycling. You are likely already cornering this way regularly without even realizing it.

Road Camber

Most roads in North America are sloped slightly toward the apex of a turn to give cars more traction and road to counteract the centrifugal forces that threaten to make a car slide out. An *off-camber* turn is one where the road slopes away from the apex like an inside-out race car track, giving less centrifugal support. Cambered roads are preferred by cyclists. If a turn appears to be off-camber, lower your speed and use more of a steering-type turn rather than relying on tire traction.

The Apex

Once you've committed to the turn, you soon go through its apex, or center. This is usually the most nerve-racking part of a turn because it is where the turn's angle is most severe. As you go through the apex remain calm and in control, riding the bike instead of allowing it to ride you. Feel your body's weight on your outside foot and the inside handlebar pressing down. Meanwhile your head remains straight up and down; avoid leaning it in the direction of the corner. If anything, lean it toward the *outside* of the turn. Stay low, and grip the bars securely, but avoid being stiff or white-knuckled. Don't stick your knee out; just let it relax or keep it naturally near the top tube.

The split second as you reach the apex is where you find out whether you've chosen a speed that you can maintain through the corner. Avoid braking in any turn once you've committed to leaning the bike unless you're sure you're going to overshoot the turn. Also, avoid changing your line inside the turn; slight jerks of steering are a frequent cause of crashes. If you have to change your line due to an obstacle, slightly straighten the bike for a moment while shifting your weight toward the inside of the turn, make the steering correction, and then smoothly return to the lean, continuing to eye the exit and beyond as you come through the apex.

The Exit

Exiting a corner is usually the easiest part of making a turn. If you've chosen a good line through the corner and maintained as much of your initial speed as possible, you just need to keep your eyes down the road for the next turn or scan of the roadway. The exit is where the forces pulling you toward the outside of the road begin to subside and you straighten up on the bike again. If you had to stop pedaling sometime before the apex, you will have to judge during the exit when you can begin pedaling again. Sooner is better.

Cornering Practice

Carefully thinking through each of these steps is impossible at speed, which is why low-speed practice is crucial. Use large, empty parking lots or quiet roads and create different cornering situations. Practice corners with a variety of entries and exits, using the painted parking spaces as road edges. Rehearse the same corners both when the pavement is dry and when it is slick with rain.

Many riders find that they are more comfortable cornering on one side than the other (right versus left, for example). Practice cornering to both the left and the right. Create turns that aren't 90 degrees, some that are barely corners, and some that are U-turns. Find two or three corners in a row and practice setting up for successive turns. Practice often and the thought process of cornering will become quicker and more natural. Eventually you might be able to stop consciously thinking about the corner and ride purely on instinct.

Cornering in a Race Pack

As discussed in chapters 10 and 14, the nature of a race pack is that it starts thin in the front, fattens out, and then thins out again near its tail, creating a diamond shape. Imagine a pack in this shape approaching a 90-degree turn and having the whole road. With the front riders starting from the farthest outside area of the turn cutting into the apex near the curb and then exiting all the way to the outside of the road again, there is simply no room for other riders to be inside or outside. The riders in those positions will have their lines cut off. Whenever a pack nears a corner, the first few riders can choose the best lines, while those behind to the inside and outside have to slow down to fall in line with the riders taking the possible lines through the turn to stay with the flow of the front riders. The overall effect is somewhat like an accordion, with the riders slowing down to fall into line slowing the progress of every rider behind them. What this means for riders in the back of the pack is that they have to slow for a corner that they wouldn't have had to if had they been in the front of the pack. Once the trailing riders get through the turn's apex, they'll have to jump to stay with the leaders, wasting precious energy.

Choosing the proper line through a turn is particularly important in group riding because riders near you expect you to be fast and safe through any corner. If you are in the very front of the pack, other riders expect you to take the best line, as if you were the only rider on the road. The rest of the riders have to adjust to what you do. If you are in the middle of the pack, you likely have to take the line that is left open for you. If you are at the rear, you can possibly choose your own line or even use gaps between riders in front of you to move up several places during the turn. Given the possibility of crashes and the wasted energy of slowing and jumping in the back of the pack, stay near the middle-front to be both conservative and safe.

Often, when a pack corners, a lot of open space exists toward the inside of the turn. All that space may tempt you to try to move up. But there is a reason why no one is riding there: if you try to approach the corner from the inside at the same speed as the other riders taking the normal line, when you reach the apex of the turn you will cut directly into the path of the other riders' lines, potentially causing a crash. Some riders attempt this maneuver by yelling "Inside!" as they try to move up in the inside of the turn. If you try this, you will likely have other riders ignore you or even purposely "close the door" to keep you from moving up or endangering them. Expect a harsh tongue-lashing if you rejoin the field at the apex, as this is considered a very sketchy move. If you do move up on the inside on a straightaway, rejoin the field before the corner. If you're not sure you'll be able to do that, don't move up on the inside.

Cornering in the Rain

Cyclists automatically use extra caution while riding in the rain, but there are a few particulars to keep in mind, especially when cornering.

Avoid painted lines, metal grates, and the center of traffic lanes, as they may be extremely slick. Of course, when you go around a corner, you often don't have a choice but to go over the slick painted lines and lanes. In this case, rely more on actually steering the bike than using countersteering. The difference is that when countersteering, you lean the *bike* more while keeping your body more upright. When steering, you lean your *body* more while keeping the bike more upright. The logic behind this is to keep from relying so much on the tire traction to get you through the turn.

To steer through a turn, avoid leaning the bike and keep it fairly upright. Shift your body weight slightly from the center of the saddle toward the inside of the turn. Then steer the handlebars step by step so the corner becomes a series of straight lines. This technique works well in the rain or in any corner where the road surface is poor. Keeping the bike more upright also allows you to pedal through the corner, a definite advantage in certain racing situations. Steering is also the method you use on tricky corners such as when going through a hairpin turn on a climb. Avoiding braking or jerking in the corner is even more important in slick or loose conditions. Your speed should be regulated before you even enter the turn, leaving you to concentrate on steering around the corner safely and smoothly.

Descending

Descending is one of the easiest yet riskiest cycling endeavors because control and safety on a descent are always relative to the surrounding conditions. As in cornering, understanding the limits of your bike and how different conditions affect it will help you stay in control. Knowing the answer to the following questions will help you understand those limits:

- At what speed does your bike begin to shimmy?
- How solidly are your brakes working?
- Is there traffic on the road?
- Is the road surface dry, wet, or loose?
- Are there riders ahead of or behind you?
- Will you need to slow for an upcoming corner?

Regardless of the conditions, there are a few general practices to follow.

- When descending anything more than a freeway overpass, put your hands in the drops. This provides quicker reaction time and better control if you need to brake or steer to avoid someone, and it allows better shock absorption if you hit a pothole or other unexpected obstacle. Being in the drops also keeps your center of gravity low and reduces wind resistance.
- Keep your eyes up, looking down the road.
- Keep a finger or two resting on each brake lever, with the remainder of your hands gripping the drops securely and your arms and shoulders relaxed. If some braking is necessary at high speed, feather both the front and back brakes, giving each a pause to keep them from heating up against the wheel's rim. Avoid jamming on either brake, as hitting the front brake too hard may cause you to lose steering ability or even vault over the handlebars, while hitting the back brake hard may cause the rear wheel to lock up and fishtail.
- Continue pedaling until you can no longer comfortably spin your largest gear. Once you begin coasting, shift your weight back slightly, unweighting the front wheel a bit and easing off the saddle. Hold the cranks horizontal, with equal weight on the two feet to allow your legs to take up most of the road vibration. Whether you go into a full tuck depends on the safety of the descent. If the descent is mainly straight and free of traffic and you are by yourself or with a few riders not immediately near you, it is probably safe enough to tuck. When in doubt, stay in the drops.
- To go into a tuck, start from a low regular coasting position and move your hands smoothly one at a time to the inside tops of the bars. Center your weight at the tip of the saddle, sharing the weight burden between both legs and the saddle. Then crouch down until your chin is just slightly above and behind your wrists. While this position is more aerodynamic, it is much more difficult to make evasive maneuvers. Move back to the drops as you approach a turn.

Descending With a Group

The main rules of group descending are *space, smoothness,* and *togetherness.* First, give yourself and others around you a comfort zone to maneuver in. The higher the speeds, the bigger the zone needs to be. While it's possible to descend while inches away from another rider, it's not necessary unless you are much lighter than your competitors. Make your movements on a descent gradual and smooth. A pack of riders drafting usually descends faster than an individual. (For that reason, it's important to stay with other riders or wait for other riders over the top of a climb.) If you are in the front of a pack on a descent, pedal until it's inefficient to continue doing so. If you are behind other riders in a training ride situation, such as a double paceline where you aren't racing, regulate your speed so that you don't overtake other riders too quickly on a mild descent. Stay in line rather than overshooting the other riders and disrupting the orderliness of the paceline.

In a race during a descent when you are working in a breakaway or chasing situation, use every advantage that the draft affords you to gain speed. To best take advantage of drafting during a descent, form a single rotating paceline where each rider continually shoots past the front rider on the wind-protected side. The paceline will have greater spacing between each bike than on flat terrain, but the basic concept is still the same.

Cornering on a Descent

The number-one rule of cornering on a descent is to regulate your speed *before* entering the turn and then complete the turn without touching the brakes. Take speed off gradually so that you can enter the corner with smooth momentum. Slamming on the brakes at the last minute risks losing your momentum going in and out of the corner and may cause you to lose traction or control. As in flat-terrain cornering, keep your center of gravity low, and stay relaxed. The tenser you are, the more likely you are to make mistakes. Scan the pavement in front of you, and then keep your eyes down the hill rather than fixating on obstacles.

When cornering on a descent with a pack of riders, remember that there are fewer lines through the corner than on flat terrain due to the higher speeds. The pack needs to thin itself out to go quickly through corners. This means regulating speed not only in relation to the corner itself, but also in relation to the other riders. You will probably find that the insides of bending descent turns are some of the easiest places to pass more timid riders. Passing this way is fine as long you aren't taking unnecessary chances. A rider crashing in a turn generally slides to the outside. If anyone ever crashes in front of you, your inclination will be to go around him to the outside, when you should really be steering to the inside or holding your line.

Part IV

Racing Strategy and Tactics

Photo by Jim & Mary Whitmer

The beauty of bike racing is that the strongest rider doesn't always win. As strong as you may be, it's incredibly difficult to ride away from other racers. Even naturally talented riders need guts, aggressiveness, opportunity, patience, and luck to win. Very few riders win races—whether road races, time trials, criteriums, or stage races—without race smarts.

Chapter 14

A Systematic Approach to Racing

Often, riders train for years, getting stronger with time, but their racing results actually plateau. Usually, it's not that they aren't capable of doing more; it's just that they are approaching their races the same way weekend after weekend, year after year, without applying the lessons they have learned. With all of bike racing's gears, terrains, conditions, racing lengths, and athlete types, it is a complicated sport even on its most basic level. So it's easy for riders to give in, follow the pack around weekend after weekend, and think they are racing well just because it hurts and they are still with a group.

However, anyone who pays attention to detail can learn and use cycling tactics. A good grasp of tactics isn't just the knowledge of when to attack, join, bridge, or chase down a breakaway. It is an entire system of approaching a race. *The overriding rule of this system—the one you must always remember—is to conserve energy during less important parts of the race so that energy can be expended toward making a winning move.* It sounds simple, but it's surprising how often racers of all levels ignore this rule by pushing too big or too small a gear, making a useless show of strength too early in the race, not taking advantage of aerodynamics effectively, or mistiming strategic moves.

The Four Cs

You can make use of tactics successfully even in your first race if you use the building blocks of strategy we call the *four Cs: course, competition, conditions,* and *confidence.*

Just as every bit of preparation you do should focus on the goals you set up for yourself in chapter 3, the races you choose and the way you conduct yourself in those races must further those goals. Applying the four Cs to each race you enter will go a long way in ensuring that you move closer to your goals with each race. In chapters 15 through 18, we apply the four Cs to each type of road racing, pointing out the nuances of each race and the preparation, skills, and practice you need to be successful.

Course

The course is one of the most important factors in how you perform in a race. Knowledge of the hills or gravel sections is strategic information. Even choosing to do the race (or not) based on its terrain is a strategic decision in your race season. Relate your strengths and weaknesses to areas of the course. Does the course have hills, flats, or windy sections that favor your strengths? In which areas might you be vulnerable and have difficulty following stronger riders?

All riders should study course information ahead of the race, but many don't bother. Knowing the course well can go a long way in improving tactics and morale. While the most effective way to scout a course is to ride it ahead of time, it won't always be possible. In that case, find a map that details the roads of the course. The race Web site may even link to a map of the course. Perhaps the promoter has provided a map of the course in the race packet or has posted a magnified version on a bulletin board near the start. There may even be a course profile showing the race's climbs and descents.

Be familiar with the course so that you will recognize major turns coming up. The misfortune of going off course, even if it is not directly your fault, is still your responsibility according to race rules. Some riders even write course landmarks onto a piece of athletic tape and then tape it to their stem before the start. This is particularly effective in longer races.

Once you have information about a race, process the facts. Knowing a course has 360 vertical feet (110 meters) of climbing per lap is a fact. But knowing that the 360 feet all occur in one 10 percent grade climb after a sharp right-hand turn, and that you need a 39 × 23 gear for it, is tactical knowledge. Ask riders who have done a particular course in the past, particularly those in your category who have done well there, to fill you in about the course's challenges. If you don't know someone who has completed the course, ask riders before the start of your race.

Once you are at a race venue, become as familiar with the course as possible, especially near the start and finish. There's no excuse for not knowing the first and last kilometers of a race; you should have arrived in plenty of time to check them out, even if you have to ride on the sidewalk while other races are in progress. Courses often have signs posted marking 5 kilometers, 1 kilometer, 500 meters, and 200 meters to go. Look for landmarks to signify these points in case you miss the signs in the heat of the finish.

Competition

While the course provides the venue, the competitors make the race. As you race, take the time to discover the strongest competitors and teams weekend after weekend. Study their strengths and weaknesses. Just as important, consider how the other teams and individuals in your race may interpret *your* strengths and weaknesses.

Being familiar with your competitors can remove some of the element of surprise in a race by helping you to anticipate their moves and to make moves of your own to isolate their weaknesses. If the same climber wins races weekend after weekend by climbing away on the main hill and riding solo to the finish, examine how this individual is allowed to get away with it race after race. Maybe one answer is to get to the hill before that rider, which would require an attempt to break away without that rider earlier in the race.

In beginning racing, individuals rather than teams often affect the outcome. However, some individuals in the same club may be organized enough in the category 4 and 5 races for you to take advantage of that team's strategy for your own benefit. More details on this are included in the upcoming chapters for each event.

Conditions

As you prepare for a race, consider the weather conditions and potential wind. When you arrive at a race venue, check the direction and strength of the wind and consider how it might affect various parts of the course. Knowing which way the wind blows will help you decide which side of the pack to be in at any point in the race. It will also help you plan ahead for the wind you will encounter after the next turn and allow you to set up ahead of time by moving up or to the protected side.

Plan ahead by bringing extra clothing for cold days and extra water for hot days. Will you need long-fingered gloves and booties for an early-season race? Why take the chance—bring them along. Check for wind strength before deciding whether to use a disk wheel. Are the time savings of a deep dish or disk wheel worth the swerving the wind might cause? Check the pavement type on the race course and consider how it might affect tire traction if rain is coming. You may have to rein in your need for speed on descents and corners. If you have the option, bring sunglasses appropriate for the light conditions—dark for sunny days, clear for rainy or nighttime racing, or amber for cloudy, dark days.

Losing to another competitor's strength or wits is honorable. Losing to the weather is inexcusable. You don't have to be a victim of wind and weather. Use the conditions to your advantage!

Confidence

Confidence is taking everything you know about yourself and tying it to the strategic fundamentals we've discussed. It is understanding your own strengths and weaknesses and gaining experience in group rides so that you know whether you are basically a climber, sprinter, time trialist, or all-around rider. Confidence is having the patience to wait for the right moment to show your strength, rather than wasting energy trying to be a different kind of rider.

Confidence is having an awareness of your current fitness level and knowing whether you are on track with your training program and goals. It is also the ability to conduct yourself in accordance with your goals. For instance, if you are using races early in the season simply for training without worrying about the outcome, make constant attempts to get away for training purposes and don't worry that you may potentially break away with other riders who can possibly outsprint you at the end. You might make a gamble, such as a long solo breakaway, just for the training—an action you might not try in a more important race if you are a good sprinter.

Confidence is knowing you are strong on the flats, for instance, and the 98-pound climber who hopes to leave you behind in the hills will struggle in the flat crosswind if you go to the front of the pack and hammer. It's knowing you thrive in the heat or suffer inordinately in the cold. It's knowing that the course where you were behind the leader by 10 minutes last year won't have you suffering nearly as much this year due to your improvement. Confidence is knowing that you mixed a weaker energy drink for this weekend's race because last weekend the stronger concoction gave you a stomachache.

While these concepts might seem vague when you consider them in general, when you apply them in a race they make sense. After you finish a race, apply the four Cs again, checking to see whether you were true to your goals and determining where you could make improvements. You will see in the following chapters how valuable this simple approach can be.

Inside the Race

Chapter 4 got us to the start line and then skipped to the finish, and now we fill in the racing details. Here we concentrate on the components common to road races and criteriums, as most of the details for time trial racing are included in chapter 16.

The Start

Once the race gun goes off, get under way as quickly and as smoothly as possible; clip into your pedal, and switch to bigger gears to go with the flow of the pack. Start in a gear that allows you to get off the line quickly so that other riders won't overtake you and squeeze you out of position before you get going. If the start terrain is flat, usually a 53 × 19 or 17 is enough to get off the line quickly and allow you to accelerate with the pack. (You typically want to start in the big chain ring, if possible, because it is easier to get to the bigger gears quickly and smoothly as the pace picks up off the line.) The longer the race, the more relaxed the start is likely to be, and vice versa. If you miss clipping in on the first try, don't panic or stare at the pedals while you try to clip in. Take a few pedal strokes with your foot just planted on top of the pedal to get up a little speed, and then try clipping in again.

Moving Down the Road

Particularly in the beginning of the race when the pack holds the most riders and everyone is jockeying for position, racers take up as much of the road (or more) as they are allowed. To keep things safe, races have a full road closure or have only half the road available to the race with a centerline rule in effect.

A full road closure will have police officers posted at intersections of the road holding up traffic and at least one police vehicle leading the race ahead of the riders and all the official race vehicles. Riders are able to use the entire road for the race without being penalized for crossing the centerline at any time. One note: despite a full road closure, never assume that any road is completely closed to traffic unless you are in a criterium where the entire course is roped off. Even then you have to keep an eye out for pedestrians crossing the road. On remote country roads, local residents may not have gotten the word or may disregard signs and directions and risk traveling toward the race pack. If your riding instincts tell you not to brave a blind corner in an oncoming lane, pay attention to them. It may end up saving your life.

While full road closures are optimal, the most common circumstance in local racing is to have the use of the right lane or lanes only. Intersections are safely blocked, but oncoming traffic heads toward the pack as on a normal road. In this case, the centerline rule is designed to protect racers. The centerline rule states that if you cross the centerline, you may be penalized in either time or placings, or you may simply be disqualified. Some races may give warnings for a first infraction, but many races that have had problems in the past will immediately disqualify riders crossing the centerline, whether intentionally or accidentally.

Another, similar form of road closure is the rolling enclosure. This is the most common type of road closure found in long professional races, where a closure of all the roads in the race would result in a lockdown of hundreds of avenues for several hours. In a rolling enclosure the police and official race vehicles travel ahead of, along with, and behind the pack, pulling over oncoming traffic and closing intersections as encountered, allowing traffic to resume in its wake. The riders have the use of the entire road, and the primary enclosure usually includes all riders within 10 minutes of contention, with separate enclosures for large chase groups. Riders too far off the back of the pack may have to contend with traffic and stop signs on their own.

Moving around in the pack and avoiding going over the centerline can be challenging at times. You want to be near the side of the pack to continually move up, but other riders have the same idea, and wind, pack speed, and aggressiveness may cause riders to cross the centerline frequently. If you are attempting to move up on the left side, be careful that you don't get pushed or forced over the centerline. You are generally allowed to ride on the yellow paint of the centerline itself, but for your own safety, it isn't recommended. If the wind direction allows, choose to move up on the right side instead; you can generally see what is coming up quite easily and take advantage of wider parts of the road or even patches of rideable gravel to move into better position.

Basic Tactical Moves

Think of the race pack as a rolling, living amoeba, changing shape to fit wherever it needs to go. The pack slims itself to pass over a narrow roadway or bridge, stretches itself out as the pace picks up and each rider seeks more effective shelter behind the rider in front, or flares out as the pace drops and riders in the back attempt to move toward the front. It is through drafting that the riders in the pack stay connected, and it usually takes the stress of a climb, wind, or sudden change in pace to break those connections. The key is learning how to break connections or maintain them, depending on whether you are making or reacting to a move.

• **Closing the gap.** Before learning to make other strategic moves, all riders need to be able to sustain or close gaps. As explained in chapter 10, the closer you are to the rider in front of you, the more effective a draft you will enjoy. Keeping the gap small is your lifeline in the pack. If a big enough gap opens, you will be working nearly as hard in the middle of the pack as the riders on the front. Closing any gaps that open in front of you is crucial at all times, even if you weren't the one who originally let the gap open. Whether you close a gap in one quick burst or in a calculated pacing effort depends on the speed of the pack, the wind conditions, and your own fitness and strength.

• **The attack.** The attack is an all-out sprint away from the pack to try to break away. The attacking rider sprints away full blast and then attempts to settle into a time trial pace she can keep up that discourages riders back in the pack from going after her. The secret of a successful attack is to charge away from the pack quickly and with enough surprise that you are able to break away cleanly, disconnecting from the riders behind and not allowing the riders in front to simply jump in behind you as you go by.

Most successful attacks are launched from the side of the pack from several riders back. This surprises the riders on the front. Those riders may be blocking others who see you going, but can't do anything about it until the riders in the front get going. Launching a full sprint from the side of the pack, on the opposite side of the road, will give you a head start; not only will the riders at the front have to close the gap you've opened, they'll also have to close a gap from side to side. The components of the attack are discussed in greater detail in chapter 15.

• **The chase.** The most natural reaction when a rider attacks is for other riders to chase him down. A chase occurs when riders go immediately after an attacking rider or continue to go after that rider as the race goes on. Chasing usually means that the connections in the pack are still intact. In other words, the riders at the front working hard to bring the escaping rider back to the pack are towing the remainder of the pack through the benefits of drafting. As a beginning racer, constantly question why you should or shouldn't help chase an attacking rider. We discuss in the following chapters the merits of chasing or not chasing in certain kinds of racing situations.

- **The bridge.** The first alternative to letting an attacking rider go, chasing yourself, or sitting in the pack being towed by someone else is to launch your own attack immediately after other attacking riders, attempting to break away with them. This is called *bridging*, and it is different from chasing because you aren't intending to bring the rest of the pack with you. Bridging is one of the most misunderstood and miscarried strategies. Many riders are under the impression that they are bridging up to another attacking rider, but if they were to simply look behind them, they would see that the rest of the pack is planted firmly on their wheel enjoying the free ride. An attempt to bridge should be as powerful as the original attack, and racers should look behind themselves frequently to make sure that they aren't just towing the rest of the field.

- **The counterattack.** The timing of an attack is as important as the force with which it is launched. The moment an attacking rider is pulled back to the pack, it is common for other riders to launch new attacks, called *counterattacks*. The value of a counterattack is that the riders at the front of the pack may be tired from chasing the previous attacker and might hesitate to go again, hoping that someone else will take up the chase. Often, a rider from an opposing team will counter with an attack once a stronger rider has been pulled back to the pack. Another strategy is to have teammates taking turns attacking in succession. As soon as one is caught, another one goes. Counterattacking is a common strategy in all levels of racing, and the smartest or most intuitive riders develop a sense of timing for the most effective opportunities to launch counterattacks, making it difficult for even the strongest riders to catch them.

- **Working together.** Whether you are off the front or off the back of the pack, taking turns in a paceline helps you conserve energy and get to the finish as quickly as possible. Make use of the other riders around you, even when you are just a group of two or three. If you are ever dropped from a pack, the first thing to do is look around for other riders getting dropped to help close the gap back to the main pack. Never chase by yourself when working with others is an option.

Often when riders are chasing back onto a pack after being dropped on a hill, you will hear a few of them shouting, "Work together!" Working smoothly in a paceline gets everyone in a group back to the pack faster, rather than attacking each other in a panicked every-man-for-himself fashion. Even waiting for other riders to catch up to you may be more worthwhile in the end than trying to hold them off behind you. This is also true when you have broken away from the pack off the front of the race and are attempting to hold off a chase group. The few seconds you may lose to the pack by waiting for another rider coming up on you will likely be gained back by the time you save working together once she reaches you.

If you find yourself to be much stronger than the group you are in, you can either take more pulls at the front or simply enjoy the ride and worry about beating everyone when you get closer to the finish line. If you find yourself to be much weaker, pull through if you feel you can, but otherwise just hang on as best you can. Remember above all that there is no rule that you have to pull in any situation. Other riders can yell all they want, but if you can't pull, don't pull.

Photo courtesy of Susan Yost

The amount of time spent pulling at the front will depend on your strength, relative to your competitors, and your tactics.

Chapter 15

Road Racing

The most beloved road racing pros are those who race the classics—one-day road races over infamous terrain on storied courses and often in extreme weather conditions. Maybe this is because of the tradition built around road racing in Europe, but likely it is because the best classic road racers are the best of the well-rounded riders, excelling on the climbs, powering over the flats, and shining in the sprints. The lore and *lure* of the road race have similar appeal to even the beginning racer. Criteriums and time trials are an integral part of racing on the road, but the road race itself is viewed as the real thing—the racing in which most racers aspire to succeed.

No two races will ever be the same, so no plan or tactic will do for every race—although the concepts you learn for road racing will apply to criterium and stage racing as well.

Saving Energy

You may have seen professional races on television where the main pack seems to roll along at a leisurely pace for as long as three hours. Without the extreme race lengths found in pro racing, amateur racing moves much more quickly—and the moves come sooner, so you have to anticipate what might come up in the race by applying the four Cs to the race course in sections. Consider the course and what kinds of obstacles occur in the first few miles.

If a substantial hill lies in the early miles, a good warm-up is necessary before the race. The pace is likely to be high as nonclimbers attack to get a head start at the hill and the climbers then dial up the pace on the hill itself. If the first miles of the race are flat and in a side wind that will stretch the pack and test your ability to stick to the wheel in front of you, this also requires a thorough warm-up. A shorter warm-up might be in order if the first miles of the course are flat, nontechnical, and in calm conditions. Table 15.1 provides a sample warm-up before a road race.

Is the race starting more quickly than you had imagined, making you wonder how you'll keep the pace for the entire distance? Plan to warm up more intensely or longer next time; but for the time being, give all you have to hold onto the wheel in front of you. It's likely that as you get more and more warmed up within the race your body will come around and you will feel better. Keep in mind that a good

Table 15.1 Sample Race Warm-Up

- 15 to 30 minutes of easy spinning in comfortable gear for whatever terrain you are on, 39 × 17 (or small chain ring × 17 rear cog); this would be a 1 to 3 effort on a scale from 1 to 10

- 1 minute, one gear bigger, slightly more intense, level 4 effort

- 1 minute, one gear bigger, slightly more intense, level 5 effort

- 1 minute, switch to big chain ring in same rear cog, slightly more intense, level 6 effort

- 1 minute, one gear bigger, slightly more intense, level 7 effort

- 1 minute, 39 × 17 (or middle chain ring and 17 rear) easy spin, reduce to level 4 effort

- 2 minutes, time trial pace in medium gear; work up to a time trial pace over the first minute and hold for the second; level 8 to 9 effort

- 1 minute, easy spin, level 4 effort

- 2 minutes, time trial pace in big gear, get up to time trial pace as soon as possible; level 8 to 9 effort

- 1 minute, easy spin, level 4 effort

- 30 seconds all-out, medium gear, level 10 effort

- 2 minutes, easy spin, level 4 effort

- 30 seconds all-out, big gear, level 10 effort

- 5 to 10 minutes cool-down, level 5 and below

warm-up will keep you ready to go for more than a half-hour. So if the race doesn't begin on time and your warm-up seems as if it is fading into history, don't panic—the warm-up time hasn't been wasted and you likely won't suffer any ill effects. Remember, too, that every other competitor is in the same boat.

Is the race starting more slowly than you had hoped, making you worry you won't even get a workout for the day? If you are one of the weaker riders in the field, enjoy the slower ride and save your energy—the hammer will go down eventually, and you need to be ready for that time. If you are one of the strongest riders, you can attack continuously until the field splits apart and you can push ahead. Whatever the tactic, do it 100 percent, but be ready to change if need be. Remember that you are never a victim of the race; you make the race. If the pace is too slow for your liking and you feel the race will wind down into a field sprint that won't favor your strength, you can always liven things up by attacking.

Keep in mind also that each effort you make is something you need to recover from. Energy wasted early on won't be available later in the race, so you need to conserve whenever possible. Drink and eat early and often, even when you aren't hungry or thirsty. If you wait until you are, it's often too late to stop an eventual bonk or dehydration that will end your race prematurely. (See chapter 8 for more on race food.) Above all, keep yourself out of the wind at all times and choose gears that allow you to spin smoothly and with as little effort as possible.

> Ride one gear lower than you think you need to on climbs, especially early in the race. No competitors will be impressed by big gear riding unless you leave them behind. Save the ability to push bigger gears for when the time counts.

Initiating and Responding to Attacks

To reach the aim of racing to leave your competition behind— whether it is long before the finish during an attack or in the final centimeters of a sprint to the line—you have to be both aggressive and responsive during the race. How you plan to get ahead depends on where you fit into the four Cs for the particular race you are competing in. Given the demanding nature of bike racing, in your first races you will just be figuring out how to hang onto the pack and get comfortable riding next to others. But eventually, as you gain a little confidence and comfort so that the timing will be right, you will launch an attack. Table 15.2 provides some guidelines for initiating and responding to attacks.

Table 15.2 Attacking and Responding to Attacks

- Your initial jump into the attack should be at full speed, as if you are going for the finish line.

- Choose a gear that allows you to move away quickly and forcefully. A gear that is too big will slow your acceleration and allow others to catch you quickly.

- Look behind you soon after your initial attack to see whether it has been successful, rather than continuing and just hoping!

- Avoid attacking just before descents or moving into straight-on headwinds. The benefit of drafting in these situations is difficult to overcome.

- Unless it is your job (within organized teamwork) to chase attacks or you plan to attack with another rider, always pause for just a moment when you see an attacking rider to see whether other riders will respond and take the responsibility to chase.

Attacking

To make your attack most effective, launch it from the edge of the first third of the field or from the back of a small group. You always want to be at least three or four riders back to gain the element of surprise. Attacks from the very front of the *peloton* are rarely successful because every single rider behind you can see what you are doing and react immediately. Your position in the field or breakaway before a strong attack varies based on the terrain and wind. Attacks are most effective from the side of the pack that is protected from the wind because every rider chasing you has to ride on the windy side. If your pack has 10 riders or fewer, you might need to be farther behind before you launch your attack.

Wait until a lull in the pack's speed before you jump. The more attacks you try, the more you will collect a sense of timing for just the right time to launch. A good time to attack is often the split second after another attacking rider has been caught (counterattacking). Often the pack breathes a collective sigh of relief once an escaping rider is brought back to the pack; a strong attack during this minuscule pause disheartens those who have just been chasing, and they refuse to chase again. At the same time, the pack will be bunching back together, and you can use the momentum you are carrying to help you rush past the front riders who have already slowed down.

Before you jump—whether it is for the line or for an attack—allow a small gap to open between you and the rider in front of you, usually about three-quarters of a bike length. Use the draft inside this gap in your initial charge from the field. As soon as you have that gap, ensure that you are in a gear in which you can accelerate quickly and jump with all your might out of the saddle, pulling against the bars and driving forward as you peel off and up the side of the pack. Once you have committed to the attack, accelerate to top speed so that you pass the riders at the front at a speed that makes it difficult for them to catch up with you immediately. Their hesitation for even a second can get you the distance necessary to encourage others to hesitate even further, and your gap has been established.

Photo courtesy of Susan Yost

As one teammate is caught by the pack, another can immediately launch a counterattack.

Once you've passed the front riders and have gained a gap from the field of up to 50 meters, settle into your saddle at a pace that you can maintain for at least 10 minutes on your own and continue to gain time ahead of the pack. It will by no means be easy. However, the hard intervals you did in training will have prepared you for this effort. Just as you go to settle in after the initial acceleration, look back and see whether your attack has been successful: Did you make a separation from the majority of the pack? If you've made a sizable separation, settle into your hard pace and keep going. If you have too many riders hanging onto your wheel in a line of riders going all the way back to the pack, ease up and be alert for counterattacks.

If you've gotten away but several riders have joined you, size up who is with you. Rerun the four Cs now on your reduced competition, the course and conditions remaining ahead of you, and the confidence you have in your own energy level and strengths. How you behave in the break depends on a variety of factors that we cover in greater depth in the following chapters.

Responding to an Attack

Since there is only one you and many other racers, you more often have to decide how to respond to attacks than how to initiate them. You will have a split second to figure out who is attacking and whether her initial jump has been successful. At the same time you need to decide whether it is your job to join the attack, sit in, or chase. Most often you sit in and wait to see what other riders do. Because so many other riders don't study up on basic strategy before their first years of racing, there is a huge "dummy factor" in individual tactics, which leads otherwise intelligent people to chase every breakaway attempt before them simply because they don't know what else to do.

When another rider attacks, usually the riders in the front of the pack respond first. The most energy-saving tactic in responding to an attack is to wait and see what others ahead of you do first. If you are at the front of the pack when an attack goes off, you can wait to see whether others move around you to chase and then take a free ride in their draft to the escaping rider. The main point is to try to find other riders to do any kind of work into the wind for you. This may seem somewhat less noble to those who come from sports in which an individual takes pride in using only one's own effort to get to the line, but in cycling, if you don't make use of others to work harder than you, you may find yourself out of gas at crucial times in a race.

In almost the same moment you pause to see whether others are immediately responding to an attack, consider the strengths and weaknesses of the attacker (if you know them) and instantly consider whether the break is worth joining and whether you are in a position to make an attack to join it. The first factors to consider are how strong the attack is and how fast the pack and the attacking riders are going. A feeble attack against a strong pack is likely to be caught quickly, and you can see almost immediately when an attack is likely to fail before it really even gets under way.

Beyond the strength of the attack itself, the factors in the decision to join or let go of a break are again tied to the four Cs. How does the upcoming course suit your strengths and weaknesses? Is there a hill coming up that you'd like to get a head start on? Perhaps you should try to join the break. Can you estimate whether you can ride time-trial pace all the way to the finish line from the current point with only one or two riders? If yes, go for it; if no, probably the pack is the best place to stay put for now. Who is in the break, and is he strong enough to last to the finish? Are other strong riders in the pack likely to let the attacking rider escape? If the answer to these two questions is yes, the break may be worth trying to join. If the attacking rider is strong but the other strong riders in the pack aren't likely to let him go, expect that they will attempt to join the attacking rider by bridging up or chasing him down, thereby towing you to the escaping riders. Is it extremely hot, cold, or windy? Riders attempting to break away in extremely hot temperatures, for example, may be unrealistic about their chances to ride at time-trial pace for more than a few minutes in the heat, and it may be better to wait in the pack and let the attackers fade on their own.

These are just a few questions that may go through your head as you consider how to react to each attack. Constantly balance them against how *you* feel, what *your* current fitness is, and what *your* original tactical plans are for the race.

If you make the commitment to join a breakaway that is already in progress, you have only a brief window of opportunity to decide whether to join the immediate attacking riders or to hold back for a moment and see whether the breakaway looks like it will gain some distance before joining. If you decide to join the immediate attackers, jump instantly and with great force to latch onto the wheel of one of the other attackers to gain an easier ride up to the forming breakaway. Once a breakaway has formed, you'll be best able to bridge up to it if the breakaway is still less than 10 seconds up the road from the pack. Once the breakaway is more than 10 seconds up the road, the ability of an individual to bridge the gap successfully diminishes significantly.

The final possible reaction when another rider attacks is to chase—take turns with other riders to pull the group into the wind to bring the attacker back to the pack. As an individual, there are very few situations where you might want to work to chase another rider. When you chase, you make yourself vulnerable to counterattacks by the riders who are drafting behind you while you work harder in the wind. Chasing also weakens you for efforts made later in the race. The only times that you as an individual might want to chase another rider are

- when you are nearing the finish and, knowing you are one of the strongest sprinters in the pack, you want to keep things together for a field sprint; or

- when you are one of the strongest riders in the field, and you can effectively chase and respond to counterattacks and still launch your own attacks after chasing.

Of course, if you are in a breakaway of only two or three riders, you will have to respond to attacks by the others in the group because there is no pack to do the work for you.

Individual Versus Team Tactics

The basics of attacking and chasing are the same whether you are in a road race, a criterium, or even a mountain bike race. How they are carried out often depends on the dynamics of the race. A large part of this dynamic is whether the racers carrying them out are individuals riding by and for themselves, or members of a team working together. An individual working alone has one objective in a bike race: to do whatever is best for that single rider at any given time during the race. In other words, that rider will never sacrifice her own energy by doing a lick of work that would benefit another rider in the race, such as chasing. An individual can try to force other racers who have teammates in the race to take up the bulk of any chase by hesitating when other riders attack. Individuals always have to be picky about when they attempt to attack or bridge to breakaways because if they are caught, they do not have a teammate to follow up with a counterattack. In the event of a necessary chase, an individual either ends up chasing alone or has to rely on other individuals in the race to help out.

If you have a description of the course with landmarks before the race, write down the mileage of feed zones, turns, and other significant markers on a short piece of athletic tape and attach it to the stem of your bike for reference during the race.

On the other hand, riders working together as teammates can often overcome their individual weaknesses and overpower even a stronger rider. The one-two punch of continued counterattacks is hard to beat when done right. The classic example of teamwork is when two teammates find themselves in a breakaway with one other single rider. As one teammate attacks, the other teammate waits for the single rider to chase the teammate and then follows in the chaser's draft, taking the free ride up to the attacking teammate's wheel. As soon as the two reach the attacking teammate, the teammate who has been sitting on the chaser takes a turn at attacking, and the individual opponent is forced to immediately respond again. This time the rider who was just caught sits on, and the cycle repeats until the lone rider can no longer react and one of the two teammates escapes. This kind of counterattacking is always useful when a number of teammates populate a pack or breakaway.

Once a breakaway is established that is favorable to one or more teams, the teammates who remain in the main pack may be able to assist their escaping teammates from behind by blocking to slow the progress of chasing riders. Unlike contact sports, where blocking may mean physically stopping other players from moving forward, blocking in cycling may mean interfering in a chase by interrupting a paceline at the front of the pack; generally being uncooperative by controlling the front of the pack, sending all the remaining team riders up there to take up space; or simply taking a turn a little slower than normal to give the escaping riders more time. The key to successful blocking is to take control without being so obvious about it that chasing riders are angered into going around you and chasing even harder. The pace has to be only slightly lower to give breakaway riders a chance to increase their gap.

Riders often debate whether it is necessary to actually interfere with a chase by other racers by getting into a paceline and interrupting it. Some maintain that it's more tactful to let the chasing riders chase away while the riders in the pack who want the break up the road to succeed simply sit on and let them take their chances. In pro racing, you will see

Savvy riders work together to close a gap

a long line of teammates chasing without interruption at the front of the pack. Actual blocking by clogging avenues with teammates or interrupting pacelines is not as common on that level of racing, where distances often take a toll on escaping riders. But in shorter amateur racing, it may be necessary to do a little blocking. Your effectiveness in blocking, however, is usually most successful when done subtly.

When teammates work together, they sacrifice energy for each another. This sacrificing may not always be equal, as the weaker members of the team may constantly work for a stronger teammate by chasing or sitting on instead of pulling during breakaways that contain a strong competitor from another team. Teammates may also sacrifice to assist a faster sprinter in the final sprint (see chapter 17, pages 201-202, for more about leadouts), ending their own chances of winning the race or possibly even placing high. If your team plans to try to work together in races, make sure that you understand each team member's role and how winnings will be split.

Dealing With a Flat

Flat tires are an inevitable part of racing, and there is no way to allow for them in the results or timing of a race. Fortunately, with quick-release wheels, replacing a flat with a good wheel can be quite fast. This fast change, however, requires that you have a spare wheel available, even though you may be in the middle of a farm road with no pit stop in sight, and that you have someone to assist you in changing it (such as a follow vehicle carrying spare wheels). Many races have neutral service vehicles, and a wheel will be near; but some races don't.

In local races, the neutral support vehicle will most often be a car or pickup driven by a volunteer (a good way for a significant other to get to watch the race up close, by the way), ideally with a mechanic or other volunteer riding shotgun to pull wheels out of the back to replace on bikes. Remember that the person getting the wheel out of the truck is probably not a professional mechanic and probably doesn't know how to do a fast wheel change, so be prepared to be patient or change the wheel yourself if necessary.

The follow vehicles with spare wheels may be *neutral*, where all riders are asked to voluntarily submit wheels before the start; *wheels in, wheels out*, where only those riders or teams who put in wheels are able to take out wheels; or *team specific*, where follow vehicles for each team are allowed to follow the race and are called up if one of their riders gets a flat. (Team-specific support is usually allowed only in elite racing.) In bigger events, wheels and race support may also be provided by professional component or wheel companies that bring their own equipment and mechanics. Regardless of the kind of support offered, always bring a set of extra wheels to every race, even if the spares are just your normal training wheels.

Once you find that you have a flat, expeditiously and safely make your way to the back of the pack. Whatever you do, *do not* slam on your brakes and stop in the middle of the pack. Instead, as you fade to the back, raise your hand to signal to the follow vehicle and officials that you have a flat. Raise your right hand to signal a rear flat; your left hand to signal a front flat. If you pass any of your teammates on the way back, be sure to let them know, calmly, that you have a flat. Once you are safely in the back of the pack, move to the right side of the road and pull over. Even if you have full use of the road, never pull to the left side of the road with a flat tire (unless you are racing in a country that drives on the left side of the road). If you get a flat on a hill within a short distance of the top, and the tire seems ridable enough for a short time, consider continuing on the flat tire until you reach the top so that you won't have to restart on a climb. See the sidebar on page 176 for tips on a fast wheel change.

Getting a Wheel Change During a Race

Professional race mechanic Vince Gee has changed wheels all over the world for riders such as Lance Armstrong. Here are his tips for a fast and efficient wheel change with the assistance of a race mechanic.

After pulling all the way over to the side of the road, unclip from both pedals and get off the bike. A common mistake by new riders is to think that keeping one foot clipped into the pedal will help them to rejoin the group more quickly. You may be able to straddle the bike while standing during a front wheel change but not for a rear change. When in doubt, simply get off the bike.

If no one is available yet to help you, open up the brakes, undo the quick release, and take out the flat wheel. For rear wheel changes, shift the rear derailleur to the smallest cog—usually either the 11- or 12-tooth cog closest to the bike's frame. This will make it easier to get the chain back on the correct cog of the new wheel.

If you have the help of a mechanic, once the wheel is on, get back on the bike and get one foot clipped in as quickly as possible and sit on the saddle. Then the mechanic will give you a hefty push to get you going again.

Be calm! Getting nervous helps no one. Hurrying the mechanic does not make the change faster. If anything, it makes the mechanic nervous and may slow the wheel change. Be calm, be quiet, and let the mechanic do her job.

Once you get going after your flat, chase back to the pack or group. If the wheel change has been a fast one and the pack isn't ripping along too quickly in front of you, you may be only several hundred meters off the back. If you are lucky enough to have teammates to work with you, it's possible that one or more of them can help pace you back on. Be careful in either dropping off to help a teammate or having one drop off to help you. If the assisting teammate isn't as strong as the rider who flatted, the rider dropping back risks getting dropped himself!

Even if you have teammates waiting, look around to see whether other riders may also be chasing back to the pack for whatever reason, and work together if it's practical. Chase back to the pack in a steady pace, giving the pedals a bit of gas if you are getting close to the pack but are still dangling on your own in the wind. Avoid drafting or pacing off the follow vehicle back to the pack. As unlucky as you've been to have a flat, most race officials, even though they'd like to look the other way, are not allowed to let you do so, and may disqualify you from the race.

Label your spare wheels with your name and phone number in case they are misplaced at a race venue. Also, write your race number on tape or a small slip of paper tucked into the spokes of your wheels contributed to the neutral follow vehicle so that you have a better chance of receiving your own race wheel during a wheel change.

Heading to the Finish

Eventually, the finish line looms closer and you have to plan your approach. Races usually end in one of three ways: A rider makes it to the line solo as a result of a successful individual breakaway, a smaller group that has broken away or dropped everyone else makes it to the line together, or the field stays together for a massive field sprint. Races that finish on hills usually result in racers finishing in a strung-out or shattered pack, with small groups or individuals struggling across the line one by one. The way the race gets to that point, of course, depends on the attacking and pacemaking that goes on during the race's more difficult terrain or conditions.

Your position in the pack is never more important than in the closing kilometers of a race. With four kilometers to go, you will need to be near the front of the pack, toward the outside, continually working to stay near the front but not placing yourself at the very front. You want to do everything you can to stay out of the middle of the pack as riders become more and more desperate to move up and stay near the front, boxing in the riders who are unlucky enough to be pushed to the middle and making it hard for them to get out again.

Saving energy until the ultimate point to jump into the final sprint is the key to a successful sprint. Many riders claim that they can't sprint, when in fact their lack of success in sprint finishes is due more to a general lack of fitness and tactical positioning. The more you develop as a total racer, the more you can make use of tactics and hold your position in the field. Road race finishes are always somewhat unpredictable because you may not get to ride the final kilometers of roadway at race speed until the actual finish. For that reason, it's imperative to memorize landmarks and locations of the 500- and 200-meter signs. (See chapter 17 for more details on sprint finishes.)

Chapter 16

Time Trialing

The time trial is the purest form of bike racing. Each rider races as fast as possible alone, and the one who rides the distance in the shortest time wins. Your bike, the clock, and the road are all you need for a time trial. You can even race a time trial against yourself, week after week, by comparing times on the same course. Time trialing is also a good way to test your fitness and progress throughout a season and from year to year.

The time trial (TT) is a popular choice for a first race because it doesn't require riding in close proximity to others. TTs are the favorite races of some riders, regardless of how skilled they become in the other kinds of racing. The straightforward suffering and all-out effort is addictive to those who love the thrill of chasing the rider in front of them while outrunning the rider behind them. Time trials are often an essential part of stage racing, so most all-around racers need to practice their time trialing regularly.

Time Trialing Basics

In time trials, riders take off one at a time, usually 30 or 60 seconds apart. The start order and times are printed on the start list. The order is usually determined randomly, with care taken to ensure that teammates aren't starting directly behind one another. Sometimes, riders known to be good time trialists are seeded in the final starting spots to make the time trial finish more exciting for spectators. In a stage race, riders doing a time trial take off in the reverse order of the general overall classification (see chapter 18).

Once you are on your way, you aren't allowed to work with or ride next to any other riders on the course for any length of time. You may catch and pass other riders or be caught and passed, but each rider just continues to the finish at the best pace he can individually maintain. Passing other riders or being passed by other riders does not affect your individual time other than the actual time you gain or lose to any particular rider.

As simple as it may seem, successful time trialing requires attention to many details.

Warming Up

Following the prerace guidelines in chapter 4 and a warm-up at least equal to that outlined in table 15.1, you should be warmed up and ready to race at the line at least three minutes before your start according to the rules (five minutes beforehand is ideal). The shorter the time trial, the more intense the warm-up needs to be. As you start your warm-up, compare the current time to that of the race clock. They may not agree, and knowing the difference can save you from missing your start time.

When you get to the start, the next three or four riders to take off will be lined up next to their bikes, ready to walk them to the start line on their turns. When you ride up to the line, ensure that your bike is in the proper starting gear. For most riders starting on flat terrain, this gear is nothing bigger than a 53 × 17. If the race starts uphill, a lower gear allows better acceleration. Experiment with different gears in practice to figure out the best one for you.

Once the rider immediately in front of you takes off, walk your bike to the start line. Remember that you have only the 30- or 60-second start interval to mount your bike and get ready to take off. While this seems like a very short time, even a 30-second start interval is enough for you to comfortably mount your bike and prepare for the final countdown.

The Standing Start

Most time trials begin with a standing start. Your bike is held so that you can ride immediately away from the line, already clipped into both pedals. A standing start begins with a race official helping you put your bike on the start mark while another grabs firm hold of the bottom of your bike's saddle so that you can mount the bike. Riders have various styles of mounting the bike for a standing start, but here is a fairly failsafe approach: First swing your leg over the bike's top tube. The official behind you will usually wait for you to do this before grabbing hold of your saddle. Then while still standing, grab your brake hoods and squeeze at least one brake while rotating the left pedal backward to the six-o'clock position with your right foot. Clip your foot in at this point, and stand up on the pedal to sit on the seat. Then roll the pedals around backward again to put your left pedal in at the six-o'clock position. Clipping in at this position helps keep the bike from rolling forward and pulling against the official who is holding you.

Once you are comfortably clipped in, place one hand at a time in the drops. Keep one finger on one brake to keep the bike from rolling. Sit on the saddle while looking forward down the road. At the same time, roll your pedals to a two-o'clock/eight-o'clock position, with your dominant foot forward. This is your power position for starting. Once you have reached this position, make sure that the official holding you has you balanced from side to side. Being off balance will be easy to detect, since it is a very unnerving feeling. If you are leaning too far to one side or the other, just tell the holder politely that you need to be leaned slightly left or right.

By the time you are all settled, the clock likely has wound down to the takeoff time. The starting official will give you a countdown with five seconds to go. As the official reaches the three-second mark, rise up out of the saddle, being careful to keep a single finger on a brake and your weight balanced on the pedals. It may seem intimidating to rise up out of the saddle like this, but standing will help you move forward more forcefully and easily once the official says *go* and the holder lets go of your saddle. At the *go* signal, let go of the brake and transfer your weight to your forward pedal as you pull back against your drops and move confidently and somewhat forcefully away from the holder. Keep your head up and continue to look down the road to where you are going. This keeps you traveling in a straight line and prevents wobbling.

More formally organized races may actually have a start ramp similar to what you may have seen for the time trials during the Tour de France. Starting on a ramp isn't too different from starting on a flat surface; as soon as you pull away from the holder, your first pedal stroke takes you down the ramp, and you may partially coast until you meet the road at the bottom of the ramp. Whatever you do, don't panic and tense up. Relax and guide the bike down the ramp. Just as important, keep looking straight ahead to where you are going, and pull decisively away from the holding official. You can practice a ramp start on the top of a driveway or other decline. If you do have troubles with a ramp start or with the standing start, don't worry—

you aren't the first, and many other riders have conquered their fears and difficulties after only a couple of tries.

Starting Speed

At the beginning of a time trial, your heart will be racing with adrenaline, and you will be ready to release all your excess energy. Mentally, this can be one of the more challenging periods of this kind of race—not because you are suffering but because you actually may need to put the reins on your surplus motivation. The moment you pull away from the start, gauge your effort. Extremely short time trials will have you pulling away from the official with nearly all your might and sprinting up to speed. But a longer, 40-kilometer (25-mile) time trial, for instance, should have you pulling away at what *feels* like a leisurely pace. The reality is that your excess energy will make even the easiest-feeling start much faster than you realize. For that reason, it's better to err on the easier side of a start than to go harder. Before a longer time trial, figure out a speed that you are confident you can maintain for the full distance. Adjust for the wind and incline at the start. In the first few minutes of the race, you will be able to easily exceed this pace, but don't do it. Just ramp up to the target pace. The lack of pain in the first minutes means you are saving energy for the second half.

Choosing a Pace

Choosing a pace that allows you to start and finish strong is the backbone of a successful time trial. The best time trial times are achieved by the steadiest effort. Regardless of the length of the time trial, the ultimate aim is to "leave everything on the course"—the moment you cross the finish line, you need to feel as though you couldn't pedal another stroke. This effort to give your all is part of what makes time trialing so challenging. If you go too hard, you slow down later in the ride and lose time. You also lose time if you start too slowly. If you aren't hurting in a short time trial or in the second half of a long time trial, you probably aren't going fast enough to win. Remember, *time trials hurt.* Even the strongest riders will produce only average TT performances if they cannot teach themselves to suffer.

The actual speeds of time trials vary because of course terrain and conditions, so it's difficult to pinpoint an effort by miles or kilometers per hour. Instead, most riders use perceived effort to guide their time trialing. Racers may also use heart rate, wattage, or cadence to help conduct their effort. As discussed in chapter 5, the different heart rate zones relate to efforts that can be sustained for a number of minutes.

© 2002 Jim Safford

Multi-national champion Dede
Demet-Barry shows how to suffer.

The anaerobic threshold (AT) is typically the breaking point where
you go into lactic-acid overload. You can maintain power over it for
only a little longer than four minutes. Your heart rate may stay up
longer, but power and speed will decrease. Therefore, time trials of
up to about seven minutes are performed at an effort mostly above
AT power and heart rate. In a time trial that is expected to last only
a few minutes, go all out from the gun to the finish.

Meanwhile, time trials lasting more than seven minutes (varying
by individual) are ridden closer to AT, other than in the final miles,
where a rider should give everything that's left regardless of what the
heart rate does or the power meter reads. When high-tech gadgets
fail, nothing beats the ability to feel how hard you are pushing
yourself. You can't ignore what your body is telling you. For that
reason, time trialing should be practiced frequently enough that you
have a refined feel for your effort.

Part of preparing to give your best effort is proper hydration and
nutrition before, during, and after the race. While most pre- and
postrace eating is covered in chapter 8, one thing to keep in mind for
time trials is that the maximal effort they require is incredibly
demanding on the entire body, including the stomach, even for very

short events. For that reason, the last major meal before the start should be a solid three to four hours in advance. You can consume snacks and tolerable race drinks up until the start if you've experimented successfully with the same products in training.

No feeding from feeders or vehicles is allowed during a TT, so you will need to carry everything you eat and drink with you during the event. What and how much to carry, if anything, is a constant source of debate because of the weight and aerodynamic concerns of carrying bottles. Studies have shown that for time trials lasting more than 20 minutes, the benefits of hydration outweigh any aerodynamic losses, so keep your bottles with you for time trials lasting longer than approximately 8 to 10 kilometers (5 to 6 miles), and drink early and often in the race. Most amateurs will never ride a time trial over 40 kilometers unless they ride the cycling portion of a long-course triathlon, so most riders will be able to time trial simply with water and carbohydrate or electrolyte drinks.

Mastering the Course

Once you are under way, take the shortest possible line over the course. Use the painted lines to help guide you, but don't be lulled into following the white line simply because it's there and you aren't focused enough on finding the fastest pavement and the shortest path through a curve in the road. Take the most direct line through each turn, all while staying to the right of the centerline on an out-and-back course. The exception to taking the shortest line is that very bumpy pavement can slow you down. It's worth taking a slightly longer line if that line is on smoother pavement. Only in the case of a one-way closed course should you ever dare to cross the centerline. Even then, you should be aware of local residents coming out of driveways or driving toward you unaware of the race.

As you glide over the course, remember that momentum is your friend. It is important to stay on top of the gear at all times and avoid getting bogged down in too big of a gear. Downshift as you slow down rather than fighting to keep the gear turning. A gear that is too large will cost you time in the initial slowing and extra energy to bring yourself back up to speed, as well as fatiguing your legs unnecessarily. Stand up over very small hills to keep your momentum going over the top. Then settle in again to your aerobars and get back into a rhythm as quickly as possible. For extended hills, change to a smaller gear, move out of your aerobars to open up your breathing and gain more leverage, and continue at the same rhythm and effort you carried over the flats. As you near the top of the climb, gradually change to bigger gears and settle smoothly back into your aerobars as the road flattens out. When rounding tight corners, always drop down into your regular bars out of your aerobars. The same goes when descending hills greater than small rollers.

Passing and Being Passed

The short time gaps between starters means that you may pass and be passed by other riders during a time trial. When you catch another rider, pass decisively and confidently, leaving no question that you are the stronger rider. The rules state that you have to keep a distance of 2 meters (6 feet) to the side as you go by and that no riders should ever ride within 25 meters (80 feet) behind another rider. Begin moving to the side when you get near 25 meters behind the rider you are passing, and then stay to the side until you are well past the rider. You will almost always pass to the left unless the rider being passed leaves room only to the right.

Occasionally, the spark of competitiveness in the rider being passed causes her to pick up speed as you attempt to pass, making it more difficult to get around and on your way. The rider will most often run out of steam, and you will eventually be able to get around without any extra effort. But once in a while the rider will really give a fight. Don't get into a sprinting duel in the middle of a time trial. If you can't get around with a moderately increased effort, it's best to back off and take another run in a few minutes. The rules state that you must drop back 25 meters before trying again.

If you are the rider being passed, continue at the speed you have been traveling, and then use the motivation of the rider now in front of you to try to maintain a faster pace, if possible, only if you are near the end of the race. It may be possible to pass the rider back again later if he fades over the final part of the course. It might also happen that you simply don't have the energy to pick up your pace. Whatever you do, don't panic or become downhearted. You never know how you may be riding in comparison to all the other riders in the race. It may be that the rider who has passed you is beating everyone by minutes and your ride may still be a strong one in the overall scheme of the race. It's also possible that a rider who rockets past you is riding faster than what can realistically be maintained. Remember that your time gap to anyone you pass or are passed by is off by at least the 30-second or 60-second start gap, so that rider may not be your closest competition timewise.

The Turnaround

Many time trials are run on out-and-back courses. This almost always means that you will need to make a U-turn on the course, usually within the two lanes of a typical road. While not all time trials have turnarounds, most do, and the time gained and lost in the turnaround can be significant in a short event. Most turnaround points are simply a cone in the center of the road with a race official standing nearby to account for each rider making the turn.

Mastering the turnaround means completing the turn as quickly, calmly, and safely as possible and then returning to speed efficiently. To do this, use the entire width of the road for your turn. Approach the turnaround from the farthest right-hand edge of the road. Just as for any other turn, bring down your speed by braking *before* the turn, and shift ahead of time into the smaller gear that you will use to exit the turn. As you near the area of the cone and are level with it, begin your turn; this actually causes you to start the turn just past the cone. It may seem natural to make a symmetrical turn around the cone, but you save a little time if you make a lopsided turn in which the first part of the turn is sharper and the last part shallower so that you can begin pedaling again sooner (see figure 16.1).

If you widen the second half of the turn, begin pedaling sooner than if you were simply to do a round turn with the cone as the center. If you are anxious about your first turnaround, be sure to stay on the road and go around the cone. As you come out of the turn, rise out of the saddle, and get on top of the gear to get yourself back up to speed. Then settle into a steady gear again and into your aerobars. If you are nervous going into the turn, it is always better to scrub off too much speed and take the turn properly than it is to come in too fast and have to both brake during the turn and try to avoid overshooting the exit.

Finishing on Empty

Time trials are most often won in the closing kilometers as riders find out how well they have rationed their energy throughout the race. Riding strong at the end of a TT requires intense focus throughout the race. Some racers chant mantras to themselves as they ride. Others go through mental checklists throughout the race, constantly ensuring that they are pushing the most efficient gear, turning the most powerful cadence, watching the road straight ahead and keeping the rider who left a minute ahead in sight and on target. Regardless, leave no ounce of energy unused as you cross the line. Never coast the last

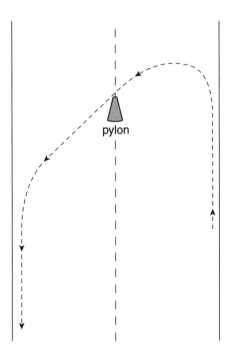

Figure 16.1 Decrease your speed, shift down to your exiting gear, and make a lopsided turn around the marker that allows you to begin pedaling as soon as possible.

few meters over the line; continue pushing through it as if every fraction of a second counts. Sometimes it does.

Aerodynamics and Positioning

While fitness and strength are required for time trial success, race-winning performance requires an aerodynamic and comfortable, powerful position on your bike. In a shorter time trial, favorable aerodynamics can yield a savings of several seconds over the same distance, while in a time trial lasting almost an hour, favorable aerodynamics can mean a savings of one or two minutes or more. If you consider that it takes a less than one-second gap to win a time trial, even a 1 percent improvement in aerodynamics can potentially mean saving time in a time trial.

Becoming "aero" means being in a position that makes the frontal area of your body and bike as low and narrow as possible to present the least amount of resistance to the wind flowing over you. It also includes using aerodynamically shaped equipment and accessories such as deep-section or disk wheels, special handlebars, a skinsuit, special helmet, booties, or other sleek equipment. Some items may make a notable difference and others a lesser or negligible difference, and the cost of these items is not always in proportion to the amount of time they save.

Finding the optimal aerodynamics for time trialing means finding a balance between ideal aerodynamic positioning and comfort as well as ease of bike handling. You may have a terrific aerodynamic position, but if it isn't comfortable, you are likely sacrificing more in performance than you are gaining in improved slipstream. Similarly, you want to time trial in a position that your body is accustomed to for intense riding. If you have a bike or position you use only for time trialing, it should be similar enough to your everyday riding position that you aren't calling on rarely used muscles that will tire sooner than those that have been honed in training.

Get Low

Typical time trialing positioning involves keeping your front area low. This means dropping your stem potentially lower than normal and bringing your forearms onto the aerobars. You can check your position by placing your bike on a turbo trainer in front of a mirror. A major limiter of getting low is your hamstring flexibility. If your shoulders drop too low, you will lose power. At some point, the muscles pushing down on one leg will be used to drive the other leg up instead of driving the bike forward. Test this by watching speed on a trainer at a constant heart rate near race pace with different shoulder heights.

Get Narrow

Aerobars are the best tool for narrowing your profile on the bike. Aerodynamic specialist John Cobb suggests that the spacing of the arms should be narrow enough out in front of you to avoid creating a scoop but wide enough to cover your thigh area. Riders should resist the temptation to move their elbows too close together, risking restricted breathing and tight neck and shoulder muscles as well as impaired bike handling. (If you do not have access to a pair of attachable aerobars, you will want to ride most flat and rolling time trials with your hands in the drops to keep low over the bike.)

The padded support area of your aerobars should cradle your arms near the elbows, not at mid-forearm. Elbow support greatly decreases tension throughout the hands, arms, and shoulders. Set up your aerobars so that the forearms (not the bars themselves) are near horizontal in the TT position, and the general extension should help keep the back flat and prevent it from being so stretched out that handling control will be lost or the back will cramp.

Riders with superb hamstring and lower-back flexibility can just attach aerobars to their regular road racing bike and make no other changes. Most riders, however, need to move the saddle forward about 5 millimeters (1/4 inch) and up about 3 millimeters (1/8 inch) and tilt the nose down a few degrees to open the hip angle and relieve pressure on the soft tissue at the pubic bone. Unless you have consistently and successfully ridden time trials in shorter triathlons where you are riding at a much steeper angle more forward on the bike, avoid moving your seat too far forward and upward. Staying closer to your current road bike position will keep you much more comfortable and efficient, and therefore faster.

Aero Equipment for the Body

Even the most inexperienced racer can improve aerodynamic effectiveness by wearing a skinsuit—a simple combination of shorts and a tight, stretchy Lycra jersey sewn together into one piece. Skinsuits are devoid of pockets or slack in the fit that will flap in the wind. Lycra or stretch rubber booties covering your cycling shoes are an additional inexpensive way to cut seconds off your time trial. The aero factor can also be improved by simply pinning on your number as flat as possible and keeping your jersey or skinsuit zipped up instead of open.

The next step up is an aerodynamic helmet made for time trialing. These helmets are generally rounder in the front and pointier in the rear and contain fewer ventilation holes than a normal helmet. They may also have an attachable eyeshield that takes the place of riding glasses. You might have seen these types of helmets worn by pros in the major tour races on television. While some of the helmets that you see the pros in Europe wear aren't approved for use in amateur racing, you can find similar helmets that do pass the local standards.

Aero Equipment for Your Bike

Leave your water bottles on your bike frame; wind tunnel studies have shown that leaving them on the bike is more aerodynamic than attaching one to the underside of your seat or using a hydropack, even when it's underneath your jersey. A worthwhile addition to your time trial setup is a set of time trial wheels such as those with few spokes and with deep-section rims, or those made of a solid disk. The differences in aero advantage between a regular 36-spoke wheel and both the deep-section and disk wheel are significant, while the differences between the deep-section and disk wheel are slight, with the disk wheel coming out slightly ahead.

If you have the opportunity to obtain a single set of time trial–specific wheels, those with deep-section rims are recommended for their versatility and handling. If you are fortunate enough to own more than one set, add a rear disk to the mix. You then have the choice of the rear disk or the deep-section rear to be used with the deep-section front. Front disks are recommended only for indoor velodrome use or for advanced racers with excellent bike-handling skills riding in zero wind conditions.

Finally, if you plan to do many time trials and have the financial means, it may be worthwhile to purchase a time trial bike. Just as with adjusting your road bike for time trials, practicality and ergonomics dictate your best choice in a time trial frame. Geometry and positioning should be not far off the position of your current road bike. Another major factor is the shape of the bike's tubing. Aerodynamic specialist John Cobb found in wind tunnel studies that tubing rounded in the front and tapered to a foil point in the rear is faster than standard one-inch round tubing, while fat round tubing is even less aerodynamic.

Beyond the bike's geometry and aerodynamics, a good time trial bike should also handle well and not be so rigid that it's simply uncomfortable to ride in any position. Even within the choices for bikes made with tapered tubing, there are many lustrous time trial bikes out there to drool over, and it can be easy to get carried away and spend thousands on a time trialing machine—so be sure to read up and ask around, then insist on trying before buying.

Much experimenting has been done in the last decade concerning the position of the rider and aerodynamic properties of the bike. There *are* more aerodynamic positions possible than what you currently see the pros riding. However, recent international rules hold riders to more standard positions to keep the competition in cycling more dependent on the rider than the technology underneath. Not all rules applicable internationally apply in North American amateur racing. Still, most bike manufacturers are only producing equipment that conforms to international rules. Before you trick out your bike, examine the rules to see whether the modifications are allowed.

Above all, run this reality check when thinking about purchasing additional aero equipment: A full time trial kit can make a difference of only a minute or two in a one-hour time trial, so if you are off the leaders by more than that without fancy stuff, it would be wiser to invest in more training than in more stuff.

Chapter 17

Criteriums

Criteriums are the flatlander's paradise. A crit is made up of multiple laps of less than a mile around city blocks, parks, or industrial parks, providing racers and spectators with fast, exciting racing showcasing bike-handling skills and plenty of sprinting action.

Crits are popular primarily in the United States and Canada, while most of the rest of the world concentrates on road racing and time trials. Anyone who has raced internationally will tell you that the North American focus on criteriums has turned U.S. riders into cornering specialists. Although crits can include small hills, they are rarely long or hard enough to drop those riders who don't climb well and who may be good sprinters and riders who thrive on going fast around corners.

To win a criterium means being the first to cross the line at the end of the final lap. The only exception is when a rider or group of riders breaks away and laps the field. In the case of a single rider lapping the field, that rider automatically wins the race no matter how she performed in the final sprint because the lap gained takes precedence over being the first across the line on the final lap. In the case of a group lapping the field, the highest-placing rider from the lapping group is the winner. Race officials may sometimes have the lapped riders or the lapped field sprint a lap earlier so that the riders who are up a lap have a fair sprint without interference.

A criterium for beginning racers is rarely longer than an hour or more than 25 miles (40 kilometers) in length. The laps are counted down with a lap board updated each lap to reflect the number of laps to go. If a time format is used, a race might be listed as "45 minutes plus two laps," for instance. Ideally, the racers race for 45 minutes, crossing the line and doing two more laps. But in the real world, racers don't always cross the finish line at the designated time. For that reason, the numbers showing on the lap board actually count down minutes for the first part of the race, then change to laps to go as the race nears its final circuits. All you really need to remember is to keep an eye on the lap board frequently during the race and listen to when the race official announces the change.

Eventually the laps count down until only the final lap remains. As the riders cross the finish line with one to go, the race officials ring a bell (or use a whistle or flag) to signify the last lap.

The Start

The start of a crit is similar to that of a road race with one exception; riders almost always go all-out from the start line in a crit to maintain or gain their position near the front of the pack. To prepare for a fast start, you need to be warmed up properly and be familiar with the course. Before the start of each race, you usually have time to do at least a couple of laps around the course, at which time you can scan the course for potholes, uneven pavement, bot dots, and other hazards. Practice taking each corner at full speed, and rehearse the ideal approach for each corner. Additionally, try riding over some of the hazards that may lie in the turns at slower speeds so that you are confident that you can ride over them in case you are forced to during the race.

> Find a teammate or other experienced rider to ride the course with before your race during the warm-up period. Someone who has either just raced on the course or who has enough experience to show you the fastest, smoothest ways through the turns can save you some anxiety during the race.

To prepare for the dash off the start line, practice some fast starts, clipping into your pedal as quickly as possible from a start with one foot in the pedal and one on the ground. Whenever you can, get a frontline starting position by getting to the line early. When the gun goes off, even if you can't get your foot in the pedal immediately keep pedaling on the top of the pedal to gain the speed necessary to avoid losing too many places, and then work your foot into the pedal. Stay calm and avoid opening a gap in front of you, and you are likely to survive even the worst start.

Often the hardest part of beginning crits is the first 10 to 15 minutes; inexperienced riders burn their nervous energy by drag racing at the front. After those initial laps, riders lose steam, and the pace tends to settle down and become more bearable, yet faster than most road races. Racers in smaller packs of riders (such as those racing in the women or junior ranks) may find keeping the pace up in a crit is more challenging than racers in large packs. With fewer riders, the gaps in ability are likely to be substantial, and it's simply more difficult to keep the pace high because some riders may be struggling to hang on while others are afraid to attack immediately and risk having to ride off the front by themselves for the greater part of the race.

As if the corners, attacks, and chases weren't enough, additional prize incentives called *primes* (pronounced "preems") are awarded on intermediate sprint laps to keep the pace high and entertain the spectators. Primes aren't tied to the overall outcome of the race and can be offered to any group on the course, such as the breakaway, main field, or even groups behind the main field. Primes are nearly always announced with the ring of the race bell for a sprint to the line on the next lap. Race announcers or officials generate excitement by yelling out the prize being offered: "Twenty dollars to the winner of the next lap!" If you win a prime during a crit, head straight to the officials' stand at the finish line after the race, as primes are often given away sooner and separately from the main race prizes.

Moving Up

Criteriums, more than any other race, are a constant fight for position in the pack. For that reason, more aggressive riders eat up the crit, blasting down the straightaways and passing the more hesitant riders through the corners. Ride gears small enough to allow you to make the constant accelerations without bogging down. Use your aerobic fitness, and spin moderate gears rather than using leg strength in big gears to jump out of corners and power down the straight-aways. Riding hard on the front of the pack drops the weakest riders in a crit but only wears down the riders pulling at the front while the other strong riders sit in and enjoy the ride.

Because of the continual turns—usually at least four per lap—being near the back of the pack is like being attached to an accordion. As the riders at the widest part of the pack slow so that all fit through each turn, the slowing riders and those behind them have to jump out of the corners to stay with the wheel in front of them while the strongest and most skilled riders drive the pace at the front of the

Staying near the front of the pack in a criterium is smoother and safer than riding near the back.

pack. Outlasting this accordion effect at the back of the pack is a huge waste of energy and should be avoided by staying nearer to the front whenever possible.

To move nearer to the front, take advantage of longer straightaways to charge up the side of the pack, tucking yourself back into the flow of the pack well before the next turn. This prevents having to brake or risking a crash by taking the corner in an unnatural line. Even if you gain only a few spots at each attempt to move up, continual tries will eventually have you in the first third of the pack, where the smoother cornering action will make you glad you made the effort to move up. Once you reach the front section of the pack, you will have to continue fighting to stay there, particularly if the pace is uneven. When the pace is high and the pack is strung out, fewer riders are able to swarm up the sides and threaten your position. But when the pace slows, the riders behind will use their momentum to move up on the outsides, potentially moving all the way to the front so that they are the first riders heading into the next corner.

Another way to move up when there aren't enough long straightaways or you simply don't have the gas to shoot up the side is to use each corner to pick off one or two places in front of you. In any cornering situation, gaps open as riders choose separate lines through the turn. It's possible to shoot these gaps without endangering yourself or the riders around you. Practice this in groups by backing off from the riders in front of you a bit as you approach the turn. Then as you see a gap open, steer toward it confidently and follow between the lines of the other riders.

Another method of moving up in corners is to go the long way. This strategy works best in races with more than four corners, where a left turn is immediately followed by a right turn, or vice versa. The idea is to stay to the inside of the first turn so that you are on the outside of the following turn. For instance, if a course turns right and then left just the width of a block later, go through the far inside of the right-hand turn and then keep pedaling on what is now going to be the far outside of the coming left turn. With other riders now braking on the other side of the road to try to tuck in before the left-hand corner, you will have time to pick up as many as 10 spots at once and will possibly even be able to continue pedaling farther into the coming turn than other riders.

Hanging On

Even when you know that you need to move up, you may sometimes feel that all you can do is hang on in the position you are occupying at the back of the pack. If you can summon the energy to make a decisive move toward the front, you will likely find that the energy spent moving up was worth it. But it's often difficult to appreciate this when you are suffering on the back. If you are stuck near the back, frequently look back to make sure that other riders are still behind you, so that if you open a gap between you and the rider in front of you, someone from behind can help close the gap and potentially help you remain in contact with the pack in front.

Use the space in the back to take runs at gaps opening between riders in the turns. Above all, don't panic. Stay relaxed and glued to the wheel in front of you during the straightaways. This is where you learn to "fight" in bike racing—gritting your teeth and suffering to hang on even when your legs and lungs feel as if they are going to explode. Hanging on a second at a time is how you do it. If you make it through one second that takes you through the exit of the next turn, you just might be able to hang on down the next straightaway too, and then possibly the pace will slow and you can recover. On top of fitness and experience, the ability to fight is what separates the riders in the front group from those behind.

Still, as often happens in a rider's first races, you may lose contact with the pack and find yourself either on your own or with a few other riders off the back. In this case, continue on at a pace you can maintain until you either reach the finish line or are lapped by a breakaway group or the main pack. Though you may feel demoralized enough to pull out of the race, don't do it! Riders who stay in and gain experience both in skills and fitness improve faster than those who drop out of races. Make a goal to stay with the pack longer in your next race, and go from there.

Race officials will pull lapped riders from the race if the course, race speeds, or pack size make leaving in the slower, lapped riders a safety concern. In the event that you are about to be lapped but are allowed to remain in the race, be alert for approaching lapping riders, and stay to the outside of the course, allowing the passing riders the faster line through any turns. If you can muster the energy, try to rejoin the pack as it passes and see whether you can hang with it. If you are dropped again, just keep going! Nobody ever improves by quitting!

Using Strategy

Nearly all riders who learn how to stay with the pack take part in the *game* of the criterium. Basic strategy for crits is mostly the same as for road races, with the exception of the free-lap rule and the ability to lap and then rejoin the field. Amateur criteriums finish in mass field sprints more often than any other outcome. For that reason, racers in a crit boil down into two camps: those who want the race to come down to a field sprint, and those who do not.

A lack of major hills forces riders to rely more on timing than terrain to launch successful attacks. Early on in the race, everyone is fresh, and those who attempt attacks are usually chased down aggressively. Attempting an early break in a crit is risky unless you know you are stronger than the majority of the pack. Even so, breakaways formed early on rarely make it to the final finish line unless the strongest teams or individuals in the race are all represented in the break. If you are unsure about your strength, it is better to wait until the second half of the race before trying an attack.

Strategic times to attack in a crit include times when the pace suddenly slows after the pack has been strung out at high speed, such as immediately after a prime sprint or just after an attack has been chased down. Using your momentum from behind the leaders to help launch you into an attack may provide the extra boost to gain a gap. Choice areas on the course to attack include right before heading into a corner or from the bottom of any hill. Attacks at these places require an all-out commitment and concentration as well as an element of surprise. Avoid giving away your intentions by shifting out of the saddle too early or looking around too much. If you attack from the outside of the course and cruise through a corner first at a higher speed than riders at the front of the pack, it is difficult for riders to adjust their pace to catch you until they are through the turn. By then you may already have a lead of several seconds. Attacking on downhills or when the pack is moving along together at only moderate speed early in the race is not recommended because of the ease the pursuers will have in chasing.

If you know you are a good sprinter, you may want to attempt breaking away. However, for anyone who excels in sprinting to make the most of the last few hundred meters of the race, it is necessary to conserve as much energy as possible throughout the race by staying out of the wind and following smooth riders in the pack. Breakaway

Criterium Racing Tips

- Bring an extra set of wheels for the pit area. If you don't have an extra set, ask someone from your club if you can borrow a set for the pit. Some clubs own wheels just for this purpose.
- Invest in an aerodynamic skinsuit to help cut down on wind drag during the race.
- Check the lap board frequently throughout your race. Even if the speed is high, the laps or minutes seem to melt slowly away at first and then fly by closer to the finish. Don't get caught too far back in the pack in the final laps because you weren't paying attention to the lap board!
- Use primes to test your legs. Even if you are feeling fantastic, back off from the final primes to save energy for the final sprint if you plan to go for the win.
- Expect the pace of the entire pack to pick up on laps where primes are offered.
- Criteriums do not allow feeding from the side of the road unless they are particularly long, hilly courses. For most races you will need to carry only water and a carbohydrate/electrolyte drink as long as you are well-fueled and hydrated before the start.
- If the leaders lap you, remember that you aren't required to finish the extra lap. You will finish on the same lap as the leaders.
- For a field sprint, put your energy on the final lap into gaining good position into the last turn. If you have good position, the sprint will take care of itself.

attempts early in the race can cost a sprinter valuable energy for the finish. If you favor your chances in a field sprint, you may want to take a chance on hoping the field will stay together, or even work to keep it together by helping to chase down any serious breakaway attempts.

Breaking Away

As in road racing, once you've made it into a breakaway, you need to decide what to do next. Some riders are so excited to be in a breakaway that they go straight to the front of the break, pull with all their might at each opportunity, and end up getting dropped back into the field behind them. Avoid doing this by remaining calm and immediately going over the four Cs in relation to your now reduced competition. Take into account the number of laps remaining, the severity of the course, the number of riders in the breakaway and their strengths and weaknesses, how the temperature may affect your stamina, the wind, the direction of the draft, and any rain affecting the traction of the pavement in the turns.

If you favor your chances in the breakaway, or if you have never placed higher in a race than the number of riders in the break, take even pulls with the other riders in the break, sitting out a turn if you are getting too tired but never pulling harder or more often than the others. If you are concerned that you may have trouble staying with the break, you may want to sit on the back of it, only pulling through if the other riders threaten to start attacking the break. Don't pull into a headwind. Remember that you'll never find any rule that mandates having to pull when you are in a breakaway. If you are getting tired and you need to sit on, or you know that if you pull you will be dropped later, simply don't pull. Even if you aren't tired, you can feign tiredness frequently to give your breakmates a false sense of security. If another rider isn't happy with your contribution to the break, it's up to him to do something about it by trying to drop you.

It's possible that if a breakaway is really moving along, it may gain so much time on the main field that it is in a position to lap the pack. Lapping the pack has advantages and drawbacks, depending on your situation. If you are off the front alone and no one is directly behind you but the pack itself, lapping the pack early in the race can help to seal your win, as once you catch the pack you can cover or chase any serious breakaway moves by other riders. However, if you have nearly a full lap lead on the field and there isn't time for other riders to lap the field, refrain from lapping the field to savor the winning moment away from the craziness of the main field sprint.

The Free-Lap Rule

The free-lap rule helps crit riders who have suffered crashes, flat tires, or legitimate mechanical failures to rejoin the race without a disadvantage by allowing them to sit out a lap while the problem is fixed.

Along each criterium course, a pit area is set up to accommodate spare wheels and provide an area where mechanics can help riders with mechanical problems during the race. In most local races, the pit area is curbside, across from the officials' stand near the start/finish area. An official also mans the pit to ensure that any rider stopping there has had a legitimate mishap. (Check the rulebook to see what is a legitimate mishap.) You are allowed a free lap for each incident of a crash or flat. On courses less than 1 kilometer (.6 mile) long, up to two free laps may be permitted per legitimate mishap.

If you flat or crash during a race, proceed directly to the pit area. You can always cut across the course or walk or run your bike backward on the course, but never *ride* backward on the course. Once you get to the pit area, begin changing the flat tire or make adjustments to anything bent during a crash. The official in the pit will look over you and your bike or flat tire to make sure that you have crashed or flatted legitimately. If the race has real mechanics in the pit to change your wheel or work on your bike, use the time there to calm down, rest for a minute, take a drink of water, wipe the sweat out of your eyes, and do a body check if you've crashed.

Once your bike is ready to go again, a mechanic or official will assist you into a standing start position and give you a large push to help you get back up to the speed of the riders coming by. You will be thrown back in alongside the group you occupied when you crashed. For instance, if you crash while in a breakaway you will be placed back into the breakaway. Likewise, if you crash while in a chase group, you will be placed back into that chase group.

If you ride tubular tires (sew-ups) it is your responsibility to ensure that the tires remain glued on firmly and properly. If a tire rolls off the rim during a crash and you head into the pit, the attending official will inspect your rim to determine whether the tire rolled because it flatted or the rolled tire caused the crash. If the official determines that it rolled before a puncture, the mishap will be ruled as not allowable for a free lap, and you will have to chase the pack.

Free laps are normally allowed until the final 8 kilometers (5 miles) of the race. If you crash after the free-lap allowance has ended, you will need to chase the pack, even if you have to visit the pit area for a repair.

If you lap the field with a small group and you are all essentially racing individually without any organized teamwork, lapping the field may still be advantageous as you can use the "dummy factor" of the main field to help chase down any of your breakmates who attempt to escape again, meaning that riders who chase just to chase and aren't paying attention to who is on which lap may help you without even realizing that they are chasing someone who is technically an entire lap ahead of them.

Lapping the field may not be such a good idea if other riders in the breakaway have teammates in the pack who will help them and lead them out in the finishing sprint once you all lap the pack. In that case, once the breakaway gap is well established, you as the lone rider should not be working to power the break all the way to lapping the field. You can help establish the gap, but after that you need to sit on and save energy for what is to come. Remember that you can work together with riders on different laps, but you can't completely drop back off the back of the pack to help a teammate gain a lap.

The Finish

Crits most often finish in mass field sprints. But carrying on from the breakaway discussion, we cover small group finishes before field sprinting. These are the two most common finish scenarios.

Small Breakaway Sprint

As a breakaway rolls toward the finish with a respectable lead on the pack, it's possible that a small break will begin to slow down as the individuals in the break cat-and-mouse around trying to conserve energy and gain the best position for the sprint finish. In this case, you need to contribute to the pace just enough, until the sprint actually starts, that you won't be caught from behind by the pack but still not give so much effort that you waste energy and sacrifice a potential race win. In terms of perceived effort, this means pulling through at a pace slightly even with or under what you have been riding up until then, and once you are sure you will still hold off the pack, setting up for the sprint as efficiently as possible. Once the sprint enters the final turns, it is like any other sprint against a mass field. Whether there are 5 or 150 riders in the final sprint, you still need to be in the top 5 riders heading into the final 500 meters or so of the race.

An alternative small breakaway finish strategy is the final lap flier. If you know you will have a difficult time winning in a sprint, the final lap flier is your last weapon. A final lap flier is a do-or-die move where you put everything you have into a surprise attack and try to hold it to the finish. In a breakaway group, if you know you would likely be near the back in a sprint anyway, you have nothing to lose by trying an attack. A final-lap flier is a 100 percent all-out effort, and when you commit to it, you are locked in and need not look back.

Focus on speed and control in the turns, and don't give up until you reach the line. In the meantime, your breakmates will hopefully be eyeing the others in the break—not wanting to be the sacrificial one to chase—and the moment's hesitation may be enough to create the gap that can't be closed. In general, the best place to launch a final-lap flier is somewhere between 500 and 800 meters to go, but individual course characteristics can influence this. A hill on the course is an optimal point to attack. If the last part of the course heads into a headwind, launch an all-out attack closer to the 500-meter mark (meaning closer to the finish than farther away). This same strategy can also work against a mass field that doesn't already have riders driving the pace at the front of the pack.

Field Sprint

Sprinting in a field of 20 or more riders can be intimidating for any new racer. But keep in mind that if you are near the front of the pack, sprinting against 150 riders can seem the same as sprinting against only 5 riders because you are concerned only about the riders immediately around you and in direct competition with you—after all, only so many riders can fit across the road. You need to fight for prime position into the final turns and sprint as fast as possible.

In a crit, you have the benefit of having covered the finish turns and straight multiple times before the final dash to the line, so most racers have an idea of where they want to begin their final sprint. For most races, the final sprint begins out of the final turn of the course. The choice position going into the final turn before the finish straight depends on how far the stretch is from the final turn to the finish line (rarely more than 300 meters). The shorter the distance, the closer you need to be to the first position in the pack. For any stretch 100 meters or shorter, you have no choice but to be the first rider through the turn. There simply isn't space or time to pass anyone in the final sprint. For a final stretch of 100 to 150 meters, you need to be no farther back than second position, and for 150 to 200 meters, you want to be no farther back than third position. For 200 to 300 meters, you can be as far back as fourth or fifth position, but no farther.

Photo courtesy of Susan Yost

The riders in this breakaway group will take turns pulling into the wind and resting behind one another as they try to outrun the pack.

Even if it costs you a lot of energy to fight for the prime position, once you turn that final corner in good position, you will find that you have the energy to do whatever you must do. Remember that you can never win if you are too far back going through the final turn, so if you focus more on the turn than the sprint, you can take some of the focus off the nerves of the sprinting and let the sprint take care of itself. It is far better to be in contention for first place and get beaten, ending up as 5th or 10th place, than it is to be fresh and be sprinting for 20th.

Leadouts

When a team working together approaches the finish intact or mostly intact, the team's members will probably try to set up their best sprint finisher for the win. This is done through a leadout in which successive teammates line up to block the wind for each other, with the sprinter in the prime position to make the most of the dash to the line. Nowhere is the beauty of the team leadout more apparent than in criterium racing.

A leadout can be conducted by one teammate leading out another in the final 500 meters of the race to deliver his teammate in prime position at the 200-meter mark, or it can be a major pro train of up to 5 or even 10 riders, beginning as far away from the finish as 4 kilometers, depending on team size and strength. The lead rider looks out for the rider being led out, guiding him at or near the front of the pack. The rider being led out is in charge of the leadout, calling to the leading rider to move right, left, or forward as needed.

Full multimember team leadouts are rare in beginning racing, but understanding them helps you to enjoy being a spectator and to know where the best sprinters hide themselves until the ideal moment to spring their final jump. A team leadout is really just an extension of a single-rider leadout, starting farther out from the finish.

A leadout typically has two stages when conducted by three or more riders. The first members of the leadout keep the speed high and smooth enough so that the competition will refrain from attacking. As each rider blows up from the effort, he simply peels off to the side and gets out of the way. The second stage sees the fastest riders on the team, often the second- and third-best sprinters or top time trialists taking over and riding all-out (even sprinting) for as long as each rider can to time the delivery of the best sprinter at top speed to the prime sprinting start point from the finish.

When a leadout is done correctly, the teammates conducting the leadout are so blown from the effort that for some the race ends as far away as an entire lap before the finish, leaving them to cross the line completely shattered and hoping that their effort paid off for their top sprinting teammate. Most times leadout riders are nowhere near the top 10 finishers. However, sometimes leadouts can be so effective that they shatter the pack so that a breakaway will occur, allowing for leadout members to place well along with their top sprinter.

Another way a team can attack the finish of any crit or road race when they don't have a top sprinter or the full numbers to do a team leadout is to take turns attacking in the final miles while the team's sprinter works to hold good position for the final sprint. If one of the attacking riders succeeds to the finish, great! But should she get caught, the speed has been kept high because other teams have chased the breakaway riders, and the team's sprinter still remains in good position in the pack to try to finish off the deal. When a team believes in the strength of its sprinter, following the standard leadout is usually more successful, while the fake leadout is much more of a crapshoot.

Chapter 18

Stage Racing

The ultimate road racing challenge is the stage race, a multiday event usually combining road races, criteriums, and time trials in a way that lets the specialists in each event showcase their talents and rewards those who excel in more than one event. Stage races add a new layer of complexity to each of their component races in that riders need to approach each race differently than they would a one-day event.

While a stage race lasts more than one day, this event is not the same as ultra-endurance racing, such as the Race Across America, where competitors ride nonstop from checkpoint to checkpoint, minimizing sleep and trudging on for days. A stage race can be anywhere from 2 to 10 days in length for amateurs, with each stage similar in length to a normal one-day race. There may be more than one stage per day. Each rider needs to finish each stage to be allowed to start the next stage and to earn an overall placing in the race. The major stage races of the men's professional peloton, called the Grand Tours, last a whopping 23 days, with only 2 days off. There are only three Grand Tours: Le Tour de France, Giro d'Italia (Tour of Italy), and La Vuelta a España (Tour of Spain).

Omniums are similar to stage races. The main difference between an omnium and a stage race is that competitors aren't required to start or finish every stage of the race. Riders gain points from each finish—for instance, 25 for first place, 23 for second, 21 for third, 20 for fourth, and so on. Riders who skip stages simply won't receive points for those stages. When you enter a multirace weekend competition, determine whether it is a timed stage race or a points omnium because different tactics are needed to win each type.

Most stage races and omniums for amateurs include two or three stages over one weekend, often including a road race, time trial, and crit. Three-day weekends often hold at least one more stage. Regardless of the number of days raced, stage racing challenges your stamina, focus, and tactical ability more than any other kind of road racing. In your first stage races, just aim to finish each stage so as to be allowed to start the next day's stage and receive a placing for the overall race. Finishing even a weekend stage race is a great accomplishment. One of the great things about stage races is that you get a time for each stage as well as a placing. You can save results from the same races year to year and, assuming similar weather and competition, directly measure your improvement.

Understanding the Stage Race

To win a stage race, you must have the lowest accumulated time over all stages. For each stage you complete, your finishing time is recorded and added to your times for the preceding stages. The list of all the riders who have completed all stages so far, sorted in order of total time, is called the *general classification*, or *GC*. You must complete every stage to be placed in the final GC. When several riders cross the line at once in a group, each is given the time of the first rider in that group. If a gap does open up, the riders who are gapped have their own time calculated off the stage winner. The first rider in a following group may be many seconds behind the first rider of a leading group and therefore may receive a time many seconds slower than a rider just ahead of the gap.

Each stage has an individual winner (or team winner, in the case of a team time trial stage), and each day has a GC leader. After the first stage, the stage winner automatically becomes the overall race leader going into the next stage and may be provided by the race with a special jersey. If that same rider either wins the next stage or finishes in close enough time to that stage's winner, she holds the lead and the leader's jersey. Time bonuses awarded for the top placings in each stage (other than time trials) can also shake things up; as much as 30 seconds can be subtracted from a stage winner's time. If the current leader loses enough time that another rider achieves the lowest cumulative time, the leader's jersey changes hands. The current stage winner is not necessarily the current overall leader. That depends on the amount of time the riders close to the lead in the GC make or lose against one another. The beauty of stage racing is that a spectacular ride by a competitor or a particularly terrible ride by the current race leader can overcome a multiminute lead even in the final stage of the race.

The most famous example of a last-stage comeback happened during the 1989 Tour de France. Frenchman Laurent Fignon was looking for his third Tour de France win, going into the final stage in Paris with the yellow leader's jersey, feeling reasonably certain that he could hang onto his 50-second lead over American Greg LeMond through the relatively short 24-kilometer (15-mile) finishing time trial. Going off the start ramp second to last for the day with only Fignon left to finish, LeMond completed the distance fastest of the day thus far and waited for Fignon to arrive, 58 seconds too late to save his jersey. LeMond won the three-week race by a mere 8 seconds as Fignon crossed the line exhausted. LeMond's look of ecstasy and Fignon's collapse off the bike in disbelief rival any great moment in sport.

Fifty seconds would have been the last thought in LeMond's mind when he went to sleep the night before that final stage and the first thing he thought of in the morning. He knew what he needed to do from the daily results provided after each stage. Individual stage results include a placing and a time for each finisher or "DNF" for those who did not finish. On the GC results page are the total time for the current leader and the total time for each rider after that. Time deficits to the leader may be listed as well. If they aren't listed, you will need to calculate each day how far you are behind the leader or by how much you are leading. Also, check the numbers and times of your closest competitors so that you can keep track of them. Riders often pore over the results of a stage race each night within the race, memorizing the relative time gaps between all the competitors for reference in the race the next day. Not having any idea of the gaps between riders going into the next stage is somewhat like riding blindly because you wouldn't have any idea why certain riders are behaving in the race the way they do.

In addition to the individual GC, stage races may also run other classifications during the race. While it is uncommon in beginning racing, stage races for higher-category riders often include a team general classification. Team GC is usually calculated from taking the time from the first three riders of a team to finish each stage. The team with the lowest cumulative time after the final stage is the winner. If the team drops below three riders, it is removed from the team GC, but the team's individual riders are able to continue and be eligible for the individual GC.

Other competitions possible within a stage race may include a mountain climbing, sprinting, or points classification. An example of the mountain competition is a *king* or *queen of the mountain* jersey awarded for points accumulated at intermediate sprint lines set at the top of the hills throughout various stages. A classification for sprint points includes various sprint lines along the route. In both cases, the locations of the sprints are listed in the race program, called the *race bible*, that you pick up at registration. The race bible lists the distances and course directions for each stage and explains any mountain or points competitions, special rules, or race changes. Usually points are awarded to only the top three or top five riders crossing the intermediate sprint line, so not all riders are contesting these classifications. A points classification might include both the mountain and sprint points in addition to points awarded for top stage placings, thereby rewarding the most consistent rider throughout the race. What to include and how to score a points classification is up to the promoter of the race.

© Empics

Although these racers are riding together, they are actually separated by a matter of seconds, minutes, and in some cases hours.

Stage Race Preparation

Because of the multiday nature of stage racing, preparation for it takes even more thought than regular weekend racing. You need to have a high volume of high-quality training behind you and be well rested, having taken it easy for at least one day—or, better yet, two or more—before the first race day. Prepare well and pay attention to details: Minimize things that you'll need to do between stages. Share logistical work with teammates: if you are not lucky enough to have a team manager, one rider can handle registration while another pumps up tires and fills water bottles. In the event of a double-stage day, the early stage will often be quite early, demanding an extremely early breakfast to allow for travel and race prep time. Between stages find a suitable and relaxing place to rest and recharge with food you can digest in time for the afternoon stage. Purchase and prepare your food before the morning stage.

Recovery is key. If you recover well from day to day, you become stronger compared to the other riders. Be conscious of conserving energy from the very first pedal stroke, both on and off the bike. You may not feel the effects of the early breakaway attempt during the first stage, but you will feel it in a later stage. This doesn't mean that you shouldn't take advantage of opportunities to break away from the peloton and potentially gain time on the majority of the field, but be choosier than normal about your attempts to attack, chase, or bridge.

Stage races often enforce a "time cut" for each stage, a certain percentage of the stage winner's time that each rider must finish within to begin the next stage. Time cuts prevent riders from sandbagging to save energy for particular stages. Unfortunately for beginners, time cuts also weed out those riders who are unprepared for longer, more demanding races. The standard time cut is 20 percent beyond the winner's time, meaning that if a rider won the stage in 2 hours, for instance, the last finishers would have to finish by 2 hours and 24 minutes. The officials may not always enforce the time cut in beginning races, but you can't count on this, so continue at a good pace, working with others to get to the line quickly. Continuing at near race pace even when you are dropped helps develop your strength and helps you avoid getting dropped in future races.

Proper hydration and fueling are especially important during a stage race. You'll need a feeder in the feed zone to hand up bottles.

Between stages sip from a water bottle constantly, stay off your feet, and trade short massages with a teammate. Stay out of the sun, carry an extra jacket for air-conditioned restaurants, keep a hat on your head and your legs covered when it's cold, and generally exercise common sense in staying warm, hydrated, and rested.

The Start

A stage race can start with a road race, crit, time trial, or a very short time trial called a *prologue.* A first-stage criterium or road race can be raced like a one-day race, with a few exceptions. One difference is that any breakaway you join or miss may make time on the pack. That time carries into the GC, whereas in a normal one-day race the actual time gaps are not important. Another difference is that while in a one-day race you lay everything you have on the line for a realistic shot at the win, going for a major breakaway or attacking incessantly in an early stage burns energy you may need in later stages. It also shows everyone your strength and makes you a mark in future stages.

When a stage race starts with a criterium or road race, riders cross the line in large packs, giving many the same GC time in the first stage. A prologue time trial, by contrast, serves to separate riders by small amounts of time before they go into the first main stage. This way, when riders cross the line in large packs in later stages, most are already separated by a number of seconds in the GC. Small gaps create more excitement and are conducive to aggressive racing.

A prologue can climb a single large hill, roll over varied terrain, or wind through challenging turns on city streets. Prologues are usually 3 miles (5 kilometers) or less. To place well, you have to go all-out for nearly the entire course. A thorough warm-up is necessary for a strong ride in a prologue. If a prologue is held in the evening, you can improve your prerace warm-up by adding a short, easy spin the morning of the prologue, loosening up your legs for the evening's effort.

For most uphill prologues, your standard road bike should be sufficient. Being able to climb efficiently out of the saddle will usually outweigh the aero advantage that you would gain in the short time spent in the aerobars of a time trial bike. If a course has a significant amount of flat and straight roadway, a time trial bike or clip-on aerobars can be an advantage. Be sure to consider the time required for attaching or taking off aerobars before the next stage.

Stage Racing Tactics

The first rule of stage racing tactics is that you must save your energy for the components of the race where you can excel and must minimize your losses where you are weakest. Competitors usually enter a stage race with one of two focuses: placing well in the GC or placing well in a particular stage or stages. Make your own decision, based on your unique talents, after talking with riders who have done the race before and after reviewing the courses in the race bible. Use the four Cs to help you choose which stages to shoot for. For instance, most time is gained and lost during time trials and hilly road stages, while criteriums and flat road stages don't usually change the standings much. While there are exceptions to this, experience shows that those who can climb and time trial well excel in stage racing.

Those who sprint well but aren't as gifted at time trialing and climbing ride more conservatively in the time trials and focus their effort on the flatter road stages or criteriums and not the overall. For those going for the GC, each time trial will have to be ridden as if it is a one-day time trial with everything on the line.

As a beginning racer, make your best effort in any time trial during a stage race—even if time trialing doesn't seem to be your specialty—so that you continue to improve. As you do more races, you'll find that you finish around the same riders again and again. Some riders head into a stage race looking to make an improvement over those riders. Noting improvement by how well you do compared to the riders you usually finish near doesn't hurt, as long as you don't get so wrapped up in beating certain riders that you overlook opportunities to place better or even win a race!

The four Cs of stage racing change slightly for each stage as the race progresses. At any given time, you need to consider what the leaders are doing and why, and how that relates to what you are currently doing in the pack. For instance, if when you make an attack the race leaders chase you immediately, you can be fairly certain that they consider your position in the GC close enough to the overall lead to be a threat. Common sense in stage racing dictates that the overall race leader needs to keep an eye on the nearest riders on GC, and the riders just below the leader on GC also watch the riders near them. For this reason, you may often see the GC leader following around the next highest placed GC rider in the pack. However, don't always expect beginning riders to follow strategy that makes the most sense aimed at winning, as many do not have a basic understanding of tactics and simply chase anyone they have the energy to chase!

Gaining Time

Chunks of time can be gained or lost on hills. How can you gain the most time on other riders on a hill? In chapter 12 we discussed the various strategies for hanging in or riding your own pace on hills when others are pushing. Now we look at the most effective ways of leaving others behind if climbing is your strength. One way is to simply attack somewhere on the climb. Attacks on climbs are most effective once the climb has had time to wear on, already shedding those riders who are too weak to stay with the leaders. The advantage of attacking is that it may allow you, and potentially a small group, to gain a large amount of time on an extended hill. Leaving competitors in your dust on the hill can demoralize them, and once you are out of sight they may ease up and give up on immediately catching you. Or they may not.

The disadvantage of attacking on a climb is that it can leave relatively large groups intact. Those groups will organize at the top of the hill to work on catching you. They will also descend together in a large group, making up time on individuals or smaller groups, especially on open descents. A better option at times may be to simply increase the tempo gradually as you roll up the climb to drop riders one by one. This way, riders are left shattered all over the climb. It takes time for them to organize into larger groups—time that may give you just the gap you need to reach the finish line first and alone.

Teamwork Tactics

Riding as an individual in a stage race is a challenging endeavor, especially if there are organized teams working together. While working together is not very common in beginning racing, as you progress through the cycling ranks teamwork becomes more of a factor. In stage racing, teams can use the relative strengths of their riders to place well in each stage and also go for the overall GC. A strong team is made up of a rounded blend of climbers, time trialists, sprinters, and riders who can do it all. For example, while one rider is off the front in the first stage, another rider can be following wheels in the pack, saving energy for the criterium the next day. Should the breakaway be caught, the wheel-sucker is ready for the sprint.

Even more tactically, a team can choose to "protect" certain riders by designating them as team leaders in the individual GC and sacrificing for those riders by chasing potential breakaways, leading those riders into hills in good position by sheltering them from the wind, or even launching attacks at strategic times to set up a counterattack for the designated teammate. Beating a rider who is protected by a strong team requires either far-superior strength or isolating the leader from his crew. If you are on your own without the benefit of a team, ride as if you are the star rider of your team, holding back from early breakaways, conserving for strategic counterattacks, and saving your strength for the hardest days of the race. If you can gain a substantial amount of time on one stage and hold your own in the rest, you have a good chance of placing well in the overall GC.

Working together, even with riders not on your team, is never more important than in stage racing. Traveling as a group will almost always get you to the finish line faster than setting out on your own or trying to hold off a group behind you. The energy you save will enable you to compete again the next day, even if saving it means not gaining time on certain riders.

Glossary

accordion effect—In the middle of a pack, the speed changes violently, up and down, in a way that is not consistent with the natural rhythm of a rider alone on the same course.

aerobars—Add-ons for handlebars to help a rider get low and narrow; also called *tribars*.

all (a)rounder—A rider who can climb, time trial, and sprint pretty well.

at the back—Riders who are in the last quarter of the field, or the last rider in the field.

attack—To accelerate suddenly in an effort to leave a group of riders.

bonk—To run out of stored glycogen, suddenly run out of riding energy.

breakaway—A rider or group of riders up the road from the main group.

bridge—To cross the gap from one group to another, leaving the first group behind.

cadence—Pedaling rate in full revolutions per minute.

category—An ability group, used to allow for more enjoyable racing.

chase—To ride hard in an effort to catch another rider or group of riders without regard to anyone who might be towing along.

chase group—A group that rides hard together to try to catch a breakaway or another group.

clinchers—Modern tires suitable for racing or training that feature an inner tube and are held to the rim by a hooked bead.

closed course—A race course on which the only traffic is other racers and official vehicles.

counterattack or counter—To attack just as another rider or group is caught by the field or chase group.

countersteering—Leaning the bike into a turn.

criterium (crit)—A multilap race, typically between .5 and 1 mile (0.9 and 1.6 kilometers).

cyclocross—A multilap offroad race, typically lasting 30 to 60 minutes, in which riders compete on a modified road bike with knobby tires.

deep dish or deep section—An aerodynamic rim section characterized by a high, triangular profile of the rim.

disk wheel—A wheel in which spokes are replaced with a complete disk to reduce aerodynamic drag.

double-butted—Term used to describe spokes or frame tubes that are thickened on the ends for strength and thinned in the middle for lighter weight.

draft—To ride close behind or beside another rider to take advantage of the hole in the wind produced by that rider.

drop—To leave behind.

dropout—The slotted portion of a bike frame to which the rear-wheel clamps.

drops—The lower portion of a traditional road racing handlebar.

echelon—A paceline that stretches out sideways so riders can take maximum advantage of the draft in a side wind.

espoire—The age group of racers from 19 to 23 years old.

false flat—A very slight uphill angle that looks flat.

field limit—The maximum number of riders allowed in a race.

final results—The official outcome of a race, determined after all protests have been accounted for and any authorized corrections have been made. Final results are immutable, even if they are wrong.

flier (take a flier)—A short, usually hopeless, breakaway or a hard attack expected to last a short while.

float (in pedal)—Freedom to change the angle of the foot in relation to the pedal.

front—The lead riders in a group. *On the front* means leading the group. *At the front* means close to the individual leaders but not pulling into the wind.

gap—A space between a rider and the rider in front of that rider. When there is a gap, the following rider is not benefiting much from the draft.

gear inches (GI)—A measure of the gear in use. To calculate, use the following formula: GI = chain-ring teeth × tire diameter (26 in. for 650c tires, 27 in. for 700c or tubular tires)/rear cog teeth.

general classification (GC)—Ranking of riders by accumulated time in a stage race.

half-wheel—To ride hard enough to keep the front wheel just ahead of the wheel of the rider next to you.

hold a line—To maintain a constant distance from the side of the road, especially in a corner.

hoods—The rubber covers on the brake levers.

indoor trainer—A device that clamps to the rear axle of a bicycle and supports it so that it can be ridden in place.

jump—To accelerate hard for a few seconds.

junior—A rider with a racing age of 18 years or less.

kermesse—A European style of exhibition racing that is typically executed on a 6- to 10-kilometer (4- to 6-mile) flat course.

lap the field—To break away from and catch up with the entire main group.

lead out—To ride hard for the benefit of a drafting rider coming into a sprint.

master—A rider with a racing age of 30 or over in some events, 35 or over in other events.

neutral wheel/vehicle—Service wheels or support vehicles available to all racers.

neutralize—To temporarily suspend active racing to ride together as a group.

off the back (OTB)—So far behind most racers as to be out of contention in the event.

omnium—A competition made up of several races in which riders score points and the best overall point score wins. Distinct from a stage race in which the overall winner is determined by accumulated time rather than points.

overreaching—Training more than the body is really ready for; leads to fatigue and a moderate decline in performance. The consequences of overreaching clear up with a few days of rest.

overtraining—Training much more or harder than the body is really ready for; leads to deep fatigue that takes weeks or months to clear up.

paceline—Group of riders lined up so that each is drafting the one in front.

pack—Group of riders.

pave—Cobblestone road.

pit—The area where wheel changes and repairs may be made in a criterium.

preliminary results—The results as the officials initially see them, subject to a 15-minute protest period.

preregistration—Signing up for a race by mail or Internet before race day.

prime (pronounced *preem*)—A prize awarded to the winner or winners of an intermediate sprint before the end of the race.

protect—To ride in front of or sacrifice for another rider who has a better chance of winning.

pull—To ride at the front, granting the benefit of the draft to other riders.

pull off—Move to the side and stop pulling.

pulled, get—Asked to leave the race by the officials

racing age—The age on the racing license; the age of a rider on December 31 of the current year.

racing license—A certificate bearing the rider's name, racing age, category, club name, and other information that helps the officials place the rider in the correct race group.

relegation—An official sanction for a minor rule infraction in which a rider receives a placing farther back in the field than where he or she crossed the line.

road race—A mass-start race held on a course; may be point-to-point or out and back, or may have one or several loops.

roll a tire—The tire comes off the rim, eliminating traction.

rollers—1. Short hills in which momentum plays a significant role in getting one over the hill. 2. A training device made up of a set of three drums in a frame on which a bicycle can be ridden.

rotate—In a paceline, to trade off taking pulls at the front so as to share the work of leading into the wind.

RPM—Revolutions per minute.

sandbagger—One who rides in a lower category than that for which he or she is or could be eligible.

senior—The group including racing ages from 19 to 30 or 35. Younger and older riders are generally allowed to ride with the seniors.

set up—To move oneself and teammates into position for a sprint or an attack.

sit in, sit on—To ride hidden in the group, drafting but taking no pulls.

skinsuit—A tight-fitting, smooth, one-piece racing uniform.

solo—To ride alone, away from a group of racers.

spin—To ride at a high cadence (typically 90 to 110 RPM) using light pressure on the pedals.

stage race—A series of several races to determine an overall winner based on accumulated time.

staging area—The area near the start line where riders are expected to meet before the start of a race.

straight gauge—Term used to describe spokes of a constant diameter or thickness; the opposite of double-butted.

suck wheel—To draft; sometimes used derogatorily.

time trial—A race in which individuals ride separately against the clock and times are compared to determine a winner.

tops—The upper, straight-across portion of a traditional road handlebar.

top tube—The horizontal or nearly horizontal upper tube in a diamond-shaped bicycle frame.

tow—To pull a group of riders by riding at the front of the group.

true—To change the relative tension on the spokes of a wheel to make the wheel round and prevent it from wobbling side to side.

tubular—A style of tire in which the inner tube is sewn into the tire, which is then held to the rim by strong contact-cement. Also called a "sew-up."

tuck—To ride with the shoulders very low to reduce wind resistance; usually done on fast, straight descents.

upgrade—To move to a higher category based on experience or racing success.

upgrade points—Points awarded for racing success; required for a category upgrade.

velodrome—Bicycle racing track.

wheel sucker—A rider who wins or places in races with minimal pulling and lots of drafting.

Resources

Organizations

International

Union Cycliste Internationale (UCI). The international cycling federation governing the road, track, mountain, BMX, and other cycling federations worldwide. Also coordinates an international calendar of racing for professional men and women racers, espoire racers, juniors, and masters.

Union Cycliste Internationale, CH 1860 Aigle, Switzerland
Ph: 41.24.468.58.11; Fax: 41.24.268.58.12
www.uci.ch
admin@uci.ch

North American

Canadian Cycling. The governing body for road, mountain, and track cycling in Canada, including racing licenses, officiating, coaching resources, and race permits.

Canadian Cycling Association, 702 - 2197 Riverside Drive, Ottawa, Ontario, K1H 7X3
Ph: 613.248.1353; Fax: 613.248.9311
www.canadian-cycling.com
general@canadian-cycling.com

United States

USA Cycling. The governing body for road, mountain, track and BMX bike racing in the U.S., including racing licenses, officiating, coaching resources, and race permits.

USA Cycling, One Olympic Plaza, Colorado Springs, CO 80909
Ph: 719.578.4581; Fax: 719.578.4628
www.usacycling.org
usac@usacycling.org

Alternative Associations to USA Cycling
(Not all areas have major alternative associations)

Midwestern area

American Bicycle Racing. A national organization that provides racing permits, licenses, and coaching resources. An alternative to USA Cycling in the Midwestern states.

American Bicycle Racing, P.O. Box 487, Tinley Park, IL 60447-0487
Ph: 708.532.7204; Fax: 708.532.7484
www.ambikerace.com
ambikerace@aol.com

Rocky Mountain area

American Cycling Association. A national organization that provides racing permits, licenses, and coaching resources. An alternative to USA Cycling, primarily in the Mountain states.

American Cycling Association, P.O. Box 7129, Denver, CO 80204
Ph: 303.458.5538; Fax: 877.702.6438
www.americancycling.org
membership1@americancycling.org

West Coast area

Northern California/Nevada Cycling Association. A regional organization that provides racing permits, licenses, and coaching resources in Northern California and Nevada. Works in cooperation with USA Cycling.

NCNCA, P.O. Box 2005, Livermore, CA 94551
Ph: 510.278.3456
www.ncnca.org
ncnca@attbi.com

Oregon Bicycle Racing Organization (OBRA). A regional organization that provides racing permits, licenses, and coaching resources in Oregon. An alternative to USA Cycling.

OBRA, P.O. Box 16355, Portland, OR 97292
Ph: 503.667.6220
www.obra.org
membership@obra.org

Publications

Bicycling Magazine. The largest monthly cycling magazine in the world, this is a good resource for training hints and interesting features.

Bicycling, Rodale, Inc., 135 N. Sixth St., Emmaus, PA 18098
800.666.2806
www.bicycling.com
bicycling@rodale.com

Cycle Sport Magazine. A British magazine that prints an American edition monthly, covering European professional racing and featuring the riders of the European peloton.

Cycle Sport, 2225 University Ave. W., Saint Paul, MN 55114
info@cyclesportmag.com

The Ride Magazine. An East coast-based magazine about racing and bike culture with excellent results, coverage, and interviews.

The Ride Magazine, 1173 Massachusetts Avenue, Arlington, MA 02476
781.641.9515
www.ridezine.com
theride@ridezine.com

VeloNews. The premier journal of American bicycle racing. Provides tips, interviews, U.S. and international race coverage.

VeloNews, Inside Communications, 1830 N. 55th Street, Boulder, CO 80301
Ph: 303.440.0601
www.velonews.com
vninteractive@7dogs.com

Web sites

BicycleCoach.com. A listing site for USA Cycling licensed coaches.
www.bicyclecoach.com

Bicyclesports.com. Provides bicycle aerodynamics research results and advice by aerodynamics specialist John Cobb.
www.bicyclesports.com

Bike.com. A site with excellent writing about racing and training. Read journals by the pros, race coverage, industry coverage, and training tips.
www.bike.com

Bikeride.com. One of the Web's best resources for links to thousands of cycling sites. Provides some race coverage.
www.bikeride.com

Cyclingnews.com. The first, and still the best, Web site for news, features and articles about bike racing. Heavy on European coverage, but provides excellent same-day results of many U.S. races, both regional and national.
www.cyclingnews.com

Dailypeloton.com. Racing news, features, racer journals, and articles.
www.dailypeloton.com

United States Anti-Doping Agency. Lists banned substances, provides medical notification forms for allowed prescriptions, explains drug-testing protocol.
www.usantidoping.org

Wobblenaught.com. Bike fitting by physiologists, coaches, and engineers through computer-aided design.
www.wobblenaught.com

Wenzel Coaching. A cool site with training information, coaching information, and profiles of athletes and coaches.
www.wenzelcoaching.com

Suggested Reading

Borysewicz, Edward, and Ed Pavelka. 1986. *Bicycle Road Racing: The Complete Program for Training and Competition.* Brattleboro, VT: Vitesse. One of the classic books on road racing and tactics. Written in the early 1980s, this book is still a valuable resource for bike racers who love the nuance of tactics and want to learn more about pro racing.

Burke, Edmund. 2002. *Serious Cycling,* 2nd edition. Champaign, IL: Human Kinetics. Excellent training and nutritional advice from one of the top authors of the sport.

Friel, Joe. 1996. *The Cyclist's Training Bible.* Boulder, CO: Velo Press. A training resource with excellent workouts and technical advice.

Lemond, Greg, and Kent Gordis. 1990. *Greg Lemond's Complete Book of Bicycling.* New York: Perigee. Another classic book on training and racing. This also contains excellent chapters on the history of bike racing in Europe and America.

Thomas, Steve, Ben Searle, Dave Smith. 2000. *The Racing Bike Book,* 2nd edition. Newbury Park, CA: Haynes. General beginning bike racing and training information, including velodrome basics.

Index

Note: The italicized *f* and *t* following page numbers refer to figures and tables, respectively.